PSYCHOLOGY OF LANGUAGE AND THO

D0409095

DATE DUE

OC 16 81			
DE 6 '99			
JR 11 '06			
JE 1 '06			

P
37
P788

Psychology of lan-
guage and thought

RIVERSIDE CITY COLLEGE
LIBRARY
Riverside, California

'81

DEMCO

PSYCHOLOGY OF LANGUAGE AND THOUGHT

Essays on the Theory and
History of Psycholinguistics

STUDIES IN APPLIED PSYCHOLINGUISTICS

Series Editor:
R.W. Rieber
John Jay College of Criminal Justice,CUNY and
Columbia University College of Physicians and Surgeons

A Continuation Order Plan is available for this series. A continuation order will bring delivery of each new volume immediately upon publication. Volumes are billed only upon actual shipment. For further information please contact the publisher.

PSYCHOLOGY OF LANGUAGE AND THOUGHT

Essays on the Theory and History of Psycholinguistics

Edited by

R.W. Rieber

John Jay College of Criminal Justice, CUNY and
Columbia University College of Physicians and Surgeons
New York, New York

PLENUM PRESS • NEW YORK AND LONDON

Riverside Community College
Library
4800 Magnolia Avenue
Riverside, CA 92506

Library of Congress Cataloging in Publication Data

Main entry under title:

Psychology of language and thought.

(Studies in applied psycholinguistics)
Includes index.
1. Psycholinguistics—History. I. Rieber, R.W. II. Series.
P37.P788   401′.9   79-25969
ISBN 0-306-40361-7

© 1980 Plenum Press, New York
A Division of Plenum Publishing Corporation
227 West 17th Street, New York, N.Y. 10011

All rights reserved

No part of this book may be reproduced, stored in a retrieval system, or transmitted,
in any form or by any means, electronic, mechanical, photocopying, microfilming,
recording, or otherwise, without written permission from the Publisher

Printed in the United States of America

CONTRIBUTORS

John W. Black • *Professor Emeritus, Department of Speech and Hearing Sciences, The Ohio State University, Columbia, Ohio*

Michael J. Clark • *Linacre College, Oxford, England*

Peter Ostwald • *Langley Porter Institute, University of California San Francisco, San Francisco, California*

W. Keith Percival • *Department of Linguistics, University of Kansas, Lawrence, Kansas*

R. W. Rieber • *John Jay College of Criminal Justice, CUNY, and Columbia University, College of Physicians and Surgeons, New York, New York*

Jules Paul Seigel • *Department of English, University of Rhode Island, Kingston, Rhode Island*

James H. Stam • *Department of Philosophy and Religion, Upsala College, East Orange, New Jersey*

John J. Sullivan • *New York University, New York, New York; University of Utah, Salt Lake City, Utah*

Karl D. Uitti • *Department of Romance Languages and Literatures, Princeton University, Princeton, New Jersey*

Harold Vetter • *University of South Florida, Tampa, Florida*

Jeffrey Wollock • *New College, University of Oxford, Oxford, England*

PREFACE

The fact that one would contemplate publication of a book such as this indicates both the maturity and the growth of activity that have taken place in the field of psycholinguistics over the past few decades. Moreover, the fact that psycholinguists and/or scholars of the history of ideas are interested in the history of their subject clearly demonstrates that much has been accomplished, and the time is indeed ripe for the reassessment of whence we have come. In addition, perhaps this interest in our historical past suggests that psycholinguistics is at a critical stage in its development. There are many scholars who believe that this critical stage manifests itself primarily in a search for a new paradigm. It would seem only reasonable to suggest that when members of a profession are searching for something new, more than likely they will take time to reflect on the past in the hope that it will facilitate the fulfillment of their quest.

This book as such reflects a wide-ranging search for historical roots over a millenium of research in the psychology of language and thought. Furthermore, it also reflects an attempt to open the context by introducing the broader perspectives of the history of ideas and the history of science together with their reassessment of the method of science motivated from within psychology itself.

We should like to thank the publishers for their encouragement and particularly the contributors of this book for their cooperation and patience. It is our hope that this book will provide the reader with a fresh perspective in his study of psycholinguistics and will help facilitate an understanding of the transition of language and thought from an earlier formative period to its present stages of maturation and development.

R. W. RIEBER

New York, N.Y.
January, 1980

CONTENTS

PART I

AN OVERVIEW

R. W. Rieber and Harold Vetter

THEORETICAL AND HISTORICAL ROOTS OF PSYCHOLINGUISTIC RESEARCH*

> *Philosophical (grammar), examining the power and nature of words, as they are the footsteps and prints of reason: which kind of analogy between words and reason is handled* sparsim, *brokenly, though not entirely, and therefore I cannot report it deficient, though I think it is very worthy to be reduced into a science by itself.*

> —Francis Bacon (*The Advancement of Learning*)

Introduction

Psycholinguistics can be said to have originated as far back in the history of philosophy as one cares to trace psychology. The widespread use of the term *psycholinguistics* and the development of a distinct discipline with that title, however, go back only to the early 1950s, when George Miller, Charles Osgood, and other psychologists introduced a knowledge of lin-

*This article is reprinted by permission of the publisher from D. Aaronson and R. W. Rieber (Eds.), *Psycholinguistic Research: Implications and Applications*. Hillsdale, N.J..: L.E.A., Inc., 1979.

R. W. Rieber • John Jay College of Criminal Justice, CUNY, and Columbia University, College of Physicians and Surgeons, New York, N. Y. 10019. *Harold Vetter* • University of South Florida, Tampa, Florida 33620.

guistics into the psychological study of language.[1] Prior to that time, psychological studies of "verbal learning" dated from the concern of Ebbinghaus (1885) with memory and are tied to a strand of theory that can be followed back to the associationism of Locke [1632–1704]. To the extent that verbal learning theorists in psychology were almost totally lacking in linguistic sophistication, it might be said that their research interests represented precisely what psycholinguistics was *not*.

In the summer of 1951, the Social Science Research Council (SSRC) sponsored an interdisciplinary seminar on language behavior at Cornell University that brought together three psychologists and three linguists.[2] Unlike many well-intentioned mutual efforts of this kind, the Cornell conference produced a number of noteworthy results. In addition to their discovery of methodological kinship, the conferees found themselves in possession of a solid foundation of shared interests in language phenomena and their systematic exploration. Two of the more influential consequences of the conference were not immediately apparent. The first of these was the establishment in the following autumn of a Committee on Linguistics and Psychology by the SSRC, which included psychologists John Carroll, James Jenkins, George Miller, and Charles Osgood, and linguists Joseph Greenberg, Floyd Lounsbury, and Thomas Sebeok. The second important consequence of the Cornell summer seminar was the grassfire rapidity with which the term psycholinguistics entered the lexicon of psychologists and linguists alike.[3]

At least part of the reason for the almost instant popularity of psycholinguistics as a term was the lack of a suitable tag or label for the variety of issues and problems encompassed by the research interests and efforts of linguists and psychologists. Roger Brown (1958) objected to the "absurd but intrusive false etymology" of the term, which tends to support the implication that a "psycho-linguist" is a mentally deranged polyglot. But his more serious concern that the term might limit the field to the traditional objectives of linguistics has fortunately been allayed by subsequent developments in psycholinguistic research. In fact, a broad range of inquiry is presently conducted under the rubric *psycholinguistic,* which fits under the more generous umbrella of the "psychology of language."

Professional interest in psycholinguistics was further stimulated by

---

[1]To the best of our knowledge, the first-modern usage of the term *psycholinguistics* appeared in Kantor (1936) as an adjective and in Pronko (1946) as a noun.
[2]For further discussion of this point, see Blumenthal (1970, p. vii) and A.R. Diebold (1965).
[3]This point is discussed further in A. R. Diebold (1965).

the publication in 1954 of a monograph entitled *Psycholinguistics: A Survey of Theory and Research Problems,* which resulted from an SSRC-sponsored conference at Indiana University. As Diebold (1965) pointed out in his editorial postscript to the reissue, this monograph provided a "charter for psycholinguistics" and quickly became a collector's item. Further SSRC conferences were held during the next several years at a variety of locations on such topics as comparative psycholinguistics, bilingualism, content analysis, associative processes in verbal behavior, dimensions of meaning, style in language, aphasia, and language universals. With the publication in 1961 of Sol Saporta's anthology entitled *Psycholinguistics: A Book of Readings,* it was apparent that psycholinguistics, both as a term and as an important area of interdisciplinary effort, was here to stay.

During most of the decade between the first SSRC conference and the appearance of Saporta's reader, language analysis was largely dominated by the structural linguistics viewpoint as it had been developed and elaborated by Bloomfield, Fries, Hockett, Pike, and others. During this "formative period" of psycholinguistics, as Maclay (1973) has called it, the harmonious relations between psychologists and linguists were enhanced by their "common commitment to an operationalist philosophy of science and a division of labor that prevented a number of difficulties from becoming overt" (p. 570). This happy state of affairs was not destined to last.

In 1957 there occurred what must be ranked among the several most important intellectual events of this century—the publication of a book entitled *Syntactic Structures* by Noam Chomsky. What Chomsky did in this single volume was nothing less than raise the flag of revolution within the linguistics camp. Much of the impact of Chomsky's critique of structural linguistics centered upon a distinction between competence and performance in language. More specifically, Chomsky challenged the proposition that it is possible to arrive at a comprehensive statement of the former by starting from a description, however detailed and specific, of the latter.

The objective linguistic theory, in Chomsky's view, is to provide a formal statement of the coherence and consistency of a language (i.e., its *grammar*). Structural linguists assumed that it was possible, given an adequate corpus of utterances by a native speaker, to *infer* the essential features of coherence and consistency that characterize the grammar of a given language. Such a statement might require a volume approaching the size of an unabridged dictionary. How, then, could we reconcile anything so voluminous and elaborate with the effective linguistic performance of the 6-year-old child? Said Carroll (1964): "Either the feat of the child is actually greater than we think it is, or there is something wrong with the assertion that a grammar of a language needs to be voluminous" (p. 23).

Each new reported study tends to deepen our appreciation for the impressiveness of the child's feat in learning his or her native language. But without detracting from the magnitude of such an accomplishment, there is the question of the relationship between linguistic behavior and linguistic theory. Is it really possible to start with the slips, false starts, hesitations, fragmentary sentences, and incomplete utterances of ordinary language behavior and arrive at the coherence and consistency of the language system?

Chomsky (1956, 1957) demonstrated that two of the three models that had been proposed up until that time as devices for generating language utterances were unsuitable for reasons involving inherent limitations on their operations: a *finite-state grammar*, which conceptualizes sentences as sequences of items selected from a large inventory and arranged in such an order that antecedent selections determine the conditional probabilities of subsequent choices (i.e., each selection that is made at some point in the sequence reduces the *potential* number of choices available at later stages); and a *phrase-structure grammar*, which makes provision for the fact that language has a hierarchical as well as a linear organization of the sentence as a series of constructions (*immediate constituents*) at successive levels.

Chomsky analyzed a number of problems such as constructional homonymity, which tax the capacities of either model, and proposed that an adequate grammar makes most parsimonious use of a small number of basic elements or *kernel* sentences from which an indefinitely large number of *derived* sentences can be generated by means of rules (called *transformations*) that rearrange the components of a word string. Such transformations involve operations like additions, deletions, permutations, and combinations which convert a sentence with a given constituent structure into a new sentence with a derived constituent structure. It adds considerably to the analytic capabilities of the grammatical model if it makes further provision for distinguishing optional transformational rules from obligatory tranformational rules.

Chomsky's views quickly attracted a group of disciples who became identified in the aggregate as *transformational*, or *generative*, grammarians. In their subsequent interactions with the structural linguists—and with the behaviorists among the ranks of the psychologists—they often seemed to display a frame of mind similar to that of St. Paul after he had experienced his encounter on the road to Damascus. Confrontation escalated into full-scale strife, so that by 1970 Hebb, Lambert, and Tucker were pleading for a DMZ—a demilitatrized zone—between the warring camps.

Thomas Kuhn, in the *Structure of Scientific Revolutions* (1970), takes issue with the traditional view of science to which every fledgling scientist is exposed as a student, namely, that scientific progress is linear, that scientific knowledge is cumulative, and that scientific research is directed toward abstract truth. Instead, Kuhn maintains, the history of any given science is revolutionary, not evolutionary. Scientific change comes about, in his view, by a process that bears a closer resemblance to the way in which regimes succeed one another in a banana republic than to the orderly process of transition from one governmental administration to another with which most Americans are familiar. The basic pattern is a clash of paradigms in which one view of nature is overthrown by another.

Much of the dispute that raged during the 1960s and the early 1970s over the issue of linguistic competence vs. performance involved a conflict between the paradigms of rationalism and empiricism. This conflict needs to be viewed in historical, as well as in theoretical, perspective. Chomsky (1966), for example, traces his own academic lineaments back to Descartes [1596–1650]; and in a recent paper, Sullivan (1977) concludes that if there had been a Cartesian linguistics, it might have borne some resemblance to what Chomsky has proposed. In particular, Descartes's transition from the doctrine of innate ideas to one of innate *powers* is consistent with Chomsky's contention that the generativity or creativity of language presupposes certain innate properties of the mind. If such properties exist, are they species-specific to the human being or are they continuously distributed across the phylogenetic scale? This is a question of considerable contemporary import, given the achievements of a number of investigators who have succeeded in teaching American Sign Language (ASL) to chimpanzees. But it was raised as long ago as the middle of the eighteenth century by La Mettrie in *L'Homme Machine* (1746, cited in Vartanian, 1960), and it has been posed in various ways and at various times by nearly every person who has seriously pondered the origins of language.

Long before psychology emerged as an autonomous discipline, with roots in both the "descriptive philosophy of experience" and biology, concern for what we would identify today as the psychology of language belonged to the philosopher and the medical practitioner. Language phenomena were often the object of study for the light they might possibly shed on the structure and process of thought or reason, rather than as legitimate objects of inquiry in themselves. When interest was shown in language phenomena *per se,* the chances were very good that the source of the concern was some type of linguistic aberration or disorder, and that the principal aim of the observer or investigator was to find some method of treatment for the disorder. Clinical preoccupation with the linguistic effects of structural disturbances led, in turn, to an interest in language and the central nervous system. Later, the initial observations of *disturbed language* (as opposed to language disturbance) in schizophrenia led to attempts to relate such phenomena to the kinds of symptoms previously noted in aphasia. Thus, the field inquiry was broadened to cover the systematic study of communication and its pathology.

We have ordered our review of the historical and theoretical perspectives in psycholinguistics with the above considerations in mind. We believe that these topic headings reflect some of the more significant recurrent themes in the psychology of language:

- Language, Thought, and Behavior
- Language and the Brain
- Communication and Its Pathology
- Comparative Study of Communication

This last section is subtitled (and we ask the reader's pardon) "Hands across the Phylogenetic Scale." Although this list makes no pretense at being comprehensive, we trust that we have managed to include a representative sample of the historical background of psycholinguistic theory and research.[4]

Language, Thought, and Behavior: Empiricism Takes a Giant Step and Falls

In language, as in so many other areas of intellectual activity, the Greeks—beginning with the pre-Socratic philosophers in the latter part of the sixth century B.C.—were the initiators of systematic inquiry. They

---

[4]The reader is referred to Robins (1967), Stam (1976), Blumenthal (1970), and Aarsleff (1967) for more detailed historical background material.

were the first language theorists; they were the first Europeans to concern themselves with the study of written texts; they founded the principles of classical European grammar. They discovered the parts of speech for Greek, and also such syntactic constructions as that of "subject and predicate, and its chief inflectional categories: genders, numbers, cases, persons, tenses, and modes. They defined these not in terms of recognizable linguistic forms, but in abstract terms which were to tell the meaning of the linguistic class" (Bloomfield, 1933, p. 5).

Hellenic interest in language was an outgrowth of philosophic pursuits. It was essentially in response to philosophical questions that Greek scholars speculated on the origin of language, the relationship between words and their meanings, and the application of principles of logic to grammar. Philosophical discussions were often directed toward linguistic problems. One of these discussions, as Ivič (1965) points out, is quite famous—the argument over whether the connection between the meanings of words and their sounds is logical and direct, or arbitrary and capricious. The "analogists" maintained that language is not dependent upon human conventions but is a gift of nature. There was perfect correspondence, in their view, between the sound of a word and its meaning; any imperfections that had arisen in this relationship in the course of time could be explained by etymological research, by systematic studies of words and their origins and derivations. The "anomalists," on the other hand, rejected the notion that there was perfect harmony between the sound and meanings of words. They drew on the existence of synonyms and homonyms, the demonstration of linguistic change over time, and the irregularity of grammar to show the imperfect nature of language.

Aristotle [384–322 B.C.] displayed the same twofold philosophical and scientific interest in language that he exhibited in other phenomena. He believed that language was found exclusively in humans, with the songs of birds the closest approximation among animals. Children, he considered, are not able to speak as adults do only because they have not yet attained control over their tongues; control is perfected through training. Human language differs biologically from the vocalization of animals, in the Aristotelian view, on the basis of a difference in the locus of sound production and the apparatus of articulation: human language is produced by the action of the tongue and animal sounds by the impact of air on the walls of the trachea. Human language articulation is unlike the expressive sounds produced by children or animals. These can neither be reduced to syllables nor combined to form syllables, as is possible with human speech.

He considered language itself as part of the natural order (*physis*) and the meanings of words as man-made (*thesis*).

Aristotle also attempted to establish a means of classifying parts of speech. The basic units of language, he felt, were nouns (*onoma*) and verbs (*rhema*), because only these words have a distinct meaning of their own; all other words merely serve to relate the logical aspects of the thinking process (*syndesmoi*).

As in so many other spheres of activity, the Romans borrowed liberally from the Greeks in matters pertaining to language. Thus, when a formal grammar was required by the Romans [100 B.C.–A.D. 200] during the period of their hegemony in order to unify the empire and compose a Latin literature, the model they chose was Greek.

The early Christian leaders considered language as God-given; and differences between languages were solely of pragmatic concern whenever a newly discovered territory needed Christianizing. Although language theorizing was dominated by the theme of divine revelation and concern for biblical exegesis, the natural basis of language was not totally abandoned. Ricobaldo of Ferrara, who believed in the separation of language capacities and languages, was supported in this belief by witnessing a miracle in 1293. When a deaf mute acquired hearing and speech after praying at the tomb of St. Anthony of Padua, he could repeat what was said to him but was unable to understand it. This was said to prove that language capacity was God-given, but that the knowledge of a particular language had to be learned.

Later Renaissance churchmen, such as Pietro Bembo [1470–1547], secretary to Pope Leo X, and Juan Luis Vives [1492–1540], maintained that language has a natural order with which no individual can tamper. Furthermore, these languages undergo changes with time, and the simplest languages are the oldest. Even the skeptic Montaigne [1533–1592] believed in the natural basis of language.

The English philosopher, essayist, and statesman Francis Bacon [1561–1626] approached the study of language as a multilevel process of communication, of which speech is only one of many possible manifestations. Discounting enquiry into the origins of names, Bacon nevertheless allows that names are "the vestiges of reason," and he envisions a philosophical grammar based on a comparison of different idioms—a theory that presupposes the possibility of creating a language entirely on the basis of convention and artifice.

The Cartesians

Marx (1967) noted that the separation between philosophy and science with respect to language began with Descartes [1596–1650]. As long as philosophy and natural science were indistinguishable, the philosophic emphasis upon language as the expression of human reason tended to confine to philosophy the consideration of all language elements. However, Descartes drew a further distinction between language and the expression of emotions, which man shares with most animals, and articulation, which he shares with parrots and magpies.

Descartes did not write extensively about language, but his conception of how the mind is related to the body influenced much of the later speculation concerning language. His resolution of the mind–body problem in terms of two substances—"extended" (all objects of the physical world, hence body) and "unextended" (not localized in space, hence mind)—and their interaction at the pineal body, generated the dualistic theory. Thus, mind can be considered as a distinct entity, apart from the body.[5]

Certainly another tenet of Cartesian philosophy that affected conceptualizatins of language was the postulation of innate ideas (e.g., God, self, conceptions of time, space, and motion).

Chomsky (1966) paraphrased Descartes to demonstrate Descartes's belief that language is a species-specific capacity, a specific human ability that is independent of intelligence. And, of course, with innate thoughts common to all men, everyone has something to talk about:

> It is a very remarkable fact that there are none so depraved and stupid, without even excepting idiots, that they cannot arrange different words together, forming of them a statement by which they make known their thoughts; while, on the other hand, there is no animal, however perfect and fotunately circumstanced it may be, which can do the same. (p. 4)

In Descartes's view, speech is not only the sign of thought, but proof of thought's existence. Descartes's remarks on language aimed to illustrate the distinctness of man as a thinking being and to establish the exemption of *res cogitans* from the mechanical laws regulating the extended world.

Despite Descartes's specification of speech as a test for humanity, it

---

[5] Margaret Wilson (1980) argues that an accurate understanding of Descartes's position leads one to the conclusion that he was not a mind–body dualist in the strict sense of that term.

fell to Geraud de Cordemoy, in his *Discours physique de la parole* (1668/1975), to offer a Cartesian analysis of human language in depth. Gaining something of the status of Cartesian orthodoxy despite various divergent expositions and conclusions, Cordemoy's works attempted to establish the congruity of the cartesian system with Christian dogma. In Cordemoy's belief, the surest sign of thought's presence is innovation—a process that displays both voice as it proceeds from the body and idea which emanates from the soul.

Locke

Locke [1632–1704] rejected the Cartesian notion of innate ideas, reasserting the Aristotelian conception of mind as a *tabula rasa*. However, he did accept a form of dualism in the mind–body postulation and went on to problems of how the mind comes to perceive the world. Locke found the relationship between ideas and words to be so close that a consideration of language became a necessary preliminary to the contemplation of knowledge (Locke, 1690/1924). The first condition of speech is a natural aptitude of the organism—a condition augmented in man by an ability to "use these words as signs of internal conceptions, and to make them stand as marks for the ideas within his own mind" (Locke, 1690/1924). The use of general terms to mark multitudes of individual experiences refines language and renders it manageable. Language arose out of the need to communicate, through external and sensible signs, ideas that are invisible. For Locke, there is no natural connection between particular articulate sounds and particular ideas—a view that he supports by noting that men do speak different languages, and, even in a common language, particular words possess various significances for different men.

Locke's theory posits that, if the human faculty for articulate expression is natural, the invention of names is conventional and arbitrary. Words originally were particular and were used to indicate individuals, only signifying notions of sensible things. General terms were gradually created to correspond to general ideas, and words which had their origin in sensible ideas were, by analogy and metaphor, transferred to spiritual notions.

Locke's influence on Condillac precipitated certain transformations in Locke's theory. Condillac "radicalized" Locke into a more consistent form of genetic sensationalism, one of the results of which was that the existence of human language as a complete entity awaiting man in the course of his development could not be taken for granted as it had been by Locke. Condillac, projecting Locke's epistemology onto a historical screen, used Locke's explanation of psychological development as a model for the historical progression of the race.

Condillac

In his *Essay on the Origin of Human Knowledge* and *Treatise on the Sensation,* Condillac [1715–1780] tries to show that all supposedly independent reflections are derivable as compositions from the data of sense—a view that is at odds with Locke's concession that not all experience is of a sensuous type. Ideas, for Condillac, are formed by a prereflective process or association requiring the use of signs. The reason that our attention focuses first on certain selected perceptions is that those perceptions are associated with our wants, all of which are interdependent and related. Thus, the connection of wants and desires produces association of ideas. But the mechanism of *liaison*—the "real cause of the progress of the imagination, contemplation, and memory"—is the use of signs that reinforce and preserve the association. These signs are the necessary precedent to human language and to the operation of reflection, because it is only at this point that the mind becomes aware of the complexity of its own operations.

Reflection and language reciprocally influence each other, leading to further progression of each and the emergence of more advanced mental faculties. In this schematism Condillac claimed to have given empiricism a more thorough going and consistent rationale than had been accomplished by Locke.

According to Condillac's theory, there is only one method, and that is the method of analysis. All thought consists in analyzing complex knowledge and extracting its simple elements and the relations between those elements. This seemingly paradoxical theory implies that what is unknown must be contained in what is known. Condillac's theory is not altogether paradoxical, however; it rests on his conception of science and of the processes of logic. We find what we do not know in what we do know, for the unknown is the known, because it is the same thing as the known. To proceed from the known to the unknown is therefore to go from the same to the same. Thought is merely a progress of expression.

For Condillac, a science is nothing more than a well-constructed language. In order for such a language to be useful, it must be simple, its signs must be precisely determined and defined, and the language must be formed in accord with the laws of analogy. "The whole art of reasoning, like the whole art of speaking, may be reduced to analogy"[6] (Condillac, 1746/1975).

The first language must have been a kind of chant, with violent inflections accompanying the action of the body. At first, language consisted only of interjections or cries in various notes according to the feelings being expressed. In the beginning, there were only the names of things; the first verbs expressed passive states of mind only. Like Locke, Condillac asserts that words expressing abstract or spiritual ideas originated in sensible ideas.

For Condillac language is not a purely arbitrary institution. The natural movements of the body provide the elements of the language of action, and the cry of passion provides the rudiments of speech. Man, impelled by need, speaks before he has willed to speak. Convention, therefore, only perfects and extends what nature has begun. Condillac believed that the elements of the language of action (i.e., the organs) were born with man. In this sense he believed that there was an innate language, but he strongly opposed the notion of innate ideas. Condillac (1809) puts the matter thus: "The language which I call innate is a language we have not learned, because it is the natural and immediate effect of our conversation. It says at once all we feel; it is therefore not an analytical method . . . it therefore affords no ideas."

Leibnitz

Leibnitz [1646–1716] maintains that words, originally, did not refer to individuals. For him, general terms would necessarily have been the first exponents of language, since it is as natural to employ general terms as it is to observe resemblances among things (Leibnitz, 1916). Moreover, Leibnitz accepts the theory of the arbitrary origin of speech only with reservation. He does maintain that some reason exists for words being what they are. He nevertheless admits the possibility that some languages are "artificial, dependent on choice, and entirely arbitrary."

Leibnitz envisioned a *"caracteristique universelle"* that would be a philosophical language analogous to the language of mathematics—a

---

[6]Humboldt's (1836/1972) contribution stressed the biological basis of language, but with an emphasis upon universality of behavior rather than individual difference (see Stam, 1977).

proposition that would call for a succinct determination of all elementary forms and a clear delineation of all the possible combinations of these rudimentary concepts. To these simple concepts and their combinations, absolute values would be applied, thus rendering a language of precise expression.

John Horne Tooke

Charles de Brosses and Antoine Court de Gébelin proposed that all vowels are interchangeable in matters of derivation; all labials are likewise similar, and so forth. Both men wrote voluminously on etymology, rendering up ultimately one original and sparsely worded language. De Brosses, the first to theorize that *fétichisme* was an important phase of pagan religion, hypothesized that the original language was formed as it had perforce to be formed under the influence of climate and the nature of speech organs. The differentiations of this *langue primordiale* owed their appearance to the changes in the vocal organs themselves and in the various climates into which speaking peoples wandered. Numerous writers took up the banner of de Brosses in France and in Germany, expanding particularly on language's accountability to climate. John Horne Tooke, in his Επεα πτεροεντα (*Diversions of Purley,* 1798), put forth a compilation of disquisitions on the importance of etymologies and innumerable derivations of individual words. Tooke believed that all linguistic progress had consisted of a tendency toward increased efficiency and atrophy of unnecessary parts. He also held that all parts of speech could be derived from original nouns and verbs. An extensive discussion of Tooke's theory of language can be found in Aarsleff (1967).

Nineteenth-Century Romantic Views

Comparative philology and the physiological theory of natural signs have engendered renewed interest in the study of language and its origins. The progress of these two theories has illustrated the inadequacy of eighteenth-century views.

The science of language delineated by Leibnitz led, by 1787, to the assertion of relationship among Sanskrit, Greek, and Latin by William Jones. In 1808, Frederick Schlegl, applying the comparative method, incorporated the languages of India, Persia, Greece, Italy, and Germany into the single category of Indo-Germanic languages. Francis Bopp, in

1816, published *System of conjugation of the Sanscrit tongue, compared with that of the Greek, Latin, Persian, and German,* a work identified as the first truly scientific comparison established between the grammars of the Indo-European languages. William Humboldt, Jacob Grimm, and Eugene Burnouf (*Studies on the Ancient Language of Persia*) completed the foundation of an experimental science of language, resulting in a genealogical classification of languages. The affiliation of languages being established, attention was turned to derivation—a process that was shown to be subject to definite and recognizable laws. By showing that languages are modified according to inevitable laws, comparative philology established that language is a natural product, subject to the laws of life.

Max Müller

Max Müller counts comparative philology among the natural sciences. Language has had a development rather than a history. "Although there is a continuous change in language, it is not in the power of any man either to produce it or to prevent it" (Müller, 1890).

Müller's theory may be substantially represented in two statements. In the first place, language is a product of nature; and secondly, man speaks by an instinct consisting of two steps—the formation of ideas and the creation of words to express them. This second thesis rests on the reduction by philosophical analysis of a language or family of languages to 400 or 500 abstract, general roots. M. Michel Breal has proved that these roots, however, cannot be regarded as constitutive elements of a first language, but are rather the remains of former substantives—originally concrete words—that have taken an abstract meaning while passing through the form of the verb.

Müller objected to evolutionary theory on the somewhat dubious basis that, if man's origins lie with some lower animal, it is futile to maintain man's distinctness from lower animals. He dismissed the matter of evolutionary transition by affirming that language is unique to humans.

William Dwight Whitney [1827–1894] attacked Müller, asserting that the latter absurdly concluded that thought and language are identical. Whitney charged that the alleged correlation between thought and language is useless unless the terms are clearly defined. The type of thought involved must be determined—whether simple mental processes, rational thought, or some less conventional type of thought. Despite his objections to Müller, Whitney did not commit himself to Darwinism or to any theory of the origin of language. While maintaining that linguistic meaning is conventionally established, he did not provide an answer to how the conventions themselves were established. In the end, he felt, the evolutionist has no contribution to make to linguistic theory.

Physiological Theory of Natural Signs

Physiology has explained the production and significance of natural signs. A gesture that expresses emotion, a sign, an expression, a facial change—each is the beginning of an action. If the face, for instance, by a particular contraction expresses a particular passion or appetite, it is because that contraction is precisely the mechanical condition necessary to satisfy that passion or appetite. This theory of Bell's was accepted and expanded by many others during the nineteenth century (see Darwin, 1873).

In his *Expression of the Emotions,* Darwin accepts Bell's principle that, because humans possessed no organs intended originally for expression, certain human movements became by long association signs of particular internal states. He goes on to account for the phenomena of expression through three principles: the principle of serviceable associative habits, the principle of antithesis, and the principle of involuntary—and to some extent nonhabitual—nervous actions.

According to the serviceable-habits principle, movements that are useful in satisfying a desire eventually emerge, after long association with the particular urging, as an independent reaction—although in a markedly less dramatic form. The somewhat hypothetical principle of antithesis provides that certain expressive movements have no other reason than an original and universal inclination to accompany a feeling with gestures contrary to those which would express an opposite feeling. The third principle—that of involuntary nervous action—is exemplified in the gestures of a furious man that may be attributed in part to an excess of nervous force and that often represent the action of striking.

Darwinian Theory

The main discussion of language in the works of Darwin was in a chapter in *The Descent of Man* (1871), in which he compares the mental powers of man and the lower animals. Here, as elsewhere, he proposed to show the genealogical links between species without obliterating specific differences. Agreeing that "the habitual use of articulate language" is peculiar to humans, Darwin goes on to qualify the statement by noting that not all human language is articulate, as in cases of human fear, surprise, and so forth. Moreover, although certain lower animals are capable of reacting to articulate speech or even of producing it to a limited extent, man is differentiated by his "almost infinitely larger power of associating the most diversified sounds and ideas."

To the extent that language is a *differentia specifica,* it is a difference of degree rather than of kind, and, as is the difficulty with all such gradualistic schemes, Darwin's final problem was to define the prior cause. He concluded that a reciprocal influence must have been in force between the development of a more efficient brain and the development of more articulate speech. Darwin also thought that the voice was first used as a means to entice and to ward off competition, and from this additional link between animal expression and human language, Darwin inferred that articulate language was preceded by music. In supporting this belief, Darwin drew heavily on the works of Herbert Spencer according to whom all nuances of the voice—loudness, quality, timbre, pitch, interval, rate of variation—are "the physiological results of variations and feeling."

Applications of the main outlines of Darwinian theory were soon made to the later and better known history of language. Sir Charles Lyell devoted a chapter of *The Antiquity of Man* to a demonstration of the law of gradual transmutation in the history of languages, and Ernst Haeckel reiterated these ideas. Frederic Bateman, who rejected evolution in *Darwinism Tested by Language* (1877), determined that material causes alone could explain neither linguistic competency nor speech failures, thus arguing the "immateriality of the faculty of speech."

Language and the Brain: The Brain's the Thing to Catch the Consciousness of the King

A group of eighteenth-century philosopher-psychologists known as *associationists*—named in accordance with their prolific writing about the "association of ideas," a phrase popularized by John Locke, and as a testimonial to their interest in the question of how simple ideas go together to form complex ones—gravitated in their studies toward the problem of how individuals learn. Their theories, with the exception of Locke's, attempted to integrate mind and body into one interrelated system. Such men as David Hartley (1749) and Erasmus Darwin (1796/1974) were extremely interested in speech and language, as well as in the normal and abnormal development of speech and language in the child.

The associationists described mental processes in terms of analysis, in light of the *law of congruity*. By this law, the basis of association was the observation that two objects, when they are perceived or thought of simultaneously or in close succession, become associated or linked together.

Hartley indicated that sensations (internal feelings stimulated by external events) are associated with simple brain states (vibrations), and ideas (internal feelings other than sensations) are also related to simple brain states. It was theorized that these bonds tie with the simple states into complex compounds. In terms of understanding language, Hartley believed that we arrive at an understanding of one another through the power of association, a process whereby simple sounds are associated into a whole (i.e., words, sentences, and so on). Hartley, who wrote about auditory images in relation to the development of speech and language in the child, believed that children learn to speak by repeating the sounds that stimulate the organism to respond. Speech disorders were interpreted in similar fashion as in the case of stuttering which, according to Hartley, develops from fear, eagerness, or a violent passion that prevents the child from using his speech mechanism correctly. The resulting confusion disrupts the vibrations traveling via neural pathways to the peripheral speech mechanism, thereby causing the individual to reiterate until he is successful. Hartley pointed out, however, that this problem would generally not develop until the child is of an age to distinguish right from wrong in the pronunciation of speech sounds. Hartley also felt that stuttering may develop from a "defect of memory from passion" and, in some cases, that it can be learned by imitation. He went on to point out that stuttering tends to spread or generalize to other words or situations. It is of interest to note that this basic phenomenon is still being explored by verbal learning theorists interested in the problem of stuttering. As Brett (1921) points out, Hartley had a strong influence on later scientists who studied language and its disorders.

Erasmus Darwin (1794/1974) was another associationist who was interested in language and its disorders. He believed that motions affecting the body might result from the following: *irritations* excited by external factors; *sensation* aroused by pleasure or pain; *volition* aroused by desire or aversion; or *associations* that could be linked with other movements.

He interpreted all disorders in terms of one or another of these processes and based his classification of diseases upon this frame of reference. Darwin's hope was that his classification would present a better understanding of the nature of illness or disease. Greatly influenced by Hartley, Darwin classified the problem of stuttering as a disease of volition, developing his theory around the idea that when the stutterer is very much preoccupied with an idea, the corresponding fear of failure is so great that the associations of the muscular motions of articulation become impaired. The stutterer then attempts in vain to gain voluntary control of these broken associations, resulting in a stuttering block that may then cause "various distortions of countenance."

The latter part of the eighteenth century and the early part of the nineteenth century saw the continuing integration of the findings of abnormal psychology with those of general psychology; in other words, the ancient relationship between physiology and pathology was now being applied to the study of the mind. This set the stage for the new "mental physiology" of the late nineteenth century. In the work of Spurtzheim and Combe, phrenology, too, became the model for the normal as well as the abnormal. These systems amount to what we might call a "divorce of convenience" or methodological monism; they deny neither mind nor body, but are centered on one or the other. Often pursued with lack of perspective, they prepared the way for the more radical monisms of extreme idealism and ultramaterialism.

The eighteenth-century faculty psychologists had placed their emphasis on the *universality* of the faculties operating on the human mind. This theme harmonized well with the drive of that age toward centralization and large-scale social and political structures which sought validity in a scientific notion of the "common man" and his capacities. Toward the end of the century, an increased interest in the individual became characteristic of a new philosophy—romanticism. A similar shift of interest took place in psychology as the study of faculties deemphasized what was common to all men and centered on the characteristics unique to each. An early prominent manifestation of this tendency was the new doctrine of phrenology instituted by Gall.

Gall's system postulated that localized physiological functions of the brain were responsible for the psychological strengths and weaknesses of the individual. These functions affected the growth of the skull and could be determined from a careful inventory of the skull's shape. Contemporary with Gall, Cabanis was doing much anatomical work in France to foster the notion of the brain as the organ of thought, from a materialist standpoint. Although not materialistic in a strict sense, phrenology obviously had a similar thrust deriving individual psychology from primarily physiological factors. What had formerly been a metaphysical category (i.e., faculty) was now an area of the brain. Phrenology was carried on after Gall's death by his colleague, Spurtzheim, by the brothers Combe in Edinburgh, and by Charles Caldwell and the Fowlers in the United States. Once Kant had raised psychology to a supreme position among the intellectual activities of man, subsequent psychological theories tended to invade every area of life with results that were often bizarre, but also often fruitful. Phrenology offered results of each variety.

As was bound to happen, phrenologists eventually applied themselves to the study of language and language disturbances, and there occurred almost unnoticed a "paradigm drift" of great importance. No longer was the focus on the static concept of pathology of the peripheral speech organ, as in Morgagni (1769); now we find the more dynamic concept of a process instituted by the brain, depending on a language faculty in the brain, and owing its weaknesses to an inadequate faculty of the brain.

Ironically, the experimental psychophysiology that stood diametrically opposed to Gall's conception of the functions of the brain and that reverted to the psychological tradition that he opposed derived its belief in cerebral localization from phrenology. Ferrier, in formulating his view of cerebral localization derived in part from phrenology, used three sources: Broca, Fritsch and Hitzig, and Hughlings Jackson. The views of Broca and Jackson, while not adhered to strictly by Ferrier, grew historically out of phrenology.

Broca's localization of a center for "the faculty of articulate language" was the first localization of a function in the hemisphere to meet with general acceptance from orthodox scientists. Even though Broca did not originate the modern doctrine of cerebral localization, it should be stressed that Broca was the first to confirm this long-suspected localization and to clarify it with clear-cut pathological evidence—although the quality of his original evidence was dubious. What Broca did contribute was a demonstration of this localization at a time when the scientific community was at last prepared to take the issue seriously.

By way of background to Broca's "discovery" and his first case, it should be noted that observations on diseases affecting speech were made as early as the Hippocratic corpus (ca. 400 B.C.), and descriptions of speech pathology are scattered throughout the history of medicine since that time. Accurate descriptions of motor aphasia were made at least as early as the end of the seventeenth century (see Benton & Joynt, 1960), but no important ideas about localization of the lesion had been advanced prior to 1800. Gall is usually credited with "the first complete description of aphasia due to a wound of the brain"—a claim based on the case of a young man who, as a result of a foil wound, was bereft of his memory of names.

While acknowledging that Gall did provide early descriptions of the symptoms of motor aphasia, it should be realized that his conception of the language faculty was hardly adequate from a contemporary point of view. He segregated apparent ability to understand questions from ability to speak voluntarily; he noted that ability to speak could be impaired while ability to move the tongue and pronounce isolated words remained intact; and he observed that ability to express ideas by gestures and to identify objects could remain intact while various modes of more formal expression are impaired.

Broca discussed in detail whether speech is an intellectual or motor function, and—though he considered the question an open one—he inclined to the former view. He believed that the pathological anatomy of aphemia[7] strongly supported the view that speech is an intellectual function. Two prevailing dogmas prevented Broca from regarding aphasia as a motor disturbance. While supporting cerebral localization, he could not believe that the cerebral convolutions were involved in motion; he considered those organs restricted to intellectual functions.

Broca had no doubt that speech was a separate faculty, the apparent discreteness of which rendered it ideal for testing the question of cerebral localization. In a report to the Société Anatomique de Paris dealing with the case of a patient, "Tan," Broca's description provided excellent data for consideration of the problems of the clinico-pathological method. The patient's history of aphemia, complicated by numerous progressive conditions, would disqualify him from modern clinico-pathological studies, but Broca was prepared to infer at autopsy that the lesion began at the third left frontal convolution—an inference he made in spite of extensive dam-

[7]Broca used the term *aphemia* for *aphasia*.

age throughout the entire hemisphere. Broca's inference was later considered highly speculative.

The same year, Broca presented a second case, basing his conclusions on a strictly limited lesion without complications. By 1863 Broca and his colleagues had collected 20 cases showing some pathological change in the left half of the brain, 19 of them in the third frontal convolution. No exact location of the cortical center was given.

Broca's major contribution was to establish that pathological data support the belief in some form of localized brain function. Hughlings Jackson recognized the impact of Broca's work and agreed with Broca that "Broca's area" was the part of the brain most often damaged in patients suffering from aphasia. However, he pointed out the danger of the trend of claiming exact localized centers. Jackson's own words described this best: "To locate the damage which destroys speech and to locate speech are two different things."

Working in the tradition of Jackson, an early twentieth-century Czechoslovakian, Arnold Pick, believed, as did Jackson, in the necessity of total cortical integration for the production of language (see Jason Brown's [1973] translation of one of Pick's important works).

Perhaps the single most important contribution to the study of language and brain mechanism was made in the work of Kurt Goldstein (1948). Goldstein, using concepts based upon Gestalt psychology, believed that "to every mental performance, there corresponds a dynamic process which concerns the entire cortex. The function of a specific region is characterized by the influence which the particular structure of that region exerts on the total process."

Current work in the neuropsychology of language continues to explore such problems as lateralization of brain function and related problems—see Rieber, *The Neuropsychology of Language* (1976). It is important to note that Marshall, writing in 1977, specifies the goal of neurolinguistic research in a way not much different than those authors cited above. This goal is "to understand the form of representation of language in the human brain." Marshall goes on to say that

> an adequate theory might be expected to pair an information processing amount of psycholinguistic functions with a detailed statement of the physiological realization of those functions in terms of neuronal circuitry (and whatever non-neural principles of electrochemical pattern formation that may be found appropriate to the description of central nervous system states). (Morton & Marshall, 1977, p. 127)

Communication and Its Pathology: Can Humpty Dumpty Be Put Back Together Again?

The pathology of speech and language has two important functions. First, it is important to the psycholinguist who is concerned with setting up and validating a fruitful theory of language and thought. Second, it specifies boundary conditions that may impose constraints on the form of both competency and performance and their mode of interaction.[8]

The state of the congenitally deaf is particularly interesting. A congenitally deaf person does not learn to speak by the processes available to normal children. It is necessary to ask what is the nature of the defect that leads to this state of affairs and what, if anything, can be done to remedy it. These questions, significant in the seventeenth and eighteenth centuries, continue to be relevant even today. The answer to the first question seems rather obvious: the congenitally deaf person does not learn to speak because he cannot hear the language being spoken around him. In the period under consideration, however, it is clear from the arguments that were advanced that this answer was not at all obvious to the majority of academicians. The solution that is obvious to us today contradicted explicit statements on the subject by Aristotle, whose influence will be briefly discussed shortly.

The answer to the second question is still interesting today because the question itself is still relevant. For the psycholinguist, the implications of any specific answers may be far-reaching with regard to the deaf person's own remedy (i.e., a sign language).

The Context of the Period

The two leading figures of this period were Francis Bacon [1561–1626], whose major works *The Advancement of Learning* (1605) and *De Augmentis Scientarium* (1622–1623) had a great influence on all the authors discussed here; and René Descartes [1596–1650], who is mentioned with suspicious infrequency but whose *Discours de la Méthode* (1637)

---

[8]Bever (1975) argues against the use of pathological data for the purpose of gaining knowledge about the normal process of language development. His polemical argument fails to appreciate that normal and abnormal communication are two sides of the same coin. Only an understanding of both facets facilitates understanding of the whole. This position is supported by Furth (1975), Morton and Marshall (1977), and others.

and *Mediationes de Prima Philosophia* (1640) were surely known in England.

Although there is no explicit reference anywhere, there is evidence for the influence of the Port Royal logic and grammar in England at this time. Wilkins in his *Essay* (1668) establishes a rather unusual system for the parts of speech in which lexical items are divided into "integrals" and "particles." The former category includes only the noun (i.e., substantive and adjective) and the "adverb derived." The latter category includes the verb and everything else (Wilkins, 1668, p. 298). On the verb, Wilkins (1668, p. 303) says that it "is really no other than an adjective, and the copula sum affixed to it or contained in it."

Funke (1965, p. 83) considers that "[this] point of view seems quite unique, and among those authorities whom Wilkins mentions we find it nowhere." While this point may be true, Wilkins may have been influenced by Dalgarno (1661, pp. 63–64), who had presented a similar scheme. The scheme becomes even less unique when we note that it can also be found in the Port Royal Grammar of 1660. Kenelm Digby, who was a follower of Descartes and a founder and member of the Royal Society, provides a link with Cartesian philosophy that needs further investigation.

Applied Psycholinguistics at the Royal Society. The rise of the experimental sciences was one of the major events of the period, clearly marking it off from the Middle Ages. The universities, as institutions, opposed any backsliding from the prevailing respect for Aristotle and his commentators. This led indirectly to the formation of the great scientific societies where academicians and amateurs alike could carry out experiments and discuss their results with people of like mind. It is surely no coincidence that two of the many authors to be discussed here, Holder and Wallis, were members of the Royal Society and another, Dalgarno, was closely associated with its founder-members. The interest in experiments extended to the attempt to teach articulation and lipreading to a deaf-mute. Holder and Wallis both published accounts of their work with the deaf in the early numbers of the *Philosophical Transactions of the Royal Society,* which first appeared in 1665.

Interest in linguistics and languages grew rapidly in the seventeenth century. The abstract study of grammar was taken up again where the medieval philosophers had left off. On the one hand, it produced such works as the Port Royal grammar. On the other hand, it attempted to design a universal philosophical language to replace Latin and to reflect more closely the "true" structure of the world. The information explosion and the need to communicate quickly and precisely on scientific topics were probably an important spur. The skepticism about language in its role as a deceiver can be traced directly to the works of Bacon.

Large polyglot dictionaries began to appear in the sixteenth century, containing usually five or six European languages. At the same time, grammars and tutors were written in English for such foreign languages as Dutch, French, Italian (1550), and Spanish for publication in England. Grammars of the vernacular also appeared that explicitly rejected the Latin model, such as Wallis's grammar (1653) (see Kemp, 1972). The modern science of phonetics can certainly trace its origins directly back to this period, and no doubt some of the trend systematization was a result of the study of new languages.

Moves toward spelling reform (by Bullokar, Gil, Hart, and Smith in England), which should be associated with such diverse events as the invention of printing and the need for a standard language consequent upon the rise of the national states, led to important work on phonetics and pronunciation. This was continued in the seventeenth century, when more works on general phonetics—such as those by Wallis (1653), Wilkins (1668), and Lodwick—and works on phonetics in the service of the deaf and dumb—such as those by Bonet, Holder, and Amman[9]—began to appear. Other books are those by Cordemoy (1668) and van Helmont (1667), but these do not really achieve as much as they claim. At this period, a rough test of the quality of a phonetician can be made by examining how he understands the nature of the voicing contrast (insofar as it is understood, even today), the function of the velum, and whether he notices the existence of, and correctly describes [ŋ], the velar nasal.

An exhaustive study of phonetics for this period is not possible here; however, additional information can be found in Dobson (1957) and Griffith (1953).

There are certainly other factors that should be considered, such as the growing interest in educational reform, and the progress made in medicine typified by Harvey's *Exercitatio anatomica de motu cordis et sanguinis in animalibus* (1628). Harvey was a student of Fabricius, professor of anatomy at Padua. The value of experiment and of the reexam-

---

[9]See reprint in English translation of this book (Amman, 1965) with an introduction by R. W. Rieber.

ination of old medical dogmas was first grasped in Italy, and from there comes the earliest note on the educability of the deaf. Above all, it is impossible to exaggerate the curiosity of men who were freeing themsevles to look at anything whatsoever that the exercise of observation, reason, and interaction might serve to illuminate or render useful. There can be no doubt that this attitude benefited at least a few deaf individuals and led ultimately to the systematic institutional training that gradually developed during the eighteenth and nineteenth centuries.

The Teaching of Speech and Language to the Deaf

> Why is it that of all the senses hearing is most liable to be defective from birth? Now language, which is a kind of voice, seems to be very easily destroyed and to be very difficult to perfect; this is indicated by the fact that we are dumb for a long time after our birth, for at first we simply do not talk at all and then at length begin only to lisp. And because language is easily destroyed, and language (being a kind of voice) and hearing both have the same source, hearing is, as it were, per accidens, thought not per se, the most easily destroyed of the senses. (Aristotle, *Problemata* XI, 1)

This short and ambiguous statement is essential to an understanding of much of the seventeenth-century discussion on the deaf. Even though it may seem superfluous nowadays, it sums up almost universally accepted beliefs at a time when Aristotle's word was law. Nobody questioned Aristotle and, because he said that the deaf could never speak or learn language, nobody tried to teach them. Because it was believed that speech was a manifestation of reason, it followed that the deaf were considered to have no ability to reason and were assigned the status of idiots.

It was not realized that the congenitally deaf person could, in most cases, not speak simply because he could not hear what people around him were saying. The chain of causation had been wrongly apprehended. If any attempts at alleviation were made, Aristotle's point of view prevailed.

The earliest major policy statement that ran counter to Aristotle's opinion and also came from a respected and famous authority is to be found in Cardano's *Paraliopomena de humanis civilibus successionibus,* Lib. III, Cap. VIII, entitled "De surdo et muta literas edocto," where it is stated that the deaf can learn to hear by reading and to speak by writing. In another work, *De utilitate ex adversis capienda,* Lib. II, Cap. VII, "De surditate" (Cardan Tom. II, pp. 73–76), Cardano describes three classes of deaf people and suggests that they should be taught to read and write to alleviate their misery. There is no mention of Aristotle. There is no attempt to validate his position apart from a reference to a story of this having already been done successfully. However, Cardano [1501–1576] was a widely read and influential sixteenth-century authority.

The first moderately well-substantiated report of the actual teaching of deaf-mutes comes from Pedro de Ponce of Spain, who died in 1584, and in a book by Francisco de Valles, which appeared in 1587. Both of these works represent an advance on Cardano's suggestions, for the students are taught to articulate. It is not known whether Ponce wrote anything on his method, but it is most likely that it did lead to the first book on the teaching of the deaf, written by Juan Pablo Bonet and published in Madrid in 1620. It does not appear that this book was known in England. However, Kenelm Digby [1603–1665] seems to have witnessed the results of Bonet's labors, probably when he visited Spain in 1622.

It had become clear that the deaf could be taught to speak. The Spanish were successful in their attempts, and the English, particularly John Bulwer, were having an equal amount of good fortune. Nothing is known of Bulwer, except that he was a physician and the author of several books, two of which were published in 1648: *Chirologia: or the Naturall Language of the Hand* and *Philocophus: or the deafe and Dumbe Man's Friend.* Bulwer should be considered the originator of the art of instructing the deaf and dumb in England. However original his work may have been, he was acquainted with some of the research done by the Spanish Benedictine monks Pedro Ponce and Juan Pablo Bonet. He had certainly heard of the case, reported from Spain by Sir Kenelm Digby, of the young boy who was taught to hear, not by listening, but by watching. The second half of his book consists of an analysis of Digby's story.

Bulwer felt that sign language was an efficient means of communication because the hand has a "discoursing facultie" that gave the deaf and dumb the ability to communicate. They can argue rhetorically by using signs. It was clear to him that signs were a perfectly adequate form of communication.

The first 13 chapters of *Philocophus* deal with articulation, interspersed with some rather weak philosophizing on the connection between voluntary actions and motion. Bulwer's knowledge of phonetics was quite limited. Some of the chapter headings give the direction of his point of view: "Of the convenience and excellent situation of the Mouth for the more visible appearance and manifestation of Speech"; "That Words are nothing else but Motion"; "That the formes of Letters, and so

consequently of Words, may be punctually observed and took notice of'';
"That the motions of the parts of the mouth in Speech are so remarkable,
that some have (not without success) attempted to imitate them by
mathematicall motions"; and finally, the conclusion: "That Articulate
Speech doth not necessarily require the audible sound of the voyce, but
may consist without it, and so consequently be seen as well as heard."
These titles outline Bulwer's argument on the feasibility of lipreading.

Voice production is explained by analogy with a pipe and he attempts
to explain the distinction between, for instance, [p], [b], and [m] by means
of varying degrees of impulsion of the air.

One other statement in the first part of Bulwer's book is of interest:

> Many of the learned are of opinion, and persuaded in their judgments, that the
> imitation of the motions of our speech may be effected by insensible creatures;
> if a Dextrous man would employ his time in contriving and making such an
> instrument to express those different sounds; _____ not having more than
> seven substantiall Differences; besides, the Vowells (as some who have care-
> fully noted them doe affirme) it would peradventure be no hard matter to
> compose such an Engine.

Compare Cordemoy, writing in 1668: "I conceive likewise, as I have
already said, that Art may go so far as to frame an Engine, that shall
articulate words like those, which I pronounce; but then I conceive at the
same, that it would only pronounce those, that were design'd it should
pronounce, and that it would always pronounce them in the same order."
The idea of a machine was prominent in certain parts of Cartesian philosophy and perhaps this was Bulwer's source.[10] It may also have been taken
from Baptista Porta whom he mentioned in this connection.

Having once established in this way that lipreading is a theoretical
possibility and having given various anecdotes about people who were
able to lipread, Bulwer presents Digby's story and carefully analyzes it.

Bulwer understood that speech represents thought and that writing
represents speech. He indicated that a deaf person could not learn to
speak because he could never imitate or understand his interlocutors.
Substantiation for his case came from the fact that people who became
deaf from illness did not as a consequence become mute and those that
became mute from illness did not grow deaf.

He further argued against a "natural" theory of language because the

---

[10]See John Bulwer, *Chirologia: or the Natural Language of the Hand* (London, 1644), with
an introduction by H. R. Gillis; reprinted in *Language, Man, and Society Series* (R. W.
Rieber, ed. A.M.S. Press, 1975).

congenitally deaf cannot speak at all. It was not conceivable to Bulwer that this alleged natural language was merely being suppressed. Man is made to learn to speak, much as he learns any of the arts and sciences. Wilkins even claimed in 1641 that man is equally disposed to learn any language in which he may be instructed. The manner in which children acquire language was a source of academic fascination for Bulwer. He could only conceive that children learned to speak by imitation yet also noted the weakness of such a theory.

Bulwer's books were, on the whole, discursive, derivative, and not necessarily consistent, yet they must have stimulated interest in England. His work is also noteworthy for the fact that he recommended the establishment of academies for the deaf. It contains a clear rejection of Aristotle's views and recommends lipreading as the remedy for the disability of the deaf-mute.

John Wallis was a mathematician and cryptographer; he invented the word "interpolation" in mathematics and the symbol ∞ for infinity. He was also a founder-member of the Royal Society and the author of the first grammar of the English language that consciously departed from Latin models. Prefixed to this grammar there is a *Tractatus prooemialis loquela, sine literarum omnium formatione et genuino sono* (Wallis, 1653, pp. 1–37), which he incorrectly claims is the first general treatise on the formation of spoken sounds. Wallis did not write a book on the teaching of the deaf, but refers back to this treatise in subsequent letters. It is, therefore, worth examining—at least his treatment of consonants—because he was certainly one of the first in England to achieve substantial results.

Wallis identified [ŋ], correctly describes it, and gives a number of minimal contrasts with [n]. He correctly analyzes [ʃ], [tʃ], and [dʒ] as composite sounds, but incorrectly describes them as [sy], [ty], and [dj], respectively. He was corrected by Amman, an important teacher of the deaf, in a letter prefixed to his *Dissertation on Speech,* first printed in 1700 in Amsterdam.

Wallis reported on his efforts at teaching the deaf and dumb to speak in three letters: to Boyle in 1670, to Brouncker in 1678, and to Beverly in 1698. In the first of these letters, actually written in March of 1661, Wallis describes his experiences in teaching Daniel Whaley to speak. Whaley, however, was not congenitally deaf; he had suffered an accident at age 5 that cost him his ability to hear and, consequently, his ability to speak. His loss of speech occurred gradually over a period of 6 months. Wallis was affirmed in his belief that the ability to speak followed the ability to hear. The loss of the latter then led to the loss of the former. Speech was not dissipated because of some inability of the organs of speech to produce sounds (i.e., Whaley's muteness was not physical). Thus, in one sense, Wallis had an ideal subject for experiment, because it was known that he was not congenitally dumb. However, the boy was in no sense a *tabula rasa*: by the age of 5 he spoke quite well. Because it is not impossible that his lack of speech did not indicate that he had "forgotten" his language, Wallis's success with Daniel Whaley was by no means a demonstration that he had succeeded in the second part of his task, namely, that of teaching him to understand a language. Wallis himself understood this; the ability to speak does not necessarily signal the ability to understand. A parrot can imitate but that is no indication that it comprehends.

He first discusses the difficulties of teaching "Understanding" (which appears to include syntax and morphology) and compares the difficulties of first- and second-language learning. His opinions are surprising, because he championed the liberation of the grammar of the vernacular from that of Latin. He felt that languages did not differ very much. Because of that, in second-language learning the teacher could use the mother tongue to explain problems in the target language. But because at some level, languages are relatively the same, the student already knows much of what he needs to learn. Nor will those universal aspects of language need to be taught in first-language learning. Deafness, however, makes this latter task more difficult to achieve. Wallis's discussion clearly reflects contemporary discussions of universal grammar.

There still remained the problem of speaking, i.e., the description of articulation. How could one teach sounds when the only language available was signing? Wallis believed that the organs of speech could be taught the proper places and manners of articulation even though these could not be seen or heard. He erred, however, by not discriminating between the congenitally deaf and those who become deaf at a later age. The latter retain their language and ability to speak. Cardano and Bulwer knew this; Wallis did not.

In *De Loquela* (1653), Wallis puts forth his methodology. By using signs, he sought to make the deaf student understand how to use the speech organs to produce sounds. If the student proceeded correctly, he would be commended; if he went about it incorrectly, he would be shown the right way to do it. Wallis was skeptical about lipreading. He believed it was necessary to master oral language first before this skill could be adequately taught. With this knowledge, linguistic redundancy and the linguistic context would facilitate learning to read lips.

After two months, Whaley had progressed so far that Wallis (1653) could claim: "There is hardly any Word, which (with Deliberation) he cannot speak [p. 40]." He was presented before the Royal Society in May of 1662 and performed much to the credit of his tutor.

The second letter (Wallis, 1678) is mainly an attempt to dismiss William Holder's priority claim, which will be discussed later. It also contains some of Wallis's most impressive observations with regard to Wilkins's discussion in his *Essay* (Wilkins, 1668). Wallis disagrees with Wilkins's treatment of the voiced-voiceless opposition, in a passage that foreshadows the clear recognition of suprasegmentals. Wilkins had treated whispering as a different kind of articulation, but Wallis ascribes it to the domain of "the whole Tenor of Speech." Included in that category are tone, time, timbre, and pitch. The difference between normal talking and whispering, then, is one of stridence not articulation. There is no need to use different phonetic symbols to characterize the two modes of speech. "Much less is this (as he makes it) the difference between V, F, or D, T, or B, P, &c. that the one is (in this Sense) Sonorous, the other Mute. For we may whisper the words, Ved, Bed, without saying Fet, Pet (Wallis, 1678, p. 18)." This is a very sound observation, but he still maintained one mistaken idea—that the difference between F and V lies "[not in the Lips, nor in the Larynx, but] in the Nostrils."

Wallis then goes on to describe what is characterized today as a difference between distinctive and nondistinctive features. He claims that Wilkins identified sounds using all the features available, not just the ones essential to the designation. With his background in mathematics, Wallis was accustomed to using only those features which were absolutely necessary to form definitions. It was the late nineteenth century before such an examination was tried again. This was probably a consequence of the fact that the study of language slipped out of the grasp of mathematicians and philosophers and into that of those interested in the history of man.

Wallis's third letter (Wallis, 1698) mentions Alexander Popham, the pupil who had occasioned the dispute with Holder. Popham had been Wallis's student about 35 years before and had learned to speak distinctly and understand a language (Wallis feared that Popham may have lost his new ability to speak, however). He also noted that there were some deaf persons whom he did not teach to speak, only to understand and to write.

This decline in amibtion is due in part to disillusionment or skepticism. At this point Wallis felt that one needs to hear himself speak in order to fully appreciate the beauty of the language he may produce.

As for writing, Wallis felt that this was just as necessary an ability as speaking. He suggests that the pupil should learn a finger alphabet [these were already known at that time Wilkins (1641, p. 59) describes a simple one] and then he taught as any child is taught his first language. He did note one difference, however: children learn sounds by the ear but deaf people learn to sign by the eye. But both of these equally signify the same things or motions and are equally arbitrary. He closes his letter with word lists as an aid to teaching English grammar.

Wallis's importance here is less as a creative phonetician than as a teacher with practical experience. He explained clearly, if in less detail than one would wish for and expect from an experimental scientist, what his aims and methods were. There is little other evidence that is so valuable (Bonet may provide some) because in England only William Holder had any practical experience and he was interested only in explaining the teaching of articulation.

William Holder was an English phonetician, music theorist, composer, mathematician, and divine. Holder was born in Nottinghamshire in 1616. Matriculating as a scholar of Pembroke Hall, Cambridge, on July 4, 1633, Holder was elected a fellow of his college and received the M.A. in 1640. About 1642 he became rector of Bletchington, Oxfordshire, and on March 21, 1643 was incorporated M.A. at Oxford. Collated by Bishop Matthew Wren to the third prebendal stall in Ely Cathedral on June 25, 1652, Holder was not actually installed until September 1660 due to the policies of the Cromwell Protectorate. In that same year of the Restoration, he received the Doctor of Divinity degree from Oxford, and on January 27, 1662 was presented by Bishop Wren to the rectory of Northwold in Norfolk and to that of Tidd St. Giles, Isle of Ely.

On May 20, 1663, Holder was elected Fellow of the Royal Society and in May of 1668 published "An Experiment Concerning Deafness" in the *Philosophical Transactions* (*3*, 665–668). Here Holder described the method he had employed in teaching the deaf Alexander Popham to speak. Unfortunately, Popham later relapsed into dumbness and was subsequently instructed by Dr. John Wallis, whom we have already discussed.

The dates are important, for what was at stake was the honor of having been the first man in England to teach a deaf person to speak.

There was no denying that Wallis had been successful with Daniel Whaley in the early 1660s. As noted, Wallis exhibited Whaley before Charles II, Prince Rupert, and the Royal Society. But when Popham afterwards came to him, Wallis belittled Holder's prior claim. Holder defended himself in *A Supplement to the Philosophical Transaction of July 1670, with Some Reflexions on Dr. John Wallis, his Letter there Inserted* (London, 1678), only to be counterattacked by Wallis in *A Defense of the Royal Society and the Philosophical Transactions . . . in Answer to the Cavils of Dr. William Holder* (London, 1678).

The *Elements of Speech* was published when Holder was 53 years old. His work on phonetics had actually begun when he undertook to teach a deaf child to speak. The connection between phonological theory and its application in teaching speech to the deaf, as well as teaching English as a second language, is a very important one, and will be developed later on.

Holder (1669) begins his *Elements* by making it clear that no other form of language but the spoken form is "natural." He states that by studying the "natural alphabet" we may discover the basic inadequacies of all other forms of communication. "Letters," or phonemes, as we would describe them today, were thought to be the most natural elements of communication. Holder was clearly writing in the tradition developed by Wilkins in his *Mercury,* as well as his *Essay towards a Real Character.* It was the belief of Holder and many of his contemporaries that the best and perhaps only way in scientific inquiry was the "natural way." This way of nature, as it were, assumed that there were phonological as well as linguistic universals.

These universals were assumed to be readily discernible through observation and experimentation. Holder began his theory by describing the organs of speech, which he divided into two classes: organs of the natural parts of letters, and organs of the formal part of letters. The former are the lungs, trachea, and larynx (pulmonary and phonotory mechanisms) and the uvula, which directs the air to either the nose or the mouth (resonance). The latter are the tongue, hard palate, lips, etc. (articulatory mechanisms). He clearly distinguised between voiced and voiceless sounds, and his description of the consonants bears close resemblance to that of Wilkins.

As for teaching articulation to the deaf, Holder points out that lipreading is limited in scope, but by analogy with the recognition of the voicing contrast in whispered speech (when it is in fact neutralized), he shows (as Wallis did) that context is a sufficient guide to make success possible. This is almost identical to what Wallis says. It is suggested that a model of the tongue and upper jaw might be made to show the articulation of [k] and [g]. After the pronunciation of the letters has been learned, the alphabet is to be taught, followed by a finger alphabet. The pronunciation of monosyllables with increasingly complex initial and final clusters, including some, such as [dla], [dna], [gna], [sdna], which do not exist in English, is suggested as good practice, to be followed by the practicing of actual words.

Holder is obviously a very important figure in the history of psycholinguistics and communication disorders. In his emphasis on articulation as a primary feature of human symbolic activity, and his attempt to work out possible articulations irrespective of their use in language, he was well ahead of his contemporaries in England.

George Dalgarno, another phonetician, was acquainted with Wallis and Wilkins. More often he was treated as one from whom to borrow ideas but not to be mentioned as their source. His treatise *Didascalocophus or the Deaf and Dumb Man's Tutor* (Dalgarno, 1680) is perhaps the most difficult of the works discussed here, chiefly because of its style, but it is also interesting and systematic.

The introduction gives several definitions. *Interpretation* is defined as an act of cognitive power, expressing the inward motions by outward and sensible signs. He lists three kinds of interpretations: supernatural, natural, and artificial or institutional, to which he gives the names of *Chrematology, Physiology,* and *Sematology.* Sematology was a general name for all interpretation by arbitrary signs. This was further divided into the three senses of hearing, seeing, and touching; he labeled the respective aspects of interpretation *pneumatology, schematology,* and *haptology.* These, too, are subdivided into *glossology,* a branch of pneumatology where the sound source is the tongue; *typology,* or *grammatology,* a branch of schematology involving the "impressing of permanent figures upon solid and consisting matter"; and *cheirology* or *dactylology,* where communication takes place "by the transient motions of the fingers."

Dalgarno's main argument is that the principal senses are exactly equivalent in interpretive ability. He bolsters this by a repeated comparison of the capabilities of the blind and the deaf. He is almost diametrically opposed to a natural language theory or an innate hypothesis. He felt that man entered the world *tabula rasa,* ready to have a myriad of different images stamped on his being. The daily experience of blind people gave him evidence of the individual ability of the ear and tongue to advance man's knowledge. An equal degree of knowledge is attainable by the eye and expressible by signing. All signs, whether written or vocal, are equally arbitrary. There is no reason why sounds should better represent an idea than hand characters. Neither is naturally symbolic of anything.

He felt that it is probably just as simple for the deaf child to connect a sign and its reference as it is for a blind child to connect a sound and its reference. The eye is intimately concerned in language learning for, when discussing whether manual signs could be easily remembered, he pointed out that transient motions can make as much of an impression on memory as immovable objects do. As proof, he offered the fact that hearing children learn a language although the movement of the tongue is transient. Signs, however, are much more readily visible.

In a rather strange conceptual experiment, we must imagine two 7-year-old boys, one deaf, one blind, both of whom can write. Both boys are taught the acquisition of a language, the blind boy, Latin, and the deaf boy, his mother's tongue. Their probable progress is estimated and compared. The deaf should have no language and the blind a mother tongue. This should give the blind boy an advantage. If writing has already been learned, then this is hardly an acceptable assumption, and Dalgarno's argument is fallacious.

Dalgarno felt it was neither impossible nor difficult to teach a blind man to write or a deaf man to speak. Teaching the suprasegmentals of speech would be hard, however. There may be simpler characters for writing to teach the blind man and there may also be easier sounds to pronounce for the deaf. He proposed that a blind man and a mute person might communicate by means of an elementary form of a reading machine.

Skepticism of lipreading was characteristic of Dalgarno, too. If lipreading and hearing were of equal value, then a deaf person and a mute person should be equally capable of understanding. But the deaf cannot learn a language as well as the mute. Therefore, not all distinctions of sound can be made in reading lips. He must conclude that the ear has certain advantages in language acquisition that the eye does not because a blind man learns to speak by listening, but a deaf man cannot learn so well by seeing. At any rate, lipreading must be complemented by context and redundancy.

In order to teach a deaf man to read and write, there are two basic ingredients: diligence and slates. A deaf man's dictionary should be ordered in three different ways: first, alphabetically; second, following the order of double consonants at both the beginning and ends of words; and third, reducing it to several classes of objects.

Dalgarno's finger alphabet is two-handed. Letters are mapped on the left hand and pointed to by the right. In order to abbreviate clusters, one may point to all the single letters of the double or triple consonant. This should not be confusing, because there is no English word where the order of double consonants is inverted in the beginning of a syllable or the end of a word. He realizes the necessity of, but makes no proposals for, a one-handed alphabet.

Much more progress was made later on in the field of language pathology. The last several scholars whom we have discussed became liberated from the early Aristotelian dogma. As should be expected, later researchers working within new and different paradigms were able to shed more light on this topic.

Dennis Diderot [1713–1784] was an eminent French philosopher, whose *Letter on the Deaf and Dumb* appeared in 1751. It was no particular interest in the problems of deaf people that prompted Diderot to write this book but rather a desire to better understand how ordinary individuals develop knowledge about things in the real world, through an analysis of language and its natural development, as well as a communication disorder known as deafness.

Diderot's *Letter* begins with the linguistic problem of inversions but ranges widely over such topics as the origin and historical development of language, epistemology, rhetoric, and so on.

Through the example of an imaginary deaf person, Diderot attempts to determine the relationship between thought and language. The deaf person represents a hypothetical prelinguistic society. Here Diderot (1751/1975) seems to anticipate modern Gestalt psychology:

> Mind is a moving scene, which we are perpetually copying. We spend a great deal of time in rendering it faithfully; but the original exists as a complete whole, for the mind does not proceed step by step, like expression. The brush takes time to represent what the artist's eye sees in an instant. (p. 56)

This statement is as provocative today as it must have been at the time it was written. Neisser (1967) has suggested that the Gestalt school of psychology is the most direct ancestor of current psycholinguistics. Others who follow the Chomskian point of view suggest Wundt, because of Wundt's emphasis upon the sentence as the basic unit of analysis. Those who think in terms of verbal behavior would probably not agree with Blumenthal (1970) but would name Watson as the most likely candidate. No doubt all the nominees have played an important part, one way or another, in setting the stage for the currently accepted version of the psychology of language.

Diderot, however, did not compromise any of his convictions regarding the psycholinguistic nature of man. He consistently assumed knowledge to be completely dependent upon the senses and, more specifically, to the number of senses actually operating. As an interacting hypothetical experiment he imagines a society made up of five persons, each having only one of the five senses; and he comes to the conclusion that each person in this society would have a view of the world determined by his own sensory modality and that each individual would relate to the others as being senseless. This new and more innovative psychology was quite different from the older, more absolute way of approaching the problem.

During the latter part of the eighteenth century, scholars continued to struggle with this important issue. Two other men (briefly mentioned earlier) are worth mentioning again before we go on to the next century: Erasmus Darwin and John Horne Tooke. Darwin's two most important works in the area of language and thought are *Zoönomia* (1794–1796) and the *The Temple of Nature* (1803). The first was Darwin's best-received work; the second, containing among other things his theory of evolution and theory of languages, was not well appreciated in his time. Darwin (1774/1974) points out carefully that "Mr. Tooke observes that the first aim of Language was to communicate thoughts, and the second to do it with dispatch, and hence he divides words into those which were necessary to express our thoughts, and those which are observations of the former." As T. Verhave points out, Darwin's psychology is a variant of eighteenth-century association theory and is, in part, a restatement of views stated by David Hartley in his *Observations on Man* (1749). Rieber and Froeschels (1966) discussed Darwin's theory of stuttering, also deriving from the theory of association. This is very similar to Mendelssohn's (1783) viewpoint, which in turn was apparently influenced by a paper written by Spalding, in the Magazine *Erfahrungsseelenkunde,* an introspective report of a case of transitory sensory motor aphasia.

We now move to the latter part of the nineteenth century. Here we shall be concerned with the work of Wilhelm Preyer [1841–1897], a German professor of physiology at the University of Jena. Preyer, although not well known today, was quite influential during the late nineteenth century. His pioneering work helped to establish the field of developmental psychology, and he also wrote significant works on hypnosis and neurophysiology. His most important work, *Die Seele des Kindes* (1881), has recently been reprinted by Arno Press in English (*The Mind of the Child*), unfortunately without an introduction.

Originally written in Germany, *Die Seele des Kindes* was translated into many other languages, including English. It had a direct influence upon two of the most influential psychological theorists of our time, Jean Piaget and Sigmund Freud. Freud rarely quoted other writers, but it has been possible to establish the fact that he was familiar with Preyer's works; indeed, Freud was under the influence of Preyer's ideas when he established as part of his theoretical system (1) the notion of *the study of abnormal development,* and (2) *the value of using stages of development as a better means of understanding the psychological growth pattern of the child.*

Freud, of course, stressed the affective, psychosexual aspect of maturation, whereas Preyer gave emphasis to the cognitive and conative. Preyer devotes the second volume of his book almost exclusively to the linguistic and cognitive development of the child. A whole chapter deals with speech and language disturbances in adults, particularly aphasia. He then draws a parallel to speech and language disturbances in childhood.

Interest in the problem of the relationship between language and thought was quite strong in the 1880s and 1890s. Max Müller was the major advocate of the notion that thinking was not possible without language. The polemics on this issue were about as bad as the polemics of the last decade regarding competence and performance. Müller, a professor of linguistics (philology) at Oxford, engaged in active debate, mainly through the journal *Nature,* with such prominent psychologists as Sir Francis Galton and George Romanes.

Galton vehemently denied Müller's contentions, arguing that a careful study of congenitally deaf individuals would prove him wrong. But Galton never carried out the study himself, and it was not until the twentieth century that experimental cognitive psychologists were able to demonstrate what Galton had anticipated. Galton's warning to Müller is worth quoting, for it is as pertinent now as when he wrote it in 1887: "Before a just knowledge can be attained concerning any faculty of the human race, we must inquire into its distribution among all sorts and conditions of men on a large scale, and not among those persons who belong to a highly specialized literary class."

Romanes used an example of a disorder of communication, namely, aphasia, to challenge Müller's thesis. He pointed out that, once attained, symbolic concept formation afterwards continued to operate without the use of words. He continues: "This is not based on one's own personal introspection which no opponent can verify; it is a matter of objectively demonstratable fact. For when a man is suddenly afflicted with aphasia, he does not forthwith become as thoughtless as a brute. Admittedly he has lost all trace of words, but his reason may remain unimpaired."

We have seen, then, even from this capsulized review, that the question of the relationship between thought and language is of long standing. In the seventeenth and eighteenth centuries, Cordemoy and Diderot were making a clear distinction between the processes of thought and language. Although language was for them a magnificent extension of thought, thought was necessary before language acquisition could even begin, even where there was no possibility of language acquisition.

The homogenized, atomistic concepts of associations such as Erasmus Darwin and Horne Tooke tended to blur distinctions between thought and language, just as they did for psychological and physiological processes.

In the nineteenth century tremendous progress in neurophysiology and the treatment of speech disorders gave a new impetus to investigations of the thought-language problem. The accumulated research, particularly on the comparison between speech development in children and adult communication disorders, points to the conclusion that language is indeed an extension of thought, rather than a prerequisite to it.

Comparative Study of Communication (Or Hands across the Phylogenetic Scale)

In his excellent critical edition of La Mettrie's *L'Homme Machine,* Vartanian (1960) notes that the eighteenth-century French philosopher rejected the long-cherished notion of man's uniqueness on the grounds that "the behavior of human beings, when traced to its instinctual sources, seems to him to differ merely in degree, not in kind, from that of the higher animals"(p. 26). La Mettrie's belief in the continuity of animal and human intelligence ("Des Animaux a l'Homme, la transition n'est pas violente") led him to propose the experiment of teaching an ape to speak. Said Vartanian (1960):

Ill-advised as this expectation was, and notwithstanding the mockery with which it was promptly greeted, it indicates an experimental approach to animal psychology which, though historically premature, was not without value for the future. More exactly, it was the structural analogy between the brain of man and that of the ape which led La Mettrie to wonder if their considerable difference of behavior might not be due less to any organic dissimilarity than to the educative merit of the environment in which each of the species had lived and developed. This in turn entails the assumption that natural—i.e., prehistoric—man must have been very much like present-day anthropoids. (pp. 26–27)

It was not until the twentieth century that La Mettrie's proposed experiment was actually carried out.

Viki

A prolonged attempt to teach a chimpanzee human language was reported by Hayes (1951). Keith and Kathy Hayes actually raised a chimp in their home, from the age of 3 days to about 6½ years. The chimp, named Viki, was treated as nearly as possible like a human child in such matters as feeding, toilet training, discipline, and play. Viki not only learned to imitate much of the behavior of the adult humans with whom she lived; she also learned to respond to spoken commands. Nonetheless, to the end of the experiment, she never managed to mouth more than three (or possibly four) words: "papa," "mama," "cup" (and possibly "up"). The various attempts to teach human language to Viki and to other primate subjects was reviewed by Kellogg (1968), just as the remarkable breakthrough of two Nevada psychologists was beginning to attract attention.

Washoe

In June of 1966, R. Allen Gardner and Beatrice T. Gardner of the University of Nevada undertook to teach a young female chimpanzee the gesture language of the deaf. They were not so much concerned with language as such, and were in fact rather naïve about the subject when they began. They were interested in the theory of learning and reasoned that in view of past failures and the natural behavior of chimpanzees, an attempt to establish interspecies communication would be more likely to succeed if it were based on gestures. To this end, they began an essentially operant technique of rewarding the animal's own gestures when these happened to resemble the gestures made in the American Sign Language (ASL).

The experiment began when Washoe (named after the county in which the University of Nevada at Reno is located) was between 8 and 14 months old, and after 22 months of training and other interaction with the investigators and their assistants, all of whom used only manual language in the presence of the animal, Washoe had a repertory of more than 30 signs. Most of the signs named objects or pictures of objects. Once Washoe had eight or ten signs in her repertory, she began to combine them:

> Among the signs that Washoe has recently acquired are the pronouns "I-me" and "you." When these occur in combinations the result resembles a short sentence. In terms of the eventual level of communication that a chimpanzee might be able to attain, the most promising results have been spontaneous naming, spontaneous transfer to new referents, and spontaneous combinations and recombinations of signs. (Gardner & Gardner, 1969, p. 672)

Combining signs in a patterned way constitutes a primitive grammar, and the observation that a rather small list of signs is typically used in combination with signs from a longer list parallels the development of two- and three-word sentences in the process of language acquisition by human children. Washoe was approximately 3 years of age at this stage, and she was a year or so behind the human schedule for language acquisition, but the experiment is a considerable accomplishment for all parties concerned, human and ape.

A year later Washoe's lexicon had increased to 85 or more signs, and the process of forming combinations had advanced slightly (Gardner & Gardner, 1971). If we think of the grammar in terms of the requirements of English, the subsequent development is rather modest—but this is not an appropriate comparison. The American Sign Language lacks many of the grammatical requirements of English (use of a copula, for example), and if we apply the usual criterion of evaluating a system in its own terms, Washoe's language should be compared with the system represented by ASL. (As far as we know, there has never been a rudimentary analysis of ASL, but see Schlesinger, 1971, for some of the problems in dealing with the grammar of Israeli Sign Language.)

The next step in the interspecific communications research was taken when Dr. Roger Fouts, who worked with the Gardners as a graduate student, took Washoe to the University of Oklahoma Institute for Primate studies. At the institute, which is under the direction of Dr. William B. Lemmon, Fouts established that Washoe is not unique in her ability to learn ASL. Several other chimps made good progress and began to use signs in communicating with one another.

Sarah

A somewhat different approach to the language capacities of the chimpanzee has been taken by Premack and Premack (1972). The Premacks taught their chimp named Sarah to manipulate plastic pieces of various colors, shapes, and sizes; each of these pieces represents a different word. As of their 1972 report, Sarah had acquired a vocabulary of some 130 terms, which she employed with a reliability of 75 to 80%. She had also learned to use and understand the negative article, the interrogative, and *wh*-questions, as well as such concepts as "name of," dimensional classes, prepositions, the conditional, and hierarchically organized sentences.

Lana

The most recent of the chimp language experiments seems to be that of the Yerkes Regional Primate Center in Atlanta, Georgia. Psychologist Duane Rumbaugh taught a chimp named Lana to read and write simple sentences by using what is, in effect, a rather grotesque typewriter (*Newsweek*, 1974, pp. 75–76). On each plastic key of her computer console, there is a hieroglyphic-type symbol that represents a word. The work was begun in 1972; essentially the same kind of conditioning techniques have been used as were employed in the other chimp experiments. After a year of mere "rote associations," Lana began to form her own sentences, with appropriate punctuation marks. As of the 1974 report, Lana had a vocabulary of some 50 words, but Rumbaugh predicted that this number would be at least doubled.

Gorilla

Next to the chimpanzee, the gorilla is generally considered to be the creature closest to man. Francine Patterson, at Stanford University, has begun to teach a young female gorilla ASL. In a 1973 personal communication to Fouts (Fouts, 1973a), she reported that the 19-month-old gorilla was using six signs and was combining the "more" sign with "food," "drink," and "out." And Fouts reports (1973b) that he was able in a brief study to teach an infant orangutan (again, somewhat more remotely related to man) several signs, and the orangutan combined them into two-sign sequences.

Conclusions

Although the work with apes has intrinsic interest, it also carries implications as to the origins of human language. Lieberman, Crelin, and Klatt (1972) have argued that language must be a recent development, because forms prior to modern man (*Homo sapiens*) lacked the necessary vocal apparatus. Whether or not Leiberman and co-workers succeed in convincing us with their argument about the human vocal apparatus, the demonstration that the great apes have at least a rudimentary language capacity and the existence of a highly developed system of manual communication among the deaf suggest that human language may have begun as a gesture system rather than as a vocal-auditory system. This argument has been suggested most strongly by Hewes (1973) and Stokoe (1972).

Even if language began as a gesture system, and even though the deaf can converse manually equally rapidly and over as wide a range of topics as those with hearing, it is customary to define language in terms of vocal symbols. By taking the vocal system as primary, we distinguish language from derived systems such as scripts. Even the manual system of ASL is derived, in the sense that the signs are supplemented by finger spelling, which is the equivalent of a script.

The most useful definition of language may still be that of Edward Sapir (1921): "Language is a purely human and non-instinctive method of communicating ideas, emotions, and desires by a system of voluntarily produced symbols (p. 8)." Washoe's accomplishments notwithstanding, language is still a distinctively human characteristic. But we may have to drastically alter this definition if Washoe and her companions establish their manual communication as a characteristic of the Oklahoma chimp community over several generations.[11]

[11]Two recent articles—one by Premack, "The Human Ape," *The Sciences,* January–February, 1977, and one by H. T. P. Hayes, "The Pursuit of Reason," *New York Times Magazine,* June 12, 1977—point to how the use of language by apes has blurred the line between species. In the Hayes article, a suggestion is attributed to a Newark attorney that intimates that the ape in question has developed a consciousness of self and a rudimentary form of language and is therefore entitled to human rights. A thorough discussion of this issue is not possible in the context of this chapter; nevertheless, this instance amply illustrates that the issue of the continuum of ape to man has assumed extreme proportions.

Retrospect and Prospect

Paradigm, as Kuhn (1970) uses the term, connotes much more than merely pattern or design: it implies a *model of reality* that not only orders the phenomena to be studied by a particular discipline but also specifies the appropriate techniques to be employed in their systematic investigation. In Kuhn's view, a scientific revolution occurs when anomalies or "counterinstances" accumulate that resist explanation in terms of the prevailing paradigm of "normal science." Does this description of paradigm clash fit the recent or current circumstances in psycholinguistics?

Charles E. Osgood does not believe it does. Although Osgood acknowledges the revolutionary impact of Noam Chomsky's work on the field of linguistics, he questions whether we are witnessing in psycholinguistics a true Kuhnian "crisis" or merely a pendulum swing between viable paradigms. As Osgood (1975) sees it, the contributions of Chomsky and their effect upon psycholinguistic research and theory fail to meet the criteria that distinguish a scientific revolution:

> (1) There has been no attempt to incorporate solutions to problems handled successfully by the old paradigm; (2) the old paradigm has not been shown to be insufficient *in principle*; (3) there has been no new paradigm to shift *to*—in the sense of a well-motivated, internally coherent alternative theory of language performance. There has been a shift *away from* behaviorism in any form, but in the absence of any alternative paradigm, this would be better termed "revulsion" than "revolution." (p. 20)

Our historical review provides support for Osgood's conclusions. Study, research, and speculation on the psychology of language and thought have been carried on simultaneously during a period that spans at least five centuries in accordance with the competing paradigms supplied by rationalism and empiricism; and whether the fires of controversy that blazed so fiercely over competence vs. performance in recent years are burnt out or merely banked, there seem to be few prospects for revolutionary change in the immediately forseeable future.

It is important to note that most of Kuhn's examples of paradigm clash leading to crisis and revolution are taken from the physical sciences (e.g., Newton/Einstein, Priestly/Lavoisier, etc.). There are ample grounds for questioning whether the social and behavioral sciences have ever developed paradigms (or "regimes") with the kind of authority enjoyed by paradigms in the physical sciences. Instead, we would have to identify broad divergences in methodological and theoretical emphasis that may reflect a continuum rather than a dichotomy.

At any rate, having ruled out the probability of an imminent revolution in psycholinguistics, Charles Osgood (1975) concludes his "Dinosaur Caper" by venturing a few predictions concerning the future prospects for psycholinguistic research and theory as we approach the year 2000:

(1) *There will be a complete shift from emphasis upon Competence to emphasis upon Performance....*
(2) As part of this shift, *there will be an increasing avoidance of dealing with sentences-in-isolation* (whether in linguistic or psychological methodologies) *and increasing dependence upon sentences-in-context* (in discourse, in ordinary conversation, and so on)....
(3) *Semantics will be moving into the foreground as syntax moves, reciprocally, into the background....*
(4) As I have already hinted, *logical, rationalist models of language will be shown to be inappropriate for ordinary speakers and will be superseded by more gutsy, dynamic psycho-logical models....*
(5) *There will be shift from ethno-linguo-centrism toward what might appropriately be called anthropo-linguo-centrism.* (pp. 23–24)

The test of these or any predictions can be provided, of course, only by the future, and Osgood acknowledges some serious doubts concerning the ability of mankind to reach the "billennium." While awaiting confirmation or refutation of Osgood's predictions—*all* of them—we should like to indicate that we find Osgood's analysis of the current state of psycholinguistics good, active, and potent.

References

Aarsleff, H. *The study of language in England, 1780–1860.* Princeton, N.J.: Princeton University Press, 1967.

Abercrombie, D. Studies in phonetics and linguistics. Oxford: Oxford University Press, 1965.

Amman, J. C. A dissertation on speech. [Reprint of the 1893 edition (R. W. Rieber, Ed.)]

Bacon, Francis (Ed.). *The works of Francis Bacon.* Spedding, London: Ellis and Heath, 1858.

Benton, A. L., & Joynt, R. J. Early description of aphasia. *Arch. Neurol.,* 1960, *3*, 321.

Bever, T. G. Some theoretical and empirical issues that arise if we insist on distinguishing language and thought. In D. Aaronson & R. W. Rieber (Eds.), *Developmental psycholinguistics and communication disorders.* New York: New York Academy of Sciences, 1975.

Bloomfield, L. *Language.* New York: Henry Holt, 1933.

Blumenthal, A. L. *Language and psychology.* New York: Wiley, 1970.

Brett, G. S. *A history of psychology* (Vol. 2). London: George Allen and Unwin, 1921.

Brown, R. *Words and things.* Glencoe, Ill.: Free Press, 1958.

Carroll, J. B. *Language and thought.* Englewood Cliffs, N.J.: Prentice-Hall, 1964.

Chomsky, N. Three models for the description of language. *Proceedings of the Symposium on Information Theory, IRE-Transactions on Information Theory,* 1956, *2*, 113–124.

Chomsky, N. *Syntactic structures.* The Hague: Mouton, 1957.

Chomsky, N. *Cartesian linguistics.* New York: Harper & Row, 1966.

Condillac, E. B. de. *An essay on the origin of human knowledge.* Introduction by J. H. Stam. Published originally in French 1746; published London 1756. [Reprinted in *Language, man, and society series* (R. W. Rieber, Ed.), A.M.S. Press, 1975.]

Condillac, E. B. de. *The logic of Condillac.* Philadelphia, Pa., 1809.

Cordemoy, G. de. *A philosophical discourse concerning speech.* Introduction by Karl Uitti, London, 1668. [Reprinted in *Language, man, and society series* (R. W. Rieber, Ed.), A.M.S. Press, 1975.]

Dalgarno, G. *Ars Signorum, vulgo Character Universalis et Lingua Philosophica,* London, 1661.

Dalgarno, G. *Didascalocophus* or *The deaf and dumb man's tutor, to which is added a discourse of the nature and number of double consonants.* Oxford: 1680.

Darwin, C. *The descent of man.* London: John Murray, 1871.

Darwin, C. *The expression of emotions in man and animals.* London: 1873.

Darwin, E. *The temple of nature.* New York: P. and J. Swords, 1804. (Originally published London, 1803.)

Darwin, E. *Zoönomia, or the laws of organic life.* Introduction by T. Verhave, London, 1794–1796. [Reprinted in *Language, man, and society series* (R. W. Rieber, Ed.), A.M.S. Press, 1974.]

Diderot, Denis. *Diderot's early works.* Introduction by Jules Paul Siegel (includes essay on the deaf and dumb), Open Court, 1916. [Reprinted in *Language, man, and society series* (R. W. Rieber, Ed.), A.M.S. Press, 1975.]

Diebold, A. R. A survey of psycholinguistic research, 1954–1964. In *Psycholinguistics: A survey of theory and research problems.* Bloomington, Ind.: University of Indiana Press, 1965.

Dobson, E. J. English pronunciation 1500–1700 (Vol. 1). Oxford: Oxford University Press, 1957.

Ebbinghaus, H. *Memory: A contribution to experimental psychology.* Dover: 1964 (English trans.). (Originally published in Germany, 1885.)

Firth, J. R. The English school of phonetics. *T.P.S.,* 1946, *12,* 69.

Fouts, R. W. The use of guidance in teaching sign language to a chimpanzee (Pan Troglodytes). *Journal of Comparative and Physiological Psychology,* 1972, *80,* 515–522.

Fouts, R. S. Acquisition and testing of gestural signs in four young chimpanzees. *Science,* 1973, *180,* 978–980. (a)

Fouts, R. S. *Capacities for language in great apes.* Paper prepared for the 9th International Congress of Anthropological and Ethnological Sciences, Chicago, September 1973. (b)

Funke, O. *Gesammelte Aufsätze zur Anglistik und zur Sprachtheorie.* Berne: 1965.

Furth, H. G. On the nature of language from the perspective of research with profoundly deaf children. In D. Aaronson & R. W. Rieber (Eds.), *Developmental psycholinguistics and communication disorders.* New York: New York Academy of Sciences, 1975.

Gardner, R. A., & Gardner, B. T. Teaching sign language to a chimpanzee. *Science,* 1969, *165,* 664–672.

Gardner, B. T., & Gardner, R. A. Two-way communication with an infant-chimpanzee. In A. Schrier & F. Strollnitz (Eds.), *Behavior of non-human primates.* New York: Academic Press, 1971.

Goldstein, K. *Language and language disorders.* New York: Grune & Stratton, 1948.

Griffith, F. G. De Italica Pronuntiatione. *Italian Studies,* 1953, *8,* 71–82.

Hartley, D. *Observations on man*. London: S. Richardson, 1749.

Hayes, C. *The ape in our house*. New York: Harper & Row, 1951.

Hebb, D. O., Lambert, W. E., & Tucker, G. R. A DMZ in the language war. *Psychology Today*, 1973, *11*, 55–62.

Hewes, G. Primate communication and the gestural origin of language. *Current Anthropology*, 1973, *14*, 5–24.

Holder, W. *Elements of speech: An essay of inquiry into the natural production of letters: With an appendix concerning persons deaf and dumb*. London: 1669.

Humboldt, W. von *Linguistic variability and intellectual development* (English trans. by G. C. Buck, F. A. Raben). University of Pennsylvania Press, 1972. (Originally published in German, 1836.)

Ivič, M. *Trends in linguistics*. The Hague: Mouton, 1965.

Kantor, J. R. An objective psychology of grammar. Bloomington, Ind.: Indiana University Publications, 1936.

Kellogg, W. N. Communication and language in the home-raised chimpanzee. *Science*, 1968, *162*, 423–427.

Kemp, J. A. *John Wallis' grammar of the English language*. London: Longman, 1972.

Kuhn, T. *The structure of scientific revolutions*. Chicago: University of Chicago Press, 1970.

Leibnitz, G. W. *New Essays concerning human understanding*. Chicago: Open Court Press, 1916.

Lieberman, P., Crelin, E. S., & Klatt, D. H. Phonetic ability and related anatomy of the newborn and adult human, Neanderthal man, and the chimpanzee. *American Anthropologist*, 1972, *74*, 287–307.

Locke, J. *An essay concerning human understanding*. Oxford: Clarendon Press, 1924. (Originally published, 1690.)

Maclay, H. Linguistics and psycholinguistics. In B. Kachru (Ed.), *Issues in linguistics: Papers in honor of Henry and Renée Kahane*. Urbana, Ill.: University of Illinois Press, 1973.

Marx, O. The history of the biological basis of language. In E. H. Lenneberg (Ed.), *Biological foundations of language*. New York: Wiley, 1967.

Mendelssohn, M. Psychologische Betrachtungen auf Veranlassung einer von spalding. *Mag. Erfahrungsseelenkunde*, 1783, *1*(pt. 3). (Berlin)

Morgagni, G. B. *The seat and causes of disease* (Book I). Letter XIV, London: 1769.

Morton, J., & Marshall, J. C. (Eds.). *Psycholinguistics: Developmental and pathological*. Ithaca, N.Y.: Cornell University Press, 1977.

Müller, F. Max. *Science of thought*. London: Longman's Green, 1887.

Müller, F. Max. *Three lectures on the science of language*. Chicago: Open Court Press, 1890.

Müller, F. Max. Three introductory lectures on the science of thought. Chicago: Open Court Press, 1909.

Neisser, U. Cognitive psychology. New York: Appleton-Century-Crofts, 1967.

Osgood, C. A dinosaur caper. In D. Aaronson & R. W. Rieber (Eds.), *Developmental psycholinguistics and communication disorders*. New York: New York Academy of Sciences, 1975.

Pick, A. Aphasia. In J. W. Brown (Ed.), *Aphasia*. Springfield, Ill.: Charles C Thomas, 1973.

Premack, A. J., & Premack, D. Teaching language to an ape. *Scientific American*, 1972, *227*, 92–99.

Preyer, W. *The mind of the child*. New York: D. Appleton & Co., 1896. (Originally published in Germany, 1881.)

Pronko, N. H. Language and psycholinguistics: A review. *Psychological Bulletin*, 1946, *43*.

Rieber, R. W. Neuropsychological aspects of stuttering and cluttering. In R. W. Rieber (Ed.), *The neuropsychology of language*. New York: Plenum Press, 1976.

Rieber, R. W., & Froeschels, E. An historical review of the European literature in speech pathology. In R. W. Rieber & R. S. Brubaker (Eds.), *Speech pathology*. Amsterdam: North Holland, 1966.

Robins, R. H. A short history of linguistics. London: Longman, 1967.

Rosenfield, L. C. *From beast machine to man machine*. New York: Oxford University Press, 1940.

Sapir, E. *Language*. New York: Harcourt, Brace & World, 1921.

Saporta, S. *Psycholinguistics: A book of readings*. New York: Holt, Rinehart & Winston, 1961.

Schlesinger, I. M. The grammar of sign language, and the problems of language universals. In J. Morton (Ed.), *Biological and social factors in psycholinguistics*. London: Logos Press, 1971.

Stam, J. H. *Inquiries into the origin of language*. New York: Harper, 1976.

Stam, J. H. The Sapir–Whorf hypothesis in historical perspective. In R. W. Rieber & K. Salzinger (Eds.), *The roots of American psychology*. New York: New York Academy of Science, 1977.

Stokoe, W. *Motor signs as the first form of language*. Paper presented at the 71st annual meeting of the American Anthropological Association, Toronto, December 1972.

Sullivan, J. On Cartesian linguistics. In R. W. Rieber & K. Salzinger (Eds.), *The roots of American psychology*. New York: New York Academy of Science, 1977.

van Helmont, F. M. B. *Alphabeti vere Naturalis Hebraici brevissima delineatio*. Sulzback: 1667.

Vartanian, A. La Mettrie's L'Homme Machine. In *A study of the origins of an idea*. Princeton, N.J.: Princeton University Press, 1960.

Wallis, J. *Grammatica linguae anglicanae cui praefigitur, de loquela sive sonorum formatione, tractatus grammatico-physicus*. Oxford: 1653.

Wallis, J. A letter of Doctor John Wallis to Robert Boyle, Esq. *Philosophical Transactions*. 1670, *5*, N. 61, 1087–97 (Page refs. to Lock, 1706.)

Wallis, J. *A defence of the Royal Society, and the philosophical transactions, particularly those of July, 1670, in answer to the cavils of Dr. William Holder*. London: 1678.

Wallis, J. A letter of Dr. John Wallis ... to Mr. Thomas Beverly concerning his methods for instructing persons deaf and dumb. *Philosophical Transactions*, 1698, *20*, N. 245, 353–60. (Page refs. to Lock, 1706.)

Whitney, W. D. *Language and the study of language*. New York: Charles Scribner, 1871.

Wilkins, J. *Mercury: or, the secret and swift messenger*. 1641. (Page refs. to Wilkins, 1802, 1–87.)

Wilkins, J. *An essay towards a real character and a philosophical language*. London: 1668.

Wilson, M. Descartes and the mind body problem. In R. W. Rieber (Ed.), *Body and mind*. New York: Academic Press, 1980.

PART II

SEVENTEENTH AND EIGHTEENTH CENTURY CONTRIBUTIONS

Karl D. Uitti

CORDEMOY AND 'CARTESIAN LINGUISTICS'

It is hard to exaggerate our debt to seventeenth-century thought. So much of what has occurred, intellectually speaking, in more recent times may be traced back to arguments developed by representatives of the *grand siè-cle*. Even the techniques of diffusion current then—learned academies, rapid translations (usually into Latin, but often into other vernaculars), exchange of correspondence—remain ours today and have been only partially supplanted. If, as is frequently the case, antiquity or the Middle Ages are also involved, the perspective taken by present-day thinkers has usually been first conditioned by viewpoints proper to seventeenth-century thought. Consequently, even philosophers of the second or third rank deserve our close attention. Next to the giants—Galileo, Descartes, Spinoza, Locke, Leibniz, Malebranche—a host of lesser figures cope, so to speak, on a day-to-day basis with an astonishingly wide variety of concepts and concerns. (These notions usually grow out of the vast philosophical systems assembled by the great thinkers.) Some examples are rather startling. We see modernity in Cyrano de Bergerac's description of travel to the moon [ca. 1649–1650], and, we must agree, Cordemoy articulates a very modern concern for what distinguishes men from the machines their techniques will one day allow them to manufacture:

> I conceive likewise, as I have already said, that *Art* may go so far as to frame an Engin, that shall articulate words like those, which I pronounce; but then I

Karl D. Uitti • Department of Romance Languages and Literatures, Princeton University, Princeton, New Jersey 08540.

conceive at the same time, that it would only pronounce those, that were
designed it should pronounce, and that it would always pronounce them in the
same order. (1668/1968 [English trans.], p. 9)

To reacquaint oneself with issues as defined by the seventeenth-
century thinkers is, of course, valuable for its own sake and, naturally,
this understanding is indispensable for disciplines like the history of science or philosophy. But I expect that readers of the present volume will
be even more interested in how the thought of early modernity formulated
the concepts and alternatives with which, to a considerable degree and
despite changes in emphasis, we still work. Thus, to give an example,
linguistics in the past two decades or so, and above all in America,[1] has
manifested new interest in its historical tradition: in what has gone into
making it what it has become. Histories of linguistics, biographical
sketches of linguists, anthologies of "current issues," and reviews of
earlier research have proliferated. Linguistics seeks to take cognizance of
its own roots, to grasp the possibilities it contains, and to serve better its
new functions. In a sense, the status of the discipline has been made to
depend increasingly on its consciousness of itself. (This has, of course,
always been at least partly true: Bloomfield's condemnation of Wundt's
mentalism constitutes an important attempt to define the purview of linguistics as Bloomfield understood it, just as Chomsky's allegation that
Whitney, in 1872, was wrong-headed concerning Wilhelm von Humboldt
forms part of the MIT scholar's attempt to redefine the perspectives. But
in our day such redefinition has become fundamentally—even functionally
—more important. The issues are no longer quite so simple as they once
were, and, it is sensed, what the past has thought itself constitutes a significant part of the issues.) Not suprisingly, then, attention has come
to focus on the seventeenth century. To be sure, the categories of ancient and medieval grammar and logic as well as of their Renaissance
counterparts (including etymology and philology) have not yet run their
course, but these categories have frequently come down to us clothed in
the rationalist garb of seventeenth-century speculation. Even the *Minerva*

---

[1] A similar revival in the history of speculation concerning language (i.e., speculation involving linguistics itself as well as other disciplines) has occurred in Europe. Especially during
the 1960s and early 1970s linguistics was considered frequently as a kind of model discipline, a source of techniques and approaches for such varied disciplines as, e.g., anthropology, literary criticism, sociology, even philosophy. An early reprint of the Port-Royal
Grammar thus boasts an introduction by the well-known French philosopher Michel
Foucault, author of *Les Mots et les choses* (1966).

(1587) of Sánchez de las Brozas (Sanctius) has been refracted through the prism of the Port-Royal *Grammar* (1660); scholastic theory has been largely reshaped by the general and philosophical grammars of Rationalism and the Enlightenment. Indeed, certain present-day theorists believe that their brand of research, in showing greater fidelity to Port-Royal principles and procedures, copes more authentically with the genuine issues of linguistics, whereas such predecessors as had rejected these principles—the "taxonomists"—reached a dead end in their research. "Linguistics" and "philosophy of mind," once again go hand in hand; indeed, for some, the former would seem to constitute the core of the latter. All the more reason, then, to reread the "Cartesians."

A number of questions come immediately to mind. Where lies the strength of these early thinkers and, at least as important, what might their weakness be? Are their strengths and weaknesses still relevant today or is their interest confined largely, as is that we feel for Cyrano's space travel, to the curiosity or the appreciation one senses on behalf of an imaginative but long-gone predecessor? Assuming there are in fact significant parallelisms between kinds of research prevalent in modern linguistics and, say, Cordemoy's *Discourse of Speech,* wherein lie the similarities and the differences, and to what extent will our reading of Cordemoy serve to help us avoid certain errors or unpromising avenues of approach? We shall look into some of these matters. But first, let us review Cordemoy's life and work, stressing above all, when the time comes, the content of his *Discourse of Speech.*

Until the critical edition of Clair and Girbal (1968) and, especially, Battail (1973), no full-scale monographic study or biography had, to my knowledge, been devoted to Cordemoy. Thus, until quite recently, one has had to glean facts about him, as best one could, from various sources.[2] (No lengthy study of Cordemoy as yet exists in English.) Indeed, only over the past decade have some of his works been reprinted; the older editions—especially those in English and Latin—are hard to

[2]In addition to Clair and Girbal (1968), the pioneering edition-study of Cordemoy, and Battail's fundamental monograph (1973), I have found the following works particularly useful: Rivaud (1950); Bréhier (1938; tr. 1966); Ueberweg (1953[13]); Bouillier (1868[3]); Damiron (1846); Boas (1957); Pellisson and D'Olivet (1858); Chomsky (1966): see Zimmer (1968), Uitti (1969), Aarsleff (1970); Rodis-Lewis (1968); Brekle (1970; 1976); Joly and Clérico (1977). Quotations from Cordemoy's *A Philosophical Discourse Concerning Speech* (= *Discourse of Speech*) are taken from the 1974 AMS reprint, the Introduction to which constituted a first version (1969) of the present article; page references in this article correspond to the photographic reprint of the English edition dated, originally, 1668.

come by. Yet in his day, judging from the speed with which his writings were translated into Latin and English, Cordemoy was a highly respected, if not an overwhelming presence, on the European intellectual scene. Here, then, are some pertinent facts as I have been able to ascertain them.

Géraud de Cordemoy was born in Paris, of an old Auvergnat family—Pascal, we recall, also had Auvergnat roots—on October 6, 1626 (though at least one biographer says, erroneously, "at the start of the seventeenth century"), some ten or eleven years, then, before the publication of Descartes's *Discourse on Method*. Little is known of his childhood. He studied law and, apparently, was a highly successful barrister, but in the mid-1650s, he began to frequent circles where the new philosophy of Descartes was discussed.[3] One recalls that many of Descartes's most fervent admirers were not professional philosophers. As Damiron (1846) has put it, they came to him from the bar, the court, the cloister, and from the church. Cordemoy was soon noticed by Bossuet, the powerful bishop of Meaux—outstanding Gallican, at once religious traditionalist and friend to Cartesians, and without doubt the greatest orator of the age. Through Bossuet's intercession, Cordemoy was named tutor (*lecteur*) to the Dauphin in 1665 and, about the same time, *conseiller du roy*. In this capacity Cordemoy began work on a study of the earliest pre-Capetian French kings, emphasizing Charlemagne. This was to have been the first part of a lengthy *History of France* which, however, Cordemoy never completed. This work would later be continued, at the king's request, by his son, the Abbé de Feniers. Volume 1 appeared posthumously in 1685 (Cordemoy died on October 15, 1684), volume 2 in 1689. Most critics judge the *History* to be by and large a dull, unoriginal work, but all evidence indicates it helped make Cordemoy's reputation in the seventeenth century. He was received into the French Academy on December 12, 1675. Racine was moved to say of him: "M. de Cordemoy . . . , with so many other talents, possessed all traits of a true Academician: wise, precise, hard-working; had not health interrupted him in the midst of his labors, he might well have carried history as far along as M. de Corneille has carried tragedy" (quoted by Pellisson and D'Olivet, 1858, p. 216; see J. Racine [1886, p. 370]). Apparently, even Pierre Bayle praised Cordemoy's trail-blazing efforts at clarifying the earliest and most obscure

---

[3]The enthusiasm in these circles was such that at least one Cartesian, Clerselier, married his sister to Chanut, "bon cartésien," and his daughter to "M. Rohault, professeur de cartésianisme"; see Damiron (1846) pp. 2, 4.

centuries of French history. In the collection of Cordemoy's *Œuvres*, published by his son in 1704, there appears a chapter entitled "De la Nécessité de l'histoire," in which Cordemoy explains why and how history should be taught to the young.

Cordemoy's philosophical works appeared as follows: *Le Discerne-ment du corps et de l'ame, en six discours, pour servir à l'éclaircissement de la physique* (1666, 2nd ed. 1670–71; Lat. tr.: *De corporis et mentis distinctione* [Geneva, 1679]); *Discours physique de la parole* (1668; Eng. tr.: *A Philosophicall Discourse Concerning Speech, Conformable to the Cartesian Principles* (= *Discourse of Speech*, [1668]; Lat. tr.: *De loquela* [Geneva, 1679]); *Lettre écrite à un sçavant religieux . . . pour montrer; I, que le systeme de Descartes et son opinion touchant les bestes n'ont rien de dangereux; II, et que tout ce qu'il en a écrit semble estre tiré du premier chapitre de la Genèse* (1668; Eng. tr.: *A Discourse Written to a Learned Frier . . . Shewing, That the Systeme of M. Des Cartes, and Par-ticularly his Opinion Concerning Brutes, Does Contain Nothing Danger-ous; and That All He Hath Written of Both, Seems to Have Been Taken Out the First Chapter of Genesis* [1670]; *Divers Traitez de métaphysique, d'histoire et de politique* (1691); of the various collected works the most important is the above-mentioned three-part collection edited by Cor-demoy's son and published in 1704.

Most historians of philosophy stress Cordemoy's "occasionalism," i.e., the doctrines outlined especially in the fourth and subsequent dis-courses of his *Discernement du corps et de l'ame*. Cordemoy observes that a body can cease to move without ceasing to be a body. And given the fact that "on n'a pas de soi, ce qu'on peut perdre, sans cesser d'être ce qu'on est" (admirably rendered by George Boas as: "Nothing which a being can lose is an essential property of it" [1957, p. 103ff.]), it follows that bodies are moved by causes superior to them. Retaining the context of Descartes's dualism and amplifying somewhat upon Descartes's oc-casionalism, Cordemoy affirms in turn that the only cause of motion in bodies must be spiritual. Yet the human soul cannot move the body, since our will is frequently powerless (e.g., death cannot be brought on by willing it, nor can one will death away, and death is cessation of move-ment). Our will is merely the occasion for both the production and the direction of movement. The cause, initial and continuous, must be God. Cordemoy (along with his contemporary, Geulincx) anticipates here Malebranche, Leibniz, and Spinoza, as well as, in some ways, Hume. We act, so to speak, in and through God (or perhaps vice versa): "Il est aussi impossible à nos âmes d'avoir de nouvelles exceptions sans Dieu, qu'il est impossible au corps d'avoir de nouveaux mouvements sans lui" (quoted by Bouillier, 1868, p. 516). However, God has endowed our will with freedom. As Cordemoy stated in his brief *Traité de métaphysique,* "Dieu fait ce qu'il y a de réel dans nos actions, sans nous *ôter la liberté"* (Damiron, 1846, p. 118f.). This is the kernel of occasionalism, the teaching that declares, in Boas's words, that "God therefore not only is the first cause of motion but the continued cause of it, and since all change is based upon motion, all change must come through the direct intervention of the Divine Will" (1957, p. 105).

It would not be useful here, however, to emphasize the generalities of Cordemoy's occasionalism so as to neglect what this basic framework allowed him to do in a number of particular matters. If, as Bréhier has stated, "Cordemoy's Cartesianism tends toward the sort of disconnected vision of the universe which caused Leibniz to censure the occasionalists" (1966, p. 115f.), if, indeed, as we shall see, this same vision leads to a curious theory of inspiration and of "spiritual communication," it is certainly no less true that Cordemoy's concerns prompted him to analyze in highly ingenious and fertile ways what today we would call *psychophysical process.* Furthermore, there is a nobility and genuine unity in Cordemoy's thought that has reminded more than one scholar of his protector Bossuet: God has made us and endowed us with a sense of, and desire for, His purpose; we exercise our will and, so long as nothing dulls our understanding, our activity tends toward Him. Not to choose Him is also movement, or action, but though this action would not be in us without God, it is not God's. Cordemoy's analysis—his "psychological method"— is confirmed by his faith, and his faith is, in a sense, justified by his "method." Or, to put it another way, Cordemoy's approach and analytic tone are woven into the fabric of his world view. This is often the case with specific bodies of theory, but let us not forget that, conversely, Cordemoy's world view permitted, indeed encouraged, that tone and that approach.

The *Discourse of Speech* is in harmony with both the tone of Cordemoy's thought and the doctrines so far outlined. Furthermore, it is probably Cordemoy's most original and, nowadays, most readable work. Let us examine it in some detail, taking care to bear constantly in mind Cordemoy's basic assumptions and beliefs.

Very helpfully, Cordemoy summarizes what he proposes to do in a ten-page Preface. The *Six Discourses,* he reminds us, discussed our

means for knowing ourselves, namely our "discerning in us the Operations of the Soul, and those of the Body." The present *Discourse*
analyzes "the means of knowing Others," i.e., speech, which Cordemoy
explains by endeavoring "exactly to distinguish what it borrows of the
Soul, from what it holds of the Body." We recognize his terms and his
procedures. Let us run through the steps of his outline.

1. He takes up where he had left off in the sixth *Discourse:* Are "all
the Bodies, which I see to be like mine, . . . united to Souls like mine?"
Whenever what a body does is imputable exclusively to the disposition of
its organs, as is the case with animals, then that body has no soul; bodies
"that resemble mine," however, do not "speak to such purpose, as they
do, without being endowed with Reason." Such bodies have a soul.

2. Speaking means "to Give signes of our Thoughts." First in order
and most universal are "motions of the Eyes or Face" and cries that
express states of the body; these are conjoined to the passions and are
best called "natural." Next are "instituted" signs, by which the soul can
"express what ever she conceives." Cordemoy goes on to show (a) how
one may invent a language; (b) how one learns a foreign tongue; (c) how
children learn to speak (especially how the order which they use to put
words together—substantives first, verbs last—closely resembles that of
grammar); and (d) finally, how in studying these matters he has met "with
so many Arguments to evince the Distinction of the Body and Soul, that
to me it seems not, there can any thing be more evidently known, than
She."

3. Here Cordemoy examines the body's role in speech. He elabo-
rates a remarkably sophisticated articulatory and acoustical phonetics,
e.g., What "is the Change of the Throat, the Tongue, the Teeth, and the
Lips, in all the Articulations?," and then, "with the same accurateness
the effect, which by sound is produced in the Ear and Brain of him, that
heareth." Sound is physical, effective thanks to nerves that link ear and
brain in animals and man. (Cordemoy's wording will be closely paralleled
by M. Jourdain's philosophy tutor in the phonetics lesson from Molière's
Le Bourgeois gentilhomme, II, iv [1670].) Cordemoy looks into a number
of "odd effects," including those produced by birds imitating other birds,
musical instruments, and even words.

4. "Brutes need no soul to cry, or to be moved by Voyces." But "in
Men, the motion of the parts, which serve for the Voyce, or of those that
are moved by it, is ever accompanied with some thoughts; and that in
Speech there are alwayes two things, viz. the Formation of the Voyce,

which cannot proceed but from the Body; and the Signification of the Idea, that is joyn'd therewith, which cannot come but from the Soul." (One is inevitably reminded of the more recent "phonetic" and "semantic" components in generative grammar.)

5. Cordemoy distinguishes: between three sorts of signs (natural; ordinary, or institutional, as in nodding one's head in confirmation and agreement; particular, or private to a few individuals); two kinds of writing, i.e., of "speaking to the Eyes" (hieroglyphics and syllabic); two types of voice (natural and institutional). Focusing on this last type of "voice," Cordemoy explains how ideas are joined to words; he describes a complex mechanism involving the idea (or image) of the thing, the sound of the word, and how these are related in the soul, as well as the "motion of the spirits and brain" that involves the body in producing the physical connection willed by the soul. He praises the "perfect correspondence, which God hath establisht between the different changes of the brain, and the different thoughts of the Soul" (p. 85). He concludes that "*Speech* indeed depends upon the relation and correspondency of many things, and that, if afterwards it becomes easie, 'tis only from the excellent composition of the brain, and the admirable commerce between its motions and our thoughts" (p. 88).

6. The way is open for a serious reexamination of eloquence; the lawyer in Cordemoy comes out in these closing sections of his work. The first part of eloquence involves "instruction." This requires in the orator ability to "discern among things" and to "well range" what he will say; he must also possess a good memory. The second part of eloquence deals with the orator's appealing to the passions of his audience. A contradiction crops up: the first part of eloquence requires calm, order, harmony; the second, it seems, "agitates the brain" and renders "the Course of the Spirits . . . impetuous." What the orator lacks in nature must be made up by art. But he must be an honest man; lies "may impair the force or the grace of his action." (One is reminded of Pascal's "Art de persuader." In various ways, however, the problems resemble those treated by Diderot in his *Paradoxe sur le comédien* [1773]).

7. Unlike Aristotelian, or traditional, rhetorical theory, which tended to concentrate on the speech, Cordemoy's Cartesian stance focuses on the orator; the speech is a function of the orator: "Eloquence depends from the Temperament." These considerations lead him to inquire as to whether communications among pure spirits (i.e., spirits not attached to

bodies) might not be easier than those involving spirits and bodies. "The difficulty we meet with in entertainments [conversations or *entretiens*] is not to conceive the thoughts of those that speak to us, but to unwrap it from the Signes they use to express it in, which often do not sute with it." Meanwhile, "the Thought of one Spirit is always clear to another from the very instant he can perceive it," and pure "Spirits can [more easily] inspire us with their sentiments, than . . . one Man can inspire his thoughts to another."

Typical of his time, Cordemoy is primarily concerned with metaphysical questions. Yet, in his *Discourse of Speech,* these lead him to discuss technical issues, even, as we noted, the physical production of sound. The bias is quite the opposite of that prevailing in many twentieth-century theorists of language; nowadays one's treatment of technical issues tends more usually to take precedence over metaphysical concerns which, nevertheless, lie implicit in one's approach and value-system. Consequently, for the most part, historians of philosophy have usually followed Francisque Bouillier in his summary of the *Discourse of Speech* and its relevance to the remainder of Cordemoy's work (my translation):

> After having proposed various means for knowing oneself, [Cordemoy] proposes in this *Discourse* the means for knowing others, namely, speech; he seeks to prove, following Descartes, that speech is the sole sign permitting us to recognize this existence of reasonable souls in souls other than ourselves. He distinguishes between natural language, which expresses passion, and institutional signs thanks to which the soul expresses all that it conceives; and he separates in speech what belongs to the soul from what belongs to the body. (p. 516)

In other words, by refining upon certain characteristically Cartesian notions,[4] Cordemoy invents what Rivaud has called his "curious" theory of language, thereby developing Descartes and also illustrating his own thought. His terms and manner of thinking gained considerable currency in the later years of the seventeenth century and throughout the Enlightenment. Condillac, for one, will speak at length of *signes naturels* or *d'institution* and will stress even more than Cordemoy had done the no-

---

[4]Though an "excellent Cartesian," Cordemoy was not unconditionally faithful to all Descartes's teachings, as Leibniz pointed out (*Système nouveau pour expliquer la nature des substances* . . . , in *Philosphischen Schriften,* 4 [Hildesheim, 1960], p. 473). He recognized bodies as "indivisible substances" and was obliged to "recourir aux Atomes, croyant d'y trouver une véritable unité." Some historians see here the influence of Descartes's great rival, Gassendi (cf. Rivaud, 1950, p. 182).

tion of psychosyntactic association (*liaison*). For Cordemoy too, just as it had been for Descartes,[5] for the Gentlemen of Port-Royal, and, indeed, for the entire Enlightenment tradition, speculation on language could not avoid the issue of what constituted proper speech; Cordemoy's rhetoric is also very much of its time.

One fundamental idea links Cordemoy's interest in language to the doctrines of the sensualist Condillac and, indeed, to the concern of many thinkers today. In her cogent study of Condillac and the French Enlightenment, Isabel F. Knight restates very well the close connection in Condillac between what language is and does, its origin and basic functions, and what she aptly calls "man's natural, instinctive, and physical capacity for expression" (1968, p. 154). As we observed, Cordemoy approaches language from the vantage point provided by his understanding of the physical and spiritual makeup of man: what man is explains what language is and, conversely, how language works helps us better comprehend what man is. Similarly, for Condillac, man's grasp of reality depends on how he operates with signs; studying these operations helps the philosopher view more clearly the nature of mental procedures. (In a sense it does not matter that in outlook Condillac is resolutely anti-Cartesian and that he would ridicule Cordemoy's occasionalism as he did the teachings of Malebranche in his scathing *Traité des systèmes* [1749, 1771]). Furthermore, human behavior is contrasted or compared with that of animals by Cartesian and empiricists alike—though in opposing ways—in their common concern for psychophysical process. For some, human beings should be likened to animals and to machines. Over time this view acquired greater importance because reliance on the Cartesian notion of soul "could only grow less and less essential as the method of psycho-physical inquiry progressively [during the eighteenth century] sought... to clarify the mechanics of mental activity without calling it [i.e., this notion of soul] into use (Vartanian, 1960, p. 58). Meanwhile, Cordemoy had so entirely adopted Descartes's doctrine concerning the incapacity of animals to speak—their mechanical nature—that his work came to be identified purely and simply with the orthodox Cartesian posi-

[5]In a letter to Father Mersenne (dated November 20, 1629), Descartes favors the creation of a "science" which would be entrusted with making men aware of the universal language they all speak and thereby enable peasants to judge better "de la vérité des choses, que ne font maintenant les philosophes" (see Descartes, 1936, p. 89ff.).

tion.[6] For Cordemoy speech was a sign of humanity, hence unmechanical and, as certain moderns would have it, "unbounded." This is why Cordemoy comes in for such considerable praise in Chomsky's *Cartesian Linguistics*; as Chomsky puts it, Cordemoy has argued "that there can be no mechanistic explanation for the novelty, coherence, and relevance of normal speech" (1966, p. 7). Given the highly theoretical bent of transformational grammar, it is not surprising that its practitioners should feel sympathy for the kind of speculation Cordemoy excels at, for, precisely, the broad theoretical base he assigns his remarks on language.[7] Thus, Chomsky describes as "important" Cordemoy's "emphasis on the creative aspect of language use," though he downplays "the Cartesian attempts to account for human abilities" (1966, p. 9). In Chomsky's view a kind of metaphysical affirmation necessarily—even ostentatiously—precedes scholarly activity concerned with language, though when experience in the field contradicts given practical modalities linked to the affirmation, these (according to generative theorists of the 1960s, e.g., J. Katz [1966, p. 282]) may be discarded in favor of new hypotheses. Man is creative and free; how his creativity and freedom are worked out in the dynamics of speech remains to be seen.

Unlike that of his modern admirers, however, Cordemoy's outlook is never determined by disciplinary concerns.[8] Quite characteristically, he stresses the art of public speaking, not a body of knowledge or a science

[6]Cf. Rosenfield (1941, p. 40), quoted by Chomsky (1966, p. 81). Needless to say, the capital text in this regard is Cordemoy's *Discourse Written to a Learned Frier* (the second of his works reprinted in 1974). I have chosen not to dwell on this relatively short text here because, quite simply, most of the ideas contained in it are reproduced or developed elsewhere, including those works I have so far summarized, and there is no space here to treat in greater detail the intricate history of beast-machines. As for Cordemoy's sincerity in finding no contradiction between Cartesian doctrine and Christian revelation, all evidence prompts one to accept what he writes at face value.

[7]Though by no means a "professional grammarian," Cordemoy stands close to the new tradition of *grammaire générale* or *philosophique*. One need only compare his generalist outlook with that of, say, Vaugelas, a grammarian whom some *philosophes* would later criticize for "giving rules but never the rules for arriving at the rules." (See François, in Brunot [1932].)

[8]These matters will be dealt with in greater detail in the closing pages of the present essay. Let us note, however, in passing that, for some, purely disciplinary concerns (i.e., "linguistics" as an autonomous discipline) have, at least to some degree, increasingly come to be subsumed into an articulated framework of consciously chosen wider philosophical speculation, e.g., several influential members of the MIT group. The late twentieth century would appear to be "wavering" in this regard.

mediating between man and language. He is no grammarian, as, say, Sánchez de las Brozas had been ("*Grammatica est ars recte loquendi. Cum Artem dico, disciplinam intelligo; est enim Disciplina scientia acquisita in discente,*" *Minerva,* I, ii), nor does he deal, as even Descartes had briefly dealt, with the "science" thanks to which we might one day understand and perhaps improve upon our language (see Descartes's above-quoted letter to Father Mersenne). Curiously, Cordemoy makes no effort to conjoin, as Condillac will do at a later date, his philosophical viewpoint and the newly budding *grammaire générale*; this is all the more astonishing in that the Port-Royal *Grammar* had appeared already in 1660. Cordemoy's linguistic speculation derives, then, entirely from his philosophical and psychophysiological interests, though he was apparently aware of other works on language (e.g., Wallis's *Grammatica linguae anglicanae* [1653]; see Rodis-Lewis, 1968, p. 32ff.).

The *Discourse of Speech* may be profitably read still as an entertaining and impressive meditation on topics that touch on issues debated even today by scholars involved in various ways with linguistic matters. Thus Cordemoy's handling of the physical production of sounds and in what manner this production is at once related to, and distinct from, "semantic" production is both amusing and instructive. A kind of "practical dualism" reflects here—though how genuinely is a matter of doubt—the well-known Cartesian "philosophical" dualism. Indeed, Cordemoy anticipates our entertainment and proudly describes the suggestive character of his book at the close of the Preface:

> I could wish, that the discourse I have made . . . , might prove as pleasant to others as the reflexions, it hath obliged me to make, have been to me. I avow, they have been all the divertisement I have enjoyed during the last Vacations; and as it is, at least in that time, permitted to comply with our inclinations, the pleasure I have found in it, sollicits me strongly to spend in the same manner all the other hours, wherein I may be permitted to divert my self. To conclude, this Argument is so pleasant and so fertile, that one needs but to propose it, and it will beget a thousand pleasing thoughts . . . so that without boasting of my Book, I may affirm, that the more Wit a man hath, the more pleasure he will find to read it.

It is perhaps the very circumscribed nature of Cordemoy's main line of reasoning that elicits, in the reader, the suggestive asides he hints at. His reader, Cordemoy affirms, "will find by occasion of the Discourse a thousand pretty things, which I have omitted." Historically speaking, then, Cordemoy's principal virtue is to have shown forcefully and at an early date in modernity the central role of language in any system of thought dedicated to explaining human mental operations (and, as Chomsky pointed out, the importance of understanding these operations if one is to grasp how language works). Yet, since he was himself unconcerned about matters that grammarians traditionally busy themselves with, he was able to let his imagination roam somewhat, begetting thereby "a thousand pleasing thoughts."

One aspect of Cordemoy's *Discourses* which, to my mind, is quite intriguing and which has hitherto received insufficient attention reflects his axiom that in—or thanks to—language one discerns souls other than oneself. The notion of dialogue—the speech act—underpins everything else, even personal "creativity": the Self is projected into its relationship with the Other. As Cordemoy repeatedly puts it, "To *speak* (in my opinion) is nothing else, but to make known what we think to that creature which is capable to understand it" (p. 14). Others "answer to my signes by other signes," indeed "it seems to me, that to *speak,* is not to repeat the same words, which have struck the ear, but to utter others to their purpose and suitable to them" (p. 13); parrots and echoes merely repeat. (In learning to speak the child utilizes the principle of association—e.g., frown = anger; sounds of words = things, actions—while participating in the speech, or dialogue, situation. He is able to do so because children "from their birth . . . have their reason [speech capacity and propensity] entire; because indeed this way of learning to speak is the effect of so great a discerning, and of so perfect reason, than a more wonderful one cannot possibly be conceived" [p. 37].) Although language serves to communicate thoughts, even though, in fact, it is sometimes difficult for us to extricate our interlocutor's thoughts from his language (p. 90), the essence of speech, it would appear, lies in the fact of interchange and in the creation of dialogue. Through dialogue we affirm our humanity, that is, we are free to incorporate into ourselves the thoughts of others and, presumably, thereby to rise above the limitations and loneliness of our individuality and to live socially. As Cordemoy states it, "men understand one another naturally" (p. 90). This is a powerful idea. It belongs to the history of modern egalitarianism and, interestingly, also to the Romantic expressionist traditions according to which human understanding no longer depends on mechanistic procedures. Rousseau, at the close of his *Confessions* (1788), is "understood naturally" by a deeply moved Mme. d'Egmont because, one supposes, she is an *âme sœur,* tuned in on his wave length. In other contexts, however, focusing upon the speech act will lead to new interpretations of what might, for lack of a better name, be termed "linguistic interpersonality." The concept is abstract and, as such, has been of considerable use in structuralist circles. One recalls Saussure's *circuit de la parole* as well as the "factors" and "functions" in Prague School theory (as, for example, Bühler or Jakobson),[9] and, more recently, the sociolinguistics developed by the late Uriel Weinreich and his Columbia team (see the important contribution by Weinreich, Labov, & Herzog, 1968). The modernist slants given to the old idea of dialogue do not perhaps originate with Cordemoy, but they are certainly present in recognizable form in his *Discourse of Speech*.

Equally imaginative and suggestive are Cordemoy's remarks on the "speech" of disembodied spirits: pure expression, as it were. We recall that, according to Cordemoy's dualist view of the matter, as "soon as there should be... necessity to borrow motions for expressing what we think, there would need no more to make other Spirits understand it, but to *will* that they should understand" (p. 115f.) Pure spirits may also communicate with men, indeed "naturally we can communicate with *meer Spirits* more easily than with *Men*" (p. 111), though, when they "would give any important advertisements to Men," spirits have usually borrowed "Bodies, and form'd Voices like those of men." Cordemoy attempts somewhat obliquely to account for Revelation; he stresses God's giving angels power to make themselves "understood by speech." "Inspiration" is consequently our being "spoken to" by spirits, the source of these "better thoughts" that "may come into our mind," although they "have no affinity to any of these, that naturally are in our Soul" (p. 114).

Cordemoy's conclusions follow quite logically from his premises. He expresses clearly and with great sobriety one of the kinds of spiritualism that seem to lie latent in doctrines that differentiate substantially between body and soul. But, quite strikingly, Cordemoy's analysis of the "speech" of spirits provides a fitting close to his meditation. In explaining inspiration, he returns to his occasionalist doctrine: "when one Soul will make known to another Soul what she thinketh, that happens foreasmuch as Almighty God brings it to pass" (p. 121). He praises God for endowing the human spirit with freedom to love Him and for having given us suffi-

---

[9]Significantly, Cordemoy comes very close to affirming, in just so many words, the arbitrary nature of the linguistic sign (or *signe d'institution*): "There is nothing less resembling our Thoughts, than is all that, which serves us to express them" (p. 21). And, as Rodis-Lewis has shown, this viewpoint is "vigorously defended" by Malebranche "contre les partisans d'une langue originelle naturellement expressive" (p. 20f.). (Cf. Brekle, 1970, p. xxviiiff.; 1976, p. 66ff.)

cient "power of *knowing,*" in order "to know the things of Nature as much as 'tis usefull to know them" (p. 123). In short, what Cordemoy has studied, namely, "all the several wayes, whereby Thoughts may be communicated, which is properly what we call Speaking," fits into a larger, still more coherent view of man in Creation. This view is also fully expressed in the *Discourse Written to a Learned Frier.* The communication of spirits, or inspiration, allows Cordemoy to tie the strands of his vision together and to locate man at his proper place in a beautifully proportioned, harmonious universe. The meditation, in drawing to a close, acquires a kind of poetic shape which serves to express Cordemoy's awe at the marvels he has just treated of and, finally, to suggest to us the reality of "things to be found, that are beyond our natural light." We understand, at last, that when one speculates seriously on the mysteries of language one is unavoidably led to touch on many other matters. Cordemoy shows his own awareness of this when he wisely shies away from "insisting on the consideration of all the great Truths, that might be collected from this whole Discourse."

These "great Truths," or, at least, discussions revolving about them, have come, in curious ways, to permeate much of the considerable debate surrounding the complex issue now known as "Cartesian linguistics." "Cartesian linguistics" provides a veritable laboratory case, then, for those of us interested in exploring the larger issues involving us and our seventeenth- and eighteenth-century "predecessors." I have already referred to Chomsky's largely sympathetic treatment of Cordemoy's thought and to his willingness—eagerness, even—to accept the sort of metaphysical assumptions proclaimed as necessary by Cordemoy. At the start of this essay we noted that as for Cordemoy so with Chomsky: "linguistics" (= speculation concerning language) and a specific variety of "philosophy of mind" go hand in hand: and their association is predicated by both thinkers on strikingly similar grounds. Indeed, some scholars have pointed out areas of agreement between Cordemoy and Chomsky that the latter himself, for one reason or another, chose not to stress. Thus, Brekle (1970, p. xxi; 1976, p. 69) remarks that Cordemoy's sketching out the possibility of a correlation between the child's linguistic apprenticeship and a general theory of grammar is taken up, without reference to Cordemoy, by Chomsky (1965, p. 59). (Chomsky's reference to Beattie [1788] on the same page, however, goes unmentioned by Brekle.) Meanwhile, critics of the notion of "Cartesian linguistics" tend to break down into two, often allied, camps: those who find Chomsky's historiography (1966) wanting (e.g., superficial, distorted, inaccurate) and those who simply reject the philosophical assumptions shared by Cordemoy and Chomsky. Even though it was perhaps in the interest of Chomsky's thesis to ignore entirely Condillac's refutation of Cartesianism—which is precisely what he did—I felt (Uitti, 1969, p. 76f.), and believe today, that his failure to account for that refutation (even to address himself to it) and to examine Condillac's having focused on Man's *creations* in order to describe more fully his "creativity" did violence both to the history of "Cartesian linguistics" and to the set of conceptual schemes Chomsky considers, essentially to be "true." It is, therefore, substantially Chomsky's fault that discussion of "Cartesian linguistics" has often taken place in a distasteful atmosphere of intellectual arrogance, of polemic and diatribe. The vulgarity of much of what passes for "thought" in certain behaviorist circles has been matched—to some degree, even, justified—by Chomsky's serious sins of omission.

Joly (1977) goes further than most critics in his denunciation of "Cartesian linguistics" as a "memorable error." Not only does he catalog Chomsky's alleged misreadings of seventeenth- and eighteenth-century texts and deplore his (to Joly) erroneous insistence upon that period's Cartesian character, he stresses the, to him suspicious, causes underlying Chomsky's affinity for Descartes and his followers. Joly professes little esteem for Descartes; he explains—and, to my mind, interestingly, though with far too much partiality—Descartes's appeal to his contemporaries (and, one assumes, to Chomsky) by underlining the autobiographical character of the *Discourse on Method* ("un essai où le philosophe, toujours présent, et davantage préoccupé de la découverte de soi que de découverte scientifique, dit ouvertement [and shamelessly?]'je'" [p. 175]). Though Chomsky was "mistaken" in not choosing his model from among the "true scientists" of the period (Bacon, Galileo) and, in consequence, failed to understand Locke, Condillac, DuMarsais, Harris, Beattie, etc. (the authentic giants, who explored, in really cogent and "modern" fashion, the relationships between language and mind), his mistake is nevertheless understandable. Chomsky, presumably sharing Descartes's concern for self-knowledge (a concern reflected in Chomsky's "typically American" need, and search, for a "father" [p. 190]), also, though confusedly, hit upon a point of genuine affinity between Descartes's "system" and his own "theory":

> Fortement marquées par le raisonnement mathématique, les deux démarches sont essentiellement déductives et elles débouchent sur le même type d'expli-

cation étroitement mécaniste des phénomènes. Car la grammaire générative
transformationnelle est une forme de néo-mécanisme. Pour reprendre une
comparaison de Molho, la description du langage que fait Chomsky est au
fonctionnement réel du langage ce que la machine volante est à l'oiseau,
c'est-à-dire, en termes cartésiens, ce que l'homme-machine est à l'homme.
(Joly, 1977, p. 190)

Thus, paradoxically, despite his ostensible rejection of Bloomfieldian linguistic "mechanism" and behaviorist psychology (one of the reasons
adduced by Joly to explain why Chomsky chose to identify his manner
with the thought of Descartes), Chomsky is essentially a ... mechanist.
Joly concludes that Chomsky has made no contribution whatsoever to
"historical epistemology," that, in fact, because of his great prestige, his
ill-starred efforts have muddied the waters

Joly's judgment derives, to be sure, from his own parti-pris. For him
not only is an accurate (i.e., "right-thinking") "historical epistemology"
a desirable thing, what is authentically "historical" in his eyes differs, at
least in practice if not in intent, from what Chomsky called "studies of a
more philosophical bent, devoted to the deep intellectual connections that
have always existed between the study of language, on the one hand, and
theoretical psychology and the philosophy of the mind, on the other"
(1966, p. xi). Thus, in Joly's view, Cordemoy, considered by Chomsky as
a predecessor whose work, one assumes, explored "deep intellectual
connections" of this sort, must be denied the "linguistic relevance" (por-
tée linguistique [p. 179]) Chomsky accords him. Joly puts Cordemoy in
his place (as he sees it), namely within the "reactionary" Cartesian
"theologico-rationalist" framework ("théologique en profondeur sous
une surface rationaliste"); this allows Joly to dismiss Cordemoy. Hence,
if I understand Joly aright, Cordemoy's "out-dated" ideological context
(= Cartesian dualism, belief in God) renders what he has to say about, and
what appears to sound like, "linguistic creativity" in human beings simply impertinent: it is nonsense, at least as far as we moderns are—or ought
to be—concerned. Unlike M. Homais, Cordemoy did not march with his
times; nor, the inference seems to run, does Chomsky the historian (or,
perhaps, Chomsky the linguist) march with *his* time. Joly's "historical
epistemology" thus differs profoundly from what one might, albeit
loosely, call intellectual history in that it (and here Joly and Chomsky do
resemble one another) picks and chooses what is relevant (= "correct")
and irrelevant (= "incorrect") in the thought of the past—the picking and
choosing to be determined by the picker and chooser's own, *a priori,*
view of the world. Similarly, G. Ryle, whose anti-Cartesian *Concept of*

Mind (1949) was criticized by Chomsky (1966, p. 12), is reported (Brekle [1970, p. xxii; 1976, p. 70]) to have responded that "Man need not be degraded to a machine by being denied to be a ghost in a machine" (Cordemoy's "Man" is here decomposed into "ghost" + "machine"). Ryle's irony reflects his own philosophical bias, his own manner of reaching, and dealing with, "great Truths," yet there is something, to my mind, reductionist about this irony, at least in intellectual historical terms. Ryle's *boutade* continues in the further suggestion that Man "might, after all, be a sort of animal, namely a higher mammal. There has yet to be ventured the hazardous leap to the hypothesis that perhaps he is a man." In a very real sense—and I mean this both positively and negatively—Chomsky, Joly, and Ryle deserve each other.

I have already alluded to the kind of poetic shape that characterizes, at least as I see it, Cordemoy's *Discourse Written to a Learned Frier* (as well as, I think, his other *Discourses*). Cordemoy possessed a highly Platonic bent of mind; this is evidenced particularly, though not exclusively,[10] in the extraordinary concern—theoretical and practical—he manifested for dialogue. The coherence of his thought, related to and yet apart from its intellectual antecedents and influences, is indissolubly linked to the expression—the form—that incarnates it. (The same may be said, indeed, of the relationship between the meaning and the autobiographical character of Descartes's *Discourse on Method*.) Cordemoy's work and its reader therefore both stand to gain from the reader's making every effort to cope with this work on its own terms, as, to use Condillac's term, an "ouvrage de l'espirit." Only when understood in this way might this work, like, e.g., Plato's *Cratylus,* be assigned its proper place in what Battail, very suggestively, called "le vieux dialogue, toujours repris et toujours à reprendre, entre le sujet et l'objet, entre la nature et la raison, entre la forme et le sens" (1973, p. 232). Cordemoy's participation in this "ancien dialogue," itself dialogic, confers a genuine "intemporelle actualité" (p. 232) upon his work; failure to understand the nature of this participation will impoverish our own participation in the dialogue every bit as much as our distortion, for whatever reason, of that work also, I suspect, would constitute an impoverishment.

---

[10]Taking up on some remarks made by the late A. Adam (1956–1962), Battail comments on specifically Platonic resonances in Cordemoy's thought, particularly the influence of the *Republic* on Cordemoy's political treatise, *De la Réformation de l'État* (contained in the 1704 edition of his collected works), and, indeed, on Cordemoy's learned circle of friends (Battail, 1973, pp. 10, 17, *passim*).

Refusing to distinguish, in absolute terms, between the "poetic" and the "scientific," Condillac, I think, put the matter very well. At the close of his *Essai sur l'origine des connoissances humaines* (1746), Condillac challenges all students of thought; his words (as the example of the dramatist Corneille shows) are particularly apt in the case of works, like those of Cordemoy and Plato himself, whose inner coherence is a predominant and indispensable characteristic:

> Je finis par proposer ce problème au lecteur. *L'ouvrage d'un homme étant donné, déterminer le caractère et l'étendue de son esprit, et dire en conséquence non seulement quels sont les talens dont il donne des preuves, mais encore quels sont ceux qu'il peut acquérir: prendre par exemple, la première pièce de Corneille, et démontrer que, quand ce poëte le composoit, il avoit déjà, ou du moins auroit bientôt tout le génie qui lui a mérité de si grands succès.* Il n'y a que l'analyse de l'ouvrage qui puisse faire connoître quelles opérations y ont contribué, et jusqu'à quel degré elles ont eu de l'exercice: et il n'y a que l'analyse de ces opérations qui puisse faire distinguer les qualités qui sont compatibles dans le même homme, de celles qui ne le sont pas, et par-là donner la solution du problème. Je doute qu'il y ait beaucoup de problêmes plus difficiles que celui-là.

Cordemoy's work—and Battail, especially, demonstrates this quite well—is very much "l'ouvrage d'un homme," and only secondarily a specific contribution to a "discipline," or to a set of disciplines, in the "modern" and even in the Aristotelian sense. That is why Joly is not entirely wrong in condemning Chomsky's (symbolic) use of Cordemoy, but that is also why, as we saw, Joly's "historical epistemology," in refusing to deal with Cordemoy on his own terms, i.e., positively, distorts—is almost literally unable to recognize—what Cordemoy wrote.

Now then, if "Cartesian linguistics" is beside the point, or to the point merely in regard to the intellectual history of the past decade or so, where does that leave us with respect to Cordemoy? After all, Chomsky's essay did a great deal to kindle a new interest—a nonantiquarian interest—in Cordemoy's work. And what, in general, of our present-day stance in regard to seventeenth- and eighteenth-century thought?

It seems clear, first of all, that one can no longer with impunity simply dismiss, say, the seventeenth-century metaphysicians because they are "out-of-date," i.e., because, one suspects, they believed in God and thought, or acted, accordingly. (Nor can Condillac be left unread because he, too, but for other reasons, has been "superseded.") At the very least, a kind of humanistically oriented critical concern for these thinkers is essential—or so many of us are increasingly prepared to believe—to the well-being of *our* thinking as linguists, philosophers, psychologists, and the like. Humanists are, or ought to be, very cautious before labeling thoughts "out-of-date." Modes of thinking have a way of making comebacks. Who, nowadays, would be willing to echo Voltaire's judgment that "Dante, Sir, was a madman"?

Secondly, the long drawn-out debate between "rationalists" and "empiricists," especially to the degree that its late-twentieth-century historians (like Joly) choose to take sides, has obfuscated a number of issues fully as much as it has helped shed light on others. Although, as we saw, Condillac, for one, made mock of the elaborate metaphysical systems constructed during the seventeenth century and clearly found the examples of Newton and Locke more congenial than, e.g., Malebranche, he participated, surely, in debates within which the "metaphysicians," including Descartes, must be viewed as his indispensable interlocutors. Indeed, the very tags "rationalist" and "empiricist" hardly do justice to the complexities of an age which, at least as far as concerns matters of linguistic speculation, includes a remarkably coherent tradition—a tradition recognized as such, though distorted by both Chomsky and Joly, and extending at least as far back as Ramus (with roots in medieval and ancient thought) and continuing up to Humboldt and Romantic comparative grammar. These labels, then, like Sapir's "grammar," have a strong propensity to leak.

G. Clérico, discussing what she calls (I hope with tongue in cheek) the "rehabilitation" of Sánchez de las Brozas and his *Minerva,* notes that the great Spanish scholar-linguist has been the victim of numerous critical interpretations and distortions, all due to the "ideological prejudices" and "intellectual preoccupations" of the various critics involved; she concludes: "Mais afin que les déviations, les déformations que l'on impose à l'œuvre ne lui soient pas trop préjudiciables, il n'est qu'un moyen: le retour au texte" (1977, p. 131). A "return to the text," as advised by Clérico, can be very informative. A close reading of, e.g., James Harris's influential *Hermes* (1751; 1765; 1786) reveals, among other things, that not only does Harris resist classification as "rationalist" or "empiricist," he is, in fact, opposed to both these trends. Yet, *Hermes* belongs body and soul to the above-named tradition of linguistic speculation (1550–1850) within which, in more or less pure state, the rationalists and the empiricists also flourished. That that tradition really existed, as such, is nowhere more clearly confirmed than in the translation with commentary made of *Hermes* (1765) by the ambitious young French *idéologue*-grammarian, François Thurot, in 1796. Thurot praises Harris, despite, for him, the aristocratic Englishman's philosophical and methodological in-adequacies. He thereupon proceeds to bring Harris up to date, outfitting *Hermes* with a full *apparatus criticus* borrowed from Condillac-inspired ideological *grammaire philosophique* (see Uitti, 1977). In a sense, Thurot did unto Harris what Chomsky, much later, was to do unto Cordemoy; but both were able to do so because of the nature of the text—Harris's and Cordemoy's, respectively—with which they (especially Thurot) were working.

Thurot and Chomsky did not "return to the text," they brought the text to themselves. (In Thurot's case this act can be justified in that, historically speaking, he and Harris did in fact belong, each in his own way, to the same tradition.) If certain readers of the present volume wish, in the case of Cordemoy, to follow their (i.e., especially Chomsky's) example, all well and good, provided they know that that is what they are doing. And provided, for the reasons I have tried to point out, that they make fully knowledgeable use—i.e., sparingly—of such categories as "rationalist" and "empiricist." Provided, moreover, that they take stock of the inner coherence of Cordemoy's work—its nature—and, finally, provided that they recognize the importance of the three centuries of linguistic speculation I alluded to above as well as its possible relevance, nowadays, to us. It simply will not do to dismiss ghosts, or God, out of hand.

As for historians (or, say, psychologists and linguists who at least temporarily doff the historian's cap), a genuine "return to the text," in Clérico's sense and following Condillac's precepts, would be highly ad-visable, particularly in the case of an *œuvre* like that of Cordemoy. Not only would a more genuine, and firm, understanding of our disciplinary underpinnings result from such an undertaking, but study of this sort would certainly lead to at least a partial remedying of the fragmentation into which, some of us suspect, our disciplines have at present fallen. For what characterizes the Ramus-Romantics tradition is at once, as in our own case, an obsession with the mediating power of language (often viewed as one or another form of "grammar") and, unlike for most of us, the necessary linking of the concern for this mediating power with a broadly conceived, general (i.e., nonspecialized) view of Man. ("Reac-tionary" rationalists and "forward-looking" empiricists, or, as Chomsky might prefer [Zimmer, 1968, p. 293], "progressive" rationalists and "reactionary" empiricists, together believed in the necessity of this link-ing, as, indeed, did the independent, "unaffiliated," Harris.) For us, specialization has become (willy-nilly?) preeminent, at least in practice; during the period 1550 to 1850, we saw, and nowhere more clearly than in matters related to linguistic speculation, specialization was thought to serve the principle of a general view. (The *principle* predominated even though, in fact, many "general views" were formulated.) The existence of the present volume proves that we are concerned with these matters, that, indeed, we have glimpsed the affinity-in-similarity that binds us to the *grands siècles* as well as—and no less importantly—the affinity-in-dissimilarity that separates our times from their's. We have a great deal to learn. By returning to texts, in all philological humility, we stand, I think, a good chance of *establishing* the texts out of which, we recognize, our own *œuvres* have grown and to which, with lucidity and more globally than in the past, we must now respond.

To be specific, rereading Cordemoy will force us, quite healthily, to meditate on these issues. And, alongside what Cordemoy wrote concerning language acquisition in children, the different kinds of signs humans use, "natural" word order, and the "creativity" inherent in human speech, we must consider the centrality, for him, of the dialogic in language as well as the centrality, within his system, of language itself for human society. All these things cohere in Cordemoy. Should they do so also for us? If so, why, and at what price? Is, indeed, this kind of coherence itself to be desired or to be avoided? To paraphrase Condillac, this, for us, is a perfectly legitimate "problème."

References

Aarsleff, H. The history of linguistics and Professor Chomsky. *Language,* 1970, *46,* 570–585.

Adam, A. *Histoire de la littérature française au XVIIe siècle.* Vols. 1–5 (especially Vol. 3). Paris: Domat, Montchrestien, 1948–1956. (Also: Paris: Del Duca, 1962–1968.)

Arnauld, A., & Lancelot, C. *Grammaire générale et raisonnée contenant les fondemens de l'art de parler.* . . . Paris: chez Pierre le Petit, 1660.

Battail, J.-F. *L'avocat philosophe Géraud de Cordemoy (1624–1684).* La Haye: M. Nijhoff, 1973.

Boas, G. *Dominant themes of modern philosophy.* New York: Ronald Press, 1957.

Bouillier, F. C. Histoire de la philosophie cartésienne. Paris: C. Delagrave, 1868₃.

Bréhier, E. *The history of philosophy: the seventeenth century.* Chicago: University of Chicago Press, 1966. (French original: Paris, 1938.)

Brekle, H. E. Forematter to reprint of G. de Cordemoy, *Discours physique de la parole.* Facsimile reprint of 1677 edition. Stuttgart-Bad Cannstatt: F. Frommann Verlag, 1970.

Brekle, H. E. Quelques aspects linguistiques et psychologiques dans le *Discours physique de la parole* (1677) de Géraud de Cordemoy. In H.-J. Niederehe and H. Haarmann

(Eds.), *Im memoriam Friedrich Diez: Akten des Kolloquiums zur Wissenschaftsges-chichte der Romanistik*. Amsterdam: J. Benjamins, 1976.

Brunot, F. *Histoire de la langue française des origines à 1900*. Vol. 6 No. 2 by A. François. Paris: A. Colin, 1932. (See, especially, "La grammaire et les grammairiens.")

Chomsky, N. *Aspects of the theory of syntax*. Cambridge, Mass.: M.I.T. Press, 1965.

Chomsky, N. *Cartesian linguistics: A chapter in the history of rationalist thought*. New York: Harper & Row, 1966.

Clérico, G. F. Sanctius: Histoire d'une réhabilitation. In A. Joly & J. Stéfanini (Eds.), *La grammaire générale des modistes aux idéologues*. Lille: Publications de l'Université de Lille, 1977.

Condillac, E. B. de. *Essai sur l'origine des connoissances humaines* (Paris, 1746). (See edition of Condillac's works prepared by G. LeRoy. Vols. 1–3. Paris: Presses Universitaires de France, 1947–1951.)

Condillac, E. B. de. *Traité des systêmes* (Paris 1749 [1771₂]). (See edition of Condillac's works prepared by G. LeRoy. Vols. 1–3. Paris: Presses Universitaires de France, 1947–1951.)

Cordemoy, G. de. *Œuvres philosophiques, avec une étude biobibliographique*. Édition critique présentée par P. Clair et F. Girbal. Paris: Presses Universitaires de France 1968. (Contains the text of the first six *Discours* [= the *Discernement*] the *Discours physique de la parole*, the *Lettre écrite au R. P. Cossart* [= "Sçavant religieux"], and other treatises.)

Cordemoy, G. de. *A philosophicall discourse concerning speech (1668) and a discourse written to a learned frier (1670)*. New York: AMS Press, 1974.

Damiron, J.-P. *Essai sur l'histoire de la philosophie en France au XVIIe siècle*. Vol 2. Paris: Hachette, 1846.

Descartes, R. *Correspondance*. Ch. Adam and G. Milhaud (Eds.). Vol. 1. Paris: Alcan, 1936.

Descartes, R. *Philosophical works*. Translated by E. S. Haldane and G. R. T. Ross. New York: Dover Publications, 1955.

Harris, J. *Hermes, or a philosophical inquiry concerning universal grammar*. Fourth, revised edition. London: C. Nourse, 1786. (A photographic reprint of this text is provided, with a Preface by K. D. Uitti, in Vol. 1 of Harris's *Works*. New York: AMS Press, 1975.)

Harris, J. *Hermès, ou recherches philosophiques sur la grammaire universelle; traduction et remarques par François Thurot (1796)*. Facsimile edition, Introduction and Notes by A. Joly. Geneva-Paris: Droz, 1972. (A superbly annotated text.)

Joly, A. La linguistique cartésienne: une erreur mémorable. In A. Joly and J. Stefanini (Eds.), *La grammaire générale des modistes aux idéologues*. Lille: Publications de l'Université de Lille, 1977.

Katz, J. J. *The philosophy of language*. New York: Harper & Row, 1966.

Knight, I. F. *The geometric spirit*. New Haven: Yale University Press, 1968.

Pellisson, P., & D'Olivet, P.-J. *Histoire de l'Académie française*. Ch.-L. Livet (Ed.), Vols. 1–2. Paris: Didier, 1858.

Racine, J. *Œuvres*. P. Mesnard (Ed.), Vol. 4. Paris: Hachette, 1886.

Rivaud, A. *Histoire de la philosophie: l'époque classique*. Vol. 3. Paris: Presses Universitaires de France, 1950.

Rodis-Lewis, G. Un théoricien du langage au XVIIe siècle: Bernard Lamy. *Français Moderne*, 1968, *36*, 19–50.

Rosenfield, L. D. *From beast-machine to man-machine*. New York: Oxford University Press, 1941.

Ryle, G. *The concept of mind*. London: Hutchinson, 1949.

Sanctius, F. [Sánchez de las Brozas]. *Minerva seu de causis linguæ latinæ commentarius* [1587], add. by G. Scoppius and J. Perizonius. C. L. Bauerus (Ed.). Leipzig: J. A. Barthius, 1793.

Ueberweg, F. *Grundriss der Geschichte der Philosphie*. Vol. 3. Basel: Schwabe, 1953₁₃.

Uitti, K. D. Descartes and Port-Royal in two diverse retrospects. *Romance Philology*, 1969, *23*, 75–85.

Uitti, K. D. James Harris' *Hermes* in the context of revolutionary France: the translations and commentaries by François Thurot. In J. Macary (Ed.), *Essays on the age of enlightenment in honor of Ira O. Wade*. Geneva: Droz, 1977.

Vartanian, A. *La Mettrie's* l'Homme machine: *A study in the origins of an idea*. Princeton: Princeton University Press, 1960.

Weinreich, U., Labov, W., & Herzog, M. I. Empirical foundations for a theory of language change. In W. P. Lehmann & Y. Malkiel (Eds.), *Directions for historical linguistics*. Austin: University of Texas Press, 1968.

Zimmer, K. Review of Chomsky (1966). *International Journal of American Linguistics*, 1968, *34*, 293.

3

James H. Stam

CONDILLAC'S EPISTEMOLINGUISTIC QUESTION*

It is arguable, but it makes good sense nonetheless, to say that Etienne Bonnot de Condillac [1715–1780] was the first thinker to give systematic consideration to "the psycholinguistic question," as that term is characteristically understood today. Perhaps "epistemolinguistic question" would be the more accurate designation. The question entailed is that of the influence or relationship between language (in particular or in general) and an individual's mental development. It is a significantly different issue from that posed by so many students of universal or rational grammar in the previous century: the relationship between language, "fully grammatical," and mind, "fully rational"—a formulation of the problem which focused the genesis neither of language nor of rationality. Nor is Condillac's epistemolinguistic question entirely the same as the problem of the origin of language *per se,* one of the most popular topics of late eighteenth-and early nineteenth-century speculation. Again, it is different

*This essay is based in part on the author's introduction to Condillac's *An Essay on the Origin of Human Knowledge,* translated by Nugent (London, 1756), reprinted in the series *Language, Man and Society: Foundations of the Behavioral Sciences,* edited by R. W. Rieber (New York: AMS Press, Inc., 1974); and in part on passages from the author's *Inquiries into the Origin of Language: The Fate of a Question* (New York; Harper & Row, Publishers, 1976).

James H. Stam • Department of Philosophy and Religion, Upsala College, East Orange, New Jersey 07019.

from the examination of *lógos* as both reason and speech among the Stoics and earlier Greek philosophers. The epistemolinguistic issue was, to be sure, adumbrated in context by sundry empiricist philosophers: Hobbes and Locke, for example, assigned an appropriate place to language in the sequence of mental faculties and operations. With the possible exception of David Hartley, however—whose *Observations on Man, his Duty, his Frame, and his Expectations* appeared after Condillac's *Essai* in any case—none had previously tried to work out the full range of consequences entailed in the correlation of linguistic and mental development (cf. Stam, 1976, pp. 32–35).

Condillac was born Etienne Bonnot in Grenoble in 1714. Sickly, of poor vision, and slow to learn, his youth was unpromising, but he pursued theological studies nonetheless at Saint-Sulpice and the Sorbonne, only to abandon any active priesthood immediately upon his ordination. His formal education was spotty, and the man whose theoretical interests in language endured throughout his life never learned any languages other than Latin and his native French. Nor was his reading impressively extensive, but his personal contacts were of the first rank: the Abbé Gabriel Bonnot de Mably, the socialist *philosophe,* was his brother; d'Alembert was his cousin; Rousseau was tutor to Condillac's nephews—and their personal friendship lasted well into Rousseau's years of madness; and by frequenting the Parisian salons he had contact with most of the luminaries of the French Enlightenment.

Condillac's first book, *Essai sur l'origine des connaissances humaines* (1746) expounded and revised the empiricist epistemology of John Locke, already popular with French thinkers. His secure position in Englightenment circles was fully established with his second book, in 1749, the *Traité des systémes,* an attack on metaphysical dogmatism and the accepted rationalism and in general on the *"esprit de système."* The *Traité des sensations* (1754) elaborated the image now most often cited in the textbooks—an inanimate, insensate statue, endowed one by one with the basic senses and higher faculties (but not including language)—an image designed to give illustrative demonstration of the theory that all human cognition can be reduced to elements of sense. A *Dissertation sur la liberté* was published as an appendix to the *Treatise on the Sensations.* In the following year, 1755, a *Traité des animaux* was published together with a *Dissertation sur l'existence de Dieu,* anti-materialist defenses of the uniqueness of man, directed against the mechanistic interpretations of beasts as automata in Descartes and Buffon. Condillac was tutor to the

Prince of Parma from 1758 until 1767, and while there, he composed a variety of works on grammar, logic, and history for his student's instruction. These works were finally published, a few years before Condillac's death, and after numerous complications and some resistance to their appearance, as the *Cours d'études*. After his return to France from Parma, Condillac was elected to the Académie française, in which he was inactive, and later to the Société royale d'agriculture d'Orléans. In 1776, he published *Le Commerce et le gouvernement considérés relativement l'un à l'autre*, a treatise in the newly fashionable area of political economy. At the request of the Polish government, which wanted to use Condillac's work in public instruction, he composed his most systematic exposition of the "method of analysis," *La Logique*, which appeared in 1780, the year of his death. Finally, *La Langue des calculs*, which was published posthumously as a fragment, explained algebra and mathematics as exemplars of methodically analytic language. These very titles betray the persistence of Condillac's interests in language and mind.

Condillac's philosophical preferences inclined toward the English, particularly Newton and Locke, all of whom he read in French summary or translation. The subtitle of the *Essay on the Origin of Human Knowledge* modestly advertised it as a "Supplement to Mr. Locke's *Essay on the Human Understanding*." Locke was, to a great extent, "The Philosopher" for the *philosophes*, but the other British empiricists, too, were embraced and appropriated by the French enlighteners. Voltaire's *Philosophical Letters*, which first appeared in English translation as *Letters Concerning the English Nation*, popularized the school for Frenchmen, and Condillac's *Essai* systematized the master as well. A whole line of British empiricists—Bacon, Hobbes, Locke, Berkeley, Hume, many minor figures and some earlier ones—had argued in varying degrees of generality that all knowledge, all contents of the mind, could be traced back to experience of some kind. Locke had argued in his own *Essay* that the full array of human knowledge was derivable from two primary sources, sensation and reflection. The former involved data acquired through any of the five senses, whereas the latter was described by Locke as an "internal sense," or the mind's awareness of its own operations (II, i, 4). Thus Locke was a consistent empiricist—all contents of the mind are derivable from experience of some sort; but he was not a strict sensationalist—not all experience is of a sensuous kind. He considered sensation a *sine qua non* for reflection and necessarily prior to it, since the mind cannot be aware of its own operations until they are actually in operation; but Locke stoutly maintained that reflection is nonetheless autonomous, because its contents cannot be reduced to more primitive data of sense. Out of the building blocks provided by these two independent and primary sources, Locke sought to assemble all the most elevated and complex functions of human understanding and affection.

Condillac not only popularized and systematized Locke, he also revised him. Condillac objected that Locke's doctrine of autonomous reflection was an unnecessary concession, an inconsistency which weakened the entire edifice (cf. Cousin, 1866, pp. 59ff.). It implied that there was something innate in the mind, incited perhaps by circumstance, but not explicable as a response to the stimulative phenomena of the world perceived by sense. Condillac tried to show, particularly in the *Essay* and in the *Treatise on the Sensations,* that all supposedly independent reflections are derivable as compositions from sensory data, since ideas are formed by a prereflective process of association requiring the use of signs. "The ideas are connected with the signs, and it is only by this means . . . they are connected with each other" (Condillac, 1756, pp. 7–8).

Condillac's emendation of the Lockean explanation of reflection helped bring problems of language and its genesis into the stage center of epistemology. Locke himself had devoted an entire book of his *Essay* to the subject "Of Words." Locke, however, was concerned almost exclusively with the classificatory and communicative functions of language, hence with its utility in scientific taxonomy and social intercourse (cf. Givner, 1962). In neither context did Locke emphasize any role of language in the cognitive development of the psyche. Language served the goal of scientific precision in properly distinguishing genera and species *after* the mind had fully evolved the capacity to make such distinctions; and, on the other hand, language was assumed as something already given when Locke treated it as a means of communication or as a parent's assistance to the child's developing mind in the formation of general concepts. Locke sometimes spoke as though little babies not only sensed, for example, a cube of sugar, but as though they recognized it *as* cubical, white, and sweet, and as though the attachment of names were simply the conventional designations for such recognitions. It is in these regards that Condillac's approach differed from Locke's by much more than a point or so of epistemological schematism. For Condillac, the seeds of language, if not its full flower, were present and well rooted prior to reflection (cf. Formigari, 1974, pp. 277ff.). Indeed, the whole mental development up to and beyond reflection would have been quite impossible in the absence of a linguistic factor—*signs*.

Signs were of such critical importance because it was in terms of the "connexion of ideas" (*la liaison des idées*) that Condillac explained the development from sensation to reflection and the higher faculties. The impressions made by sense upon the mind are not neutral or even in their force. Instead they are regulated, patterned, and brought into relief by the progressive operations of *perception* (the mind's reception of the sense datum), *consciousness* (the mere awareness of perceptions), *attention* (concentration on certain perceptions over others), *reminiscence* (recognition that some of the perceptions so heeded have occurred before)—and beyond these, *Imagination* (the ability to revive some perceptions as recollected images in the mind), *contemplation* (the power to preserve "the perception, the name or the circumstances of an object which is vanished out of sight"), and *memory* (which retains only the name or circumstances of perceptions, because it is impossible to revive the image itself). The last group of these—imagination, contemplation, and memory—come into operation on account of the connection or association of ideas (cf. Condillac, 1756, pp. 26–50). But the mechanism of *liaison*, the "real cause of the progress of the imagination, contemplation, and memory" (p. 51) is the use of signs, which reinforce and preserve the associations.

The critical role of signs for Condillac led him to criticize Locke on still another point. Locke did not recognize the deeper epistemological relevance of signs, or of language generally for that matter, because he saw the main purpose of language in the communication of already formed ideas and overlooked its role in the very process whereby such ideas are formed. According to Condillac, the function of signs is so basic that deaf-mutes or isolated children would, in order to reason, have to contrive some system of internal signs. He distinguished three types of signs: *accidental* (when the circumstances or part of an experience evokes association with the whole), *natural* (cries or gestures expressive of passionate response), and *instituted* (conventional words or other arbitrary means of signification) (p. 51). In imagination and contemplation all three kinds may be operative, and for memory all three are necessary. Thus, the brutes, who have no instituted signs, cannot advance beyond reminiscence or, at most, imagination. The use of signs puts the mind in command of itself and raises it to a human level, so that it is no longer a merely passive receiver. Instead, it can recall ideas at will, compound and decompound them, distinguish and abstract and compare, affirm and deny, and ultimately reason. On the other hand, the necessity for signs stems, in part, from the limitations of human understanding: signs assist the finite mind when ideas involve such a manifold of qualities that it is impossible to grasp them all at once. Condillac even remarked that an infinite being would have no need of any language or sign system. It is only through the use of signs that mere consciousness can pass over into meaningful reflection, and that the mind can become aware of its true strengths as well as its limits.

The role assigned to linguistic signs in Condillac's epistemological system tended to force the question of language origin (cf. Harnois, 1928; Kuehner, 1944; Stam, 1976). If the recourse to signs is already required at the earliest stages of the evolution of the human mind, then how did the use of signs itself develop? The *Essay* was published during a decade and early in a period somewhat longer than a century when speculations about the first beginnings of language were rife. Vico, La Mettrie, Rousseau, Herder, Hamann, Fichte, the Schlegels, British romanticists, French conservatives, numerous comparative linguists, and pioneering evolutionists—to mention only the most prominent—placed critical emphasis on the interpretation of linguistic origins (cf. Stam, 1976). The entire second half of Condillac's *Essai* was devoted to language and method, beginning with a lengthy section, "Of the Origin and Progress of Language." Here again Condillac departed from Locke, to whom this whole area of interest was foreign. Locke virtually took for granted a language which had somehow or other fully developed, and his real concern in the *Essay* was not with the origin of language but with "the original of all our notions and knowledge" (III, i, 5).

In approaching the problem, Condillac made use of a device occasionally employed by eighteenth-century explicators of primitive obscurities. He affirmed—perhaps sincerely, but in any case conveniently—that the gift of speech was bestowed upon Adam and Eve supernaturally by the Deity (Condillac, 1756, p. 169); but he quickly went on to suppose how two children, alone and astray after the Deluge, might have gone about the creation of signs without such divine intervention. (A similar device had been used by Bishop William Warburton, whom Condillac acknowledges, in his *The Divine Legation of Moses* IV, 4; and, though direct influence cannot be substantiated, Bernard de Mandeville took a parallel approach in his *Fable of the Bees;* cf. Kaye, 1922, 1924.)

Such a supposition would allow investigation of the way in which language *might have been* invented by man. The remainder of the Second Part, of course, was an elaboration of the supposition with no regard to the initial affirmation of miraculous origin. Condillac's epistemology already postulated the necessity of "inward language," the use of signs for the advancement of thought; but the device of an isolated boy and girl allowed him to sketch a conjectural account of the way in which external language, language for interaction and communication, might come about.

Like other living creatures, the isolated children would have expressed their states of pleasure or pain, fear or satisfaction, with natural cries, facial expressions, and emotive gestures. Because human beings are innately compassionate, according to Condillac (as later for Rousseau), such gesticulations would gradually become the basis for mutual understanding. The first of the hypothetical children might have moved his arms and hands in a certain way in pressing need or danger. The second child would have responded with automatic sympathy and assistance. This combination of pressing need and instinctive compassion would transform some of the cries and gestures into functional signs.

> Thus by instinct alone they asked and gave each other assistance. I say *by instinct alone;* for as yet there was no room for reflexion. One of them did not say to himself, *I must make such particular motions to render him sensible to my want, and to induce him to relieve me;* nor the other, *I see by his motions that he wants such a thing, and I will let him have it;* but they both acted in consequence of the want which pressed them most. (Condillac, 1756, pp. 172–173)

It took some time before fully articulate language developed. First, some of the manual gestures and bodily movements must have come to be associated with particular causes of concern, sources of contentment, or objects of the world. Condillac lingered long on the theme of chironomic and pantomimic media of expression—a theme which became important for aesthetic theories of the day, was taken up by Diderot in his *Letter on the Deaf and Dumb for the Use of Those Who Hear and Speak* (1751), and was given practical application in the sign language devised for the instruction of deaf-mutes (cf. Josephs, 1970; Seigel, 1969, 1980; see also Seigel's Introduction in Diderot, 1916/1973). Once reflection was activated by the use of signs, the hypothetical children (or the actual children of the human race) would have become aware that vocal sounds can serve as easily as conventional gestures to convey meaning. Language then became a mixture of articulated voice with the "language of action." Gradually, articulate speech came to predominate and nearly replace gesture and mimicry, because it was economical and convenient—all of which the mind would not have recognized in its prereflective state. In primitive understanding and communication, linguistic signs were already created, and without them the mind would never have progressed.

Since the role of signs was so important for him, Condillac was not only led to a concern with linguistic beginnings, but also to a much different understanding of the very function of language from that which had been implied by Locke. Bishop Berkeley, in several works, had anticipated the objection to Locke's narrow view of language as an instrument for the expression of already formed ideas: Berkeley had suggested that all sensation is akin to a form of language and he spoke especially of "visual language" (cf. Vol. I, p. 231, pp. 264ff.; Vol. III, pp. 149ff.). It is difficult to ascertain, however, whether Berkeley's criticisms were known to Condillac—Berkeley was still untranslated—since Condillac read no English and seems to have relied heavily on comments by Voltaire (cf. Knight, 1968, p. 95; Salvucci, 1957, pp. 117–119). Regardless, the basic point common to Berkeley and Condillac was that the importance of language extended beyond the communication of thoughts arrived at independently of language and prior to it. Rather, they saw language as a necessary component in the very formation of ideas and particularly in the advancement of the "higher faculties." It would become one of the commonplaces of German theories of language from Herder on that language cannot adequately be understood as a tool or instrument (cf. Stam, 1976, p. 304).

Language and its origin was of more than psychological interest: for Condillac, psychogenesis was a near perfect recapitulation of phylogensis. The progression of mental powers could be temporally projected as a tableau of the historical advancement of the human mind. Genetic epistemology in the style of Locke—the derivation of more complex from the more simple mental operations—was seized as the key which might unlock riddles of the forward movement of humanity. The progression from the sensate to the rational in the individual mind had its correlative in the progress from a primitive poetry of vague but concrete images to a modern science of abstract but precise formulas. Primitive language was metaphorical and sensuous, like the primal operations of the psyche. Early speech featured the visual and active along with the articulate; highly figurative and rhythmic, it was a medium well suited to poetry. Verbs, the most active elements, probably came first, then nouns representing undifferentiated wholes, and so on. The evolution of writing followed similar course: first picture writing, then hieroglyphics in which a partial image represented a complete idea, and finally the more abstract and entirely conventional use of alphabets. With the growing domination of abstract rationality, language became characteristically prosaic. Poetry was lost, but knowledge gained. As the art of reasoning is inseparable from that of speaking, so every language is itself a kind of method. Improvements in language and the advancement of science move in parallel progression, for, as Condillac commented in *La Langue des calculs,* "it is the method that does the inventing, just as telescopes do the discovering" (II, iv).

The history of language, as Condillac perceived it, provided the irrefutable documentation of progressive illumination. It was a picture drawn in more exact detail by Turgot and Condorcet. And it implied an outline of world history lifted out of the enlighteners by a majority of continental and English romanticists and their precursors, though these generally transvalued the terms involved and—to exaggerate and simplify their tendencies crudely—despaired of "cold" modern abstraction while they pined for the "warmth" of ancient poetic metaphor. This "historicization" of epistemology and psychology corresponded to the widely recognized "temporalizing of the great chain of being," whereby the ontological scale of classical metaphysics was reinterpreted in terms of cosmic origins, biological evolution, and human change (cf. Lovejoy, 1936; Sampson, 1956, pp. 86ff.). Later authors would fill in details of system and adjustments of value, but Condillac's picture of man's development of language is clearly intended as a miniature of the progress of human rationality (cf. Frankel, 1948, pp. 51–56; Knight, 1968, pp. 144ff.; Schaupp, 1926, pp. 59ff.).

Condillac's documentation for this historicolinguistic sketch was, to be sure, rather meager. He lifted a few examples from Hebrew out of his reading of Warburton; otherwise all his evidence for "primitive language" was taken from classical Latin, the only foreign language he knew. And he assumed without question that Hebrew, Greek, and Latin were the most original forms of human speech. But he was modest and acknowledged the speculative character of his endeavors. He took the motto for the entire *Essai* from Cicero's *Tusculan Disputations* (I, 9):

> As far as I am able, I will explain; not, however, like Pythian Apollo, as though the things which I will say are certain and fixed; but simply as a limited man, following probable conjectures.

Condillac did not claim to deal with necessary truths, but with reasonable possibilities. And although a stiff dogmatism would eventually develop out of sensationalist epistemology, Condillac himself was cautious.

In his *Letter on the Blind for the Use of Those Who See* (1749), Denis Diderot, though generally full of praise for Condillac, intimated that in the end his principles were "the same as those of Berkeley," since we are left with no way of getting beyond our own ideas and our own signs for them (Diderot, 1916/1973, p. 105; cf. Le Roy, 1937). In response to this and other critiques, Condillac began to revise somewhat his views on language. In a letter to Maupertuis of June 25, 1752, he conceded that he had perhaps "given too much to signs" (1947–1951, Vol. II, p. 536). Of all Condillac's works, the *Treatise on the Sensations* shows the shift most obviously. The statue which the Pygmalion-philosopher brings gradually to sensate life never does acquire language or even need it, and Condillac makes hardly a reference to the function of signs. Instead, the animated statue is led to general ideas simply through the repeated experience of particular ones, unaided even by especial powers of association (1930, pp. 217–220). The statue, to be sure, never becomes a significantly social being; but that is beside the point, since Condillac had argued earlier that even for the isolated child the use of signs would be a necessary prerequisite of mental development. In the *Treatise on the Animals* Condillac also downplayed somewhat the role of language, even though one of his objectives in that work was the differentiation of animal and human natures, a logical context in which to introduce some of the points made so emphatically in the *Essai* (nf. Knight, 1968, pp. 126–128). Since, however, Descartes had made his own differentiation to hang upon the human capacity for language, perhaps Condillac was reluctant to take his fire from the enemy.

In later works, however, particularly in the *Grammaire, La Logique,* and *La Langue des calculs,* Condillac renewed his emphasis on language, now with particular reference to the correlation between language and method and his interest in the construction of a logically perfected language. The correlation was already implied in the Second Part of the *Essai,* "Of Language and Method." Condillac refers to the method he proposes as "analysis," a procedure which would come to have dogmatic status among the *idéologues* of the French Revolution (cf. Acton, 1959; Boas, 1925/1964, pp. 30ff.). A synthetic method, according to Condillac, proceeds from ideas already compounded—but if there is any fallacy in the composition, that fallacy will be preserved in the deductions from it; whereas an analytic method begins from the simple idea, where that is accessible, or else reduces the compound to its simpler constituents. Analysis then recomposes these simples only as clarity and distinctness dictate and allow—and the similarity of these methodological principles to the Cartesian ones has often enough been noted (cf. Bréhier, 1967, pp. 76ff.; Knight, 1968, pp. 43–48).

Unlike Descartes, however, who rejected the notion that any certain knowledge could derive from history, Condillac tied his explication of method to his own conjectures about linguistic history. Whatever may have been his faith in doctrinaire Enlightenment teachings about progress, Condillac sought instruction in the primitive as well. It was in the primordial and "natural" sequence of things that Condillac thought to find a corrective against future error. Mankind had advanced in many ways, but metaphysics and some other sciences had gone far astray because they did not adhere to the natural order of development. The mind progresses through the association of ideas, but such compounding turns to disadvantage whenever men lose the power to decompose their ideas. All too easily they become attached to words, abstractions, and composite figments, as though these were the very substance of life itself. The mind moves forward through processes of synthesis, but once error has occurred or has come to prevail, it is a method of analysis that is required. By decomposing composite ideas into their original components and individual elements, analysis brings the mind "back to its senses," reawakening awareness of the sensory elements with which mental processes began. In this way the obfuscations of pseudo-metaphysics and false science can be dispelled once and for all. Reductions of this kind will reveal that properly all languages are analytic methods and that "the art of reasoning amounts to a well-constructed language" (Condillac, 1809, p. 96). The abuse of language and consequent promulgation of error derive from the lazy tendency to take synthetic ideas and words as though they themselves were the foundations on which to build. The future of science—both "natural" and "social," as we should say today—is fully dependent on analytic method, for linguistic precision is as important to every scientist as is the telescope to the astronomer and the microscope to the biologist. In dealing with political economy in *Le Commerce et le gouvernement* it was this kind of a linguistic-analytic method that Condillac tried to apply. Anarchical fallacies, as Bentham would later call them, could be avoided if political slogans and ideals were reduced to their original elements as a test of their substance. On the other hand, in the posthumous *Langue des calculs,* Condillac explicated algebra as a clarified language with its own grammar and vocabulary. Although more limited in some ways than those human languages more spontaneously developed, algebra and other mathematical systems and notations stood unassailably as models of *langue bien faite* (cf. Gillispie, 1960, pp. 166ff.; Lévy-Bruhl, 1899/1924, pp. 280ff.). Unlike Condorcet and other proponents of universal characteristics, Condillac doubted the possibility that mankind would ever arrive at a single perfected idiom, but he nonetheless firmly believed that the clarification of language could lead to a more general and popular enlightenment. Thus, the search for the elementary and original in language was, for Condillac, inseparable from the preparation for a more perfect human future.

We asserted at the outset that Condillac was the first major thinker specifically to pose the psycholinguistic or epistemolinguistic question. Others before him had been led to conclusions about language and knowledge, language and reason, language and mind; but he was the first to make a genetic epistemology hinge upon the development of language and the use of signs. Despite its unassuming title, Condillac's *Essai,* and the whole of his philosophy, was more than a supplement of addenda to Locke; it entailed a fundamental shift of orientation in which considerations of language were decisive. Condillac anticipated the insight of Kant that there is in Locke's empiricism an unacknowledged but subtle form of *innatism.* The different faculties are really not so many potentialities given by the nature of the mind, which must inevitably actualize themselves at the proper point in the normal course of development. Rather the mind must come upon these powers and each individual must first learn to use them; and it is the utilization of signs, according to Condillac, which enables us to do this. Questions of the genesis of intellect led to the problem of linguistic origins on the one hand, and to the proposal of an analytic method on the other. And elaboration of these themes, in turn, led Condillac to more general considerations of history and of the hopes and means of future improvement. In this way the problem of language became critical for epistemology and psychology and for inquiries into history and society as well.

References

Acton, H. B. The philosophy of language in revolutionary France. *Proceedings of the British Academy,* 1959, *45,* 199–219.
Aarsleff, H. The tradition of Condillac: The problem of the origin of language in the eighteenth century and the debate in the Berlin Academy before Herder. In D. Hymes

(Ed.), *Studies in the history of linguistics: Traditions and paradigms.* Bloomington: Indiana University Press, 1974, pp. 93–156.

Berkeley [Bishop] G. *The works* (A. A. Luce and T. E. Jessop, Eds.) (10 vols.). London: Nelson, 1948–1957.

Boas, G. *French philosophies of the Romantic period.* Baltimore: the Johns Hopkins University Press, 1925; New York: Russell & Russell, 1964.

Bréhier, E. [*The eighteenth century* (The history of philosophy, vol. V)] (W. Baskin, Trans.). Chicago: University of Chicago, 1967.

Condillac, E. B. de. [*An essay on the origin of human knowledge: Being a supplement to Mr. Locke's Essay on the human understanding*] (Mr. Nugent, Trans.). London: 1756. Reprinted with an Introduction by J. H. Stam, in *Language, man and society: Foundations of the behavioral sciences* (R. W. Rieber, Ed.). New York: AMS, 1974.

Condillac, E. B. de. *Oeuvres* (Abbé de Mably, Ed.) (23 vols.). Paris: 1798.

Condillac, E. B. de. *Oeuvres complètes* (31 vols.). Paris: 1803.

Condillac, E. B. de. [*The Logic*] (J. Neef, Trans.). Philadelphia: 1809.

Condillac, E. B. de. [*Treatise on the sensations*] (G. Carr, Trans.; H. Wildon Carr, Intro.). Los Angeles: University of Southern California, School of Philosophy, 1930.

Condillac, E. B. de. *Oeuvres philosophiques* (G. Le Roy, Ed.) (3 vols). Paris: Presses Universitaires de France, 1947–1951.

Cousin, V. *Philosophie sensualiste au xviii*ᵉ *siècle* (5th ed.). Paris: Librairie Académique, 1866.

Diderot, D. [*Early philosophical works*] (M. Jourdain, Trans. and ed.). Chicago: Open Court, 1916. Reprinted with an Introduction by J. P. Seigel in *Language, man and society: Foundations of the behavioral sciences* (R. W. Rieber, Ed.). New York: AMS, 1973.

Formigari, L. Language and society in the late eighteenth century. *Journal of the History of Ideas,* 1974, *35,* 275–292.

Frankel, C. *The faith of reason: The idea of progress in the French Enlightenment.* New York: King's Crown Press [Columbia University], 1948.

Gillispie, C. C. *The edge of objectivity: An essay in the history of scientific ideas.* Princeton: Princeton University Press; London: Oxford University Press, 1960.

Givner, D. A. Scientific preconceptions in Locke's philosophy of language. *Journal of the History of Ideas,* 1962, *23,* 340–354.

Harnois, G. *Les théories du langage en France de 1660 à 1821* (in *Études françaises*). Paris: [1928].

Hartley, D. *Observations on man, his frame, his duty, and his expectations* (2 vols.). London: 1749.

Josephs, H. *Diderot's dialogue of language and gesture: Le Neveu de Rameau.* Columbus: Ohio State University Press, 1969.

Kaye, F. B. The influence of Bernard Mandeville. *Studies in Philology,* 1922, *19,* 86–89.

Kaye, F. B. Mandeville on the origin of language. *Modern Language Notes,* 1924, *39,* 136–142.

Knight, I. F. *The geometric spirit: The Abbé de Condillac and the French Enlightenment* (Yale Historical Publications, Miscellany 89). New Haven: Yale University Press, 1968.

Kuehner, P. *Theories on the origin and formation of language in the eighteenth century in France.* Unpublished doctoral dissertation, University of Pennsylvania, 1944.

Le Roy, G. *La psychologie de Condillac.* Paris: Boivin, 1937.

Lévy-Bruhl, L. *History of modern philosophy in France.* Chicago: Open Court, 1899/1924.

Locke, J. *An essay concerning human understanding.* (A Campbell Fraser, Ed.) (2 vols.). Oxford: Oxford University Press, 1894.

Lovejoy, A. O. *The great chain of being: A study of the history of an idea.* Cambridge: Harvard University Press, 1936.

Mandeville, B. de. *The fable of the bees; Or, private vices, publick benefits* (F. B. Kaye, Ed.) (2 vols.). Oxford: Oxford University Press, 1924.

Salvucci, P. *Linguaggio e mondo umano in Condillac* (Pubblicazioni dell'Università di Urbino, Serie di Lettere e Filosofia, Vol. V). Urbino: S. T. E. U., 1957.

Sampson, R. V. *Progress in the age of reason: The seventeenth century to the present day.* Cambridge: Harvard University Press, 1956.

Schaupp, Z. *The naturalism of Condillac* (University of Nebraska Studies in Language, Literature, and Criticism, No. 7). Lincoln: University of Nebraska Press, 1926.

Seigel, J. P. The enlightenment and the evolution of a language of signs in France and England. *Journal of the History of Ideas,* 1969, *30,* 96–115.

Seigel, J. P. The perceptible and the imperceptible: Diderot's speculation on language in his letters on the deaf and blind. In R. W. Rieber (Ed.), *Psychology of language and thought.* New York: Plenum, 1980.

Stam, J. H. *Inquiries into the origin of language: The fate of a question.* In N. Chomsky & M. Halle (Eds.), *Studies in language.* New York: Harper & Row, 1976.

Voltaire. [*Philosophical letters*] (E. Dilworth, Trans. and intro.) (Library of Liberal Arts, Vol. 124). Indianapolis: Bobbs-Merrill, 1961.

Warburton, W. *The divine legation of Moses* (2 vols.). London: 1738–1741.

4

Jules Paul Seigel

THE PERCEPTIBLE AND THE IMPERCEPTIBLE: DIDEROT'S SPECULATION ON LANGUAGE IN HIS LETTERS ON THE DEAF AND BLIND

The study of language has always been interrelated with the study of philosophy, rhetoric, and epistemolgy, but now, more than ever, it has become integrally related with the social and behavioral sciences, as well as with the study of the poetic process. Recently the problem raised by Descartes and others regarding the creative aspect of language (that uniquely human property of ordinary language use which is "both un-bounded in scope and stimulus-free") has been revived (Chomsky, 1966, pp. 5, 30–31). The importance of the seventeenth-, eighteenth-, and early nineteenth-century studies is that they raised fundamental questions regarding the character of language and its relationship to human be-havior, questions which still command a genuine interest and which have yet to be answered satisfactorily.

In the eighteenth century, in particular, the emphasis in epistemology shifted from metaphysics toward psychology, from the "metaphysics of the soul" to the "history of the soul." John Locke's *Essay Concerning*

Jules Paul Seigel • Department of English, University of Rhode Island, Kingston, Rhode Island 02881.

Human Understanding (1690) was to become the official text for the French *philosophes* Condillac, Diderot, and La Mettrie, in their consideration of the correspondence between ideas and reality. In moving away from Cartesian rationalism, Locke concerned himself with practical solutions to practical problems. He avoided the problems of epistemological dualism, which Descartes had raised, and concentrated on describing the unique ways in which man knows or thinks he knows. As Voltaire cogently noted (*Lettres Anglaises ou philosophiques,* 1734), Locke "set forth human reason just as an excellent anatomist explains parts of the body." Central to Locke's philosophy was the relationship between sensation and reflection, which he allowed was independent of the senses. However, he did not trace the most complex functions of the mind—distinguishing, judging, and willing—to their source. Although he led the attack upon innate ideas, he was content to accept these important functions as fundamental powers of the mind itself.[1] Locke's French disciple, Condillac, extended his theories to their obvious conclusions by having his famous statue come to life; that is, come to a knowledge of ideas through the senses alone (*Traité des sensations,* 1754). For Condillac, reflection itself could be traced to the association of data received through the senses themselves. In part, this was Condillac's answer to this vexing, if not insoluble, problem.

The shift in philosophy to empiricism precipitated a good deal of interest in the study of language: Condillac's psychology led to his theory of language that made the progress of the human intellect basically a study of the growth and development of language—a theory which Turgot used in his own observations on progress. Rousseau dealt with language at great lengths in his *Discourse of Inequality* and in his *Progress of the Human Mind,* the latter to which Condorcet appended a detailed discussion of language. Indeed, the interest in the genesis of language—whether natural or supernatural—spilled over into related areas both pragmatic and philosophical.

One such area for the eighteenth-century thinker was the education of the deaf. For the first time in history, learned and intelligent men turned to the systematic education of the deaf and dumb. What before had been the province of quacks and charlatans now became the laboratory for

---

[1] *The Philosophy of the Enlightenment,* translated by Fritz C. A. Koelln and James P. Pettegrove (Princeton: Princeton University Press, 1951), pp. 99–101. See especially Chapter 3, "Psychology and Epistemology."

serious thinkers, many of whom were deeply concerned with the psychological and social implications of their studies. In France *l'esprit philosophique* precipitated a whole range of psychological as well as philosophical speculations on the origins of knowledge and the connection between sounds and ideas, between visual sight and intellectual concepts. This inquiring spirit was soon directed to those unfortunates who were born deaf, dumb, or blind. It may be said that the speculations of the *philosophes* prepared the way for the growth of the great systematic teacher and linguist, the Abbé l'Epée, who, by 1760, had founded his famous school for the deaf. L'Epée, often referred to as the father of education of the deaf, would not have been able, it seems, to develop such a system had not the climate for intellectual speculation been so favorable in France. In an atmosphere charged with *l'esprit philosophique,* with new theories of drama, epistemology, gesture, literary criticism, and aesthetics springing up, it was no wonder that the education of those deprived of their senses received its first philosophical and deeply humane attention. The second half of the eighteenth century witnessed the renaissance of education of the deaf and the beginning of what deaf educators called the *silent system;* a system using a series of signs to communicate—that is, *sign language.*

Although the deaf had been communicating for centuries with a system of "natural" signs in what might be called a "subculture," it was the brilliant l'Epée who recognized that this language of natural signs was insufficient for communicating the complexities of the French language and culture. With analysis and innovation he brought forth an elaborate system of natural signs buttressed by *"signes méthodiques."* His concern with those deprived of the normal senses was neither a startling one nor one that had not been considered seriously before by the *philosophes.* The two works of Diderot which preceded the research of l'Epée, and which contributed to this rich intellectual atmosphere, were his *Lettre sur les aveugles* (1749) and his *Lettre sur les sourds et muets à l'usage de ceux qui entendent et qui parlent* (1751). Diderot's creative speculations on language—found throughout his works—reflect many of the current ideas of his contemporaries; yet, he gave them an original turn, moving away from the purely scientific treatise to eclectic and thought-provoking methods.

In both works, Diderot is concerned with the process of learning and the relationship of language to thought. In the manner of the brilliant intellectual synthesizer and speculator that he was, it was characteristic of his genius to question the limits of human understanding.[2] By studying the abnormalities inherent in the world of the deaf and dumb, Diderot attempted to draw conclusions regarding normal man and society. The microcosm of the blind and the deaf and dumb characterizes a society which can only be released from darkness and silence by some form of communication, a language, a means of accurately communicating one's sentiments. An analogy may be seen in the normal culture in which all men are essentially deaf, dumb, and blind. However, man has that distinctly human ability to create and perceive symbols of communication. He is, in fact, continually trying to express himself as well as to discover the world in which he lives. This essential relationship of thought to language was central to Diderot's intellectual posture. In his article "Encyclopédie" (for the fifth volume of the *Encyclopédie*)—following Condillac's idea (*Essai sur l'origine des connaissances humaines* [1746]) that language arose from man's need to communicate his emotions—Diderot suggests that language could liberate man's psychic energies, free him for the present, and allow him to take command over objective reality. This led him to propose a language intelligible to all mankind. However optimistic he was regarding the idea of a universal language, he was aware that language was imperfectly connected with thought and could never truly reflect the deepest human feelings. In his illuminating study of Diderot's use of language and gesture, Herbert Joseph (1969) indicates that Diderot was certain that

> Man was too poorly equipped to justify an outmoded faith in his capacity to grasp and to communicate the truth of the world: his imperfect senses limited his means of knowing; his imperfect instrument of speech limited his means of expressing. In the *Lettre sur les aveugles* (1749) and the *Lettre sur les sourds et muets* (1751), Diderot studied the data of the various senses separately and found each one inconsistent and deceptive; he studied them together and discovered that no necessary correspondence existed between them. The God-like ideal man of Descartes, who possessed the powers of mind to arrive at a complete conception of the universe, appeared to Diderot as if he were blind or deaf-and-dumb. Any statement of knowledge based on perception revealed more about the peculiar organization of the perceiver than about the nature of objective reality. By the very imprecision and contingency of its signs, human language stands as a constant reminder of the uncertainty of knowledge and of its own failure to grasp a fleeting, uniquely personal truth. (pp. 10–12)

In the two *Letters,* Diderot adopts two somewhat different stances regarding language: that of the empirical sensationist who saw language as

---

[2]See Arnolds Grava (1963, pp. 73–103) for a discussion of the synthesizing power of Diderot's thought.

a medium of communication and analysis (*Letter on the Blind*) and that of the poet, the creative artist who saw language as a possible means of representing the deepest complexities and subtleties of the human imagination (*Letter on the Deaf and Dumb for the Use of Those Who Hear and Speak*). In fact, Diderot suggests that the surest way to destroy the perceptions of the artist would be to force them into completely rational constructs; he acknowledges that categorizing and defining deny flexibility.

In the *Letter on the Blind,* Diderot is concerned with what was known as the *Molyneaux problem,* a matter of philosophical interest around which much of the discussion of eighteenth-century psychology and epistemology centered. Bishop Berkeley, Voltaire, Condillac, and others were concerned with the basic question first raised by Molyneaux in his *Optics:* Would a person born blind who has learned to discriminate among forms by touch have the immediate ability to distinguish those same forms if he regained his sight? For example, could a blind man distinguish a cube from a sphere by sight alone or must he go through a certain period of adjustment so that he could make the necessary connections between his new visual perceptions and his older tactile experiences?[3] The problem raised fundamental questions for the *philosophes* as they attempted to move from the psychological to the philosophical, asking if there were some physiological or neuropsychological inner connection between the senses.[4] Furthermore, the problem was at the very heart of the question regarding the nature of perception and the perceived universe. Condillac (*Traité des sensations*) saw the Molyneaux problem as the basis for all psychological investigation in that it questioned the role of judgment in its relation to perception and in the development of a consciousness of the external world; that is, do the senses translate the objective world or do other faculties cooperate?

Diderot's *Letter on the Blind* is, in essence, a metaphorical elaboration of the Molyneaux question, and it is also an attempt to explore the imagination of the blind, their ethos, their morality. Furthermore, it conveys a true sense of a world of complete darkness as imagined by those who actually see. The *Letter* is at once imaginative and scientific: the factual interview with the blind man of Puisaux is neatly balanced by the imaginary death-bed revelations of the blind Saunderson, a polemic which

---

[3]See also John Locke, An *Essay Concerning Human Understanding* (1690), Book I, Chapter 9, pp. 8–15.
[4]Twentieth-century investigation has verified Diderot's speculations that man would not immediately recognize the object (see Crocker, 1966, p. 103).

Diderot invented for the occasion. The essay, then, is not as loose and discursive as many commentators have suggested. Framed by the novelistic technique of the letter, it is held together from within as Diderot develops variations on the theme of the Molyneaux question. First, there is Diderot's interview with the blind man from Puisaux, to whom he puts a series of questions regarding his perceptions and values. Second, there is Diderot's discussion of the accomplishments of Nicholas Saunderson, the blind Cambridge mathematician. Finally, there is Diderot's "Addition" to the original *Letter on the Blind,* written thirty-three years later, which we may consider, with some reservations, part of the *Letter* in that it further develops the Molyneaux question. In the "Addition," Diderot discusses the accomplishments of the blind but brilliant and talented Mademoiselle Mélanie de Salignac, the niece of Sophie Volland. Important to the discussion is the observation made by Diderot that this blind woman is able to make internal connections between senses; that she is, in fact, able to connect color with space, a crucial matter which Diderot considered in the original *Letter.* But the basic question is left unanswered:

> Was her cube formed by memories of sensation of touch? Had her brain become, as it were, a hand within which substances were realized? Had a connection between two senses been established? Why does this connection not exist in my case, and why do I picture nothing that is not coloured in my mind's eye? What is the imagination of a blind man? This phenomenon is by no means easy of explanation. (p. 153)[5]

In the *Letter,* Diderot claimed that since there seemed to be no internal connection between the senses of touch and sight, the relationship was dependent upon experience. Despite the lack of interdependence between sight and touch, their "services are mutual." That is, one sense may be perfected and helped by the other, but each sense is empirical and self-contained. That Saunderson had a different "idea" of God than those who saw from birth is a logical conclusion of Diderot's sensationism. Indeed it is through the senses that one's morality and metaphysics are formed.[6] The high point of the *Letter* is the announcement by the blind Saunderson that he would believe in God if he could touch him. Saunder-

---

[5] See Denis Diderot, *Diderot's Early Philosophical Works,* translated by Margaret Jourdain (Chicago: Open Court, 1916), reprinted with an introduction by Jules P. Seigel (New York: AMS Press, 1973). All references to Diderot's work are from this translation.

[6] The late Pierre Villey (1930), blind professor of literature at the University of Caen, praises Diderot's attempts to deal with the blind but questions his conclusion that the imagination of the blind is different from those who see. The blind can, in fact, conceptualize spatial synthetic images; this Villey calls *"tactile sight"* (pp. 179–190).

son's argument, which ranges from an empirical morality to a Lucretian view of evolution, represents Diderot's criticism of Newton's rational universe. For the blind, the universe has no observable teleological elements. Moreover, the blind Saunderson, like the blind prophet Tiresias ("who had penetrated the secrets of the gods") is able to question the natural theology of Newton, the meaning of the observed order (totally unobservable by him) of the universe. The Christian clergyman, Gervase Holmes, who obviously can see, is unable to convince the blind mathematician, a man of science, of the wonders of nature, of its rational design. One sees here two worlds both dependent upon the senses as a medium to conceptualize reality. The seeing world of Holmes is "blinded" by its own conventions, by its deductions drawn from seeing the traditional order of nature. The unseeing world of Saunderson must, inductively, through the sense of touch, build its own system without ever seeing the "magnificent spectacle" of nature. Diderot rhetorically asks: "Was not the true God more completely veiled by the mists of paganism for a Socrates, than for the blind Saunderson, who never enjoyed the spectacle of nature?" The metaphorical content of the *Letter on the Blind*—as well as that of the *Letter on the Deaf and Dumb*—raises the most profound questions on the nature of "other" worlds, and points toward the modern philosophical crisis of self and identity.

Taking a more practical turn, Diderot suggests a method of communication with blind deaf-mutes, a system of touch symbols that foreshadows the method developed by Louis Braille [1809?–1852] and which has been used successfully in the education of Helen Keller and Laura Bridgeman. Such a system was very similar to the polished steel alphabet developed by Abbé l'Epée and his disciple, Abbé Sicard—both dedicated and imaginative educators of the deaf—in order to teach those who were born blind deaf-mutes. Sicard realized that such a system was certainly practical after he and his deaf student, Massieu, had been able to communicate in the dark by touch.[7] Indeed Pierre Villey acknowledged Diderot's pioneering speculations on the nature of the psychology of the blind. The *Letter* with its scientific construct of the universe and its attempt to formulate a theory of knowledge was a "source book for nineteenth-century materialism and naturalism" (Crocker, 1966, p. 104).

The *Letter on the Deaf and Dumb* (1751) continues Diderot's specu-

---

[7]Abbé Roch-Ambroise Sicard, *Cours d'instruction d'un sourd-muet de naissance* (Paris, 1800), pp. lvi–lvii; compare a discussion of this same by Dugald Stewart (1829, pp. 314ff.).

lations on language and the formation of knowledge begun in the *Letter on the Blind*. It is his most provocative work on the subject and deals with language both as a social and a psychological phenomenon as well as an artistic one. In part, it is an outgrowth of the whole intellectual ferment of the middle 1740s as well as of conversations which Diderot had with Rousseau and Condillac over dinner at the Hôtel du Panier Fleuri.

The *Letter on the Deaf and Dumb* is explicitly concerned with refuting Abbé Batteaux's well-known *Les Beaux-arts réduites à un même principe* (1746), a classical analysis of the levels of language which drew heavily upon standard French critics and on Aristotle's principle of mimesis. The *Letter* begins with the linguistic problem of inversions but ranges widely over such topics as the origin and development of language, epistemology, rhetoric, and poetics. In his discussion of hieroglyphs and emblems, Diderot advances an expressive theory of poetry which anticipates the symbolist theories of Baudelaire, Mallarmé, and T. S. Eliot (Abrams, 1958, pp. 21–26).

Through the use of an imaginary deaf-mute, Diderot tries to determine the relationship between thought and language. The deaf-mute represents a hypothetical society before conventional language was developed, a method for investigation common among the *philosophes:* Condillac, of course, had used a statue-man in his *Traité des sensations,* but the idea had also been used by Buffon and was later to be used by Charles Bonnet and others. The statue or deaf-mute allowed the *philosophes* to hypothesize about the mechanics of psychology. Diderot, using the deaf-mute to trace the natural development of language, at one point writes that our mind is

> a moving scene, which we are perpetually copying. We spend a great deal of time in rendering it faithfully; but the original exists as a complete whole, for the mind does not proceed step by step, like expression. The brush takes time to represent what the artist's eye sees in an instant. (p. 161)

The concept is analogous to that advanced by Gestalt psychologists. As perceived by Lester Crocker, it anticipates "Bergson's history of the total life of the mind spilling over the limitations of successive and detailed attention, and of his distinction between intuition and intelligence" (Crocker, 1966, p. 109; see also Hunt, 1938, p. 226). Conventional language, as it were, is the language of intelligence and is primarily for analysis, for breaking down original perceptions into orderly sequences.

As James Doolittle (1952) has observed, the "fundamental problem posed in the *Sourds et muets* is that of a medium of communication between man and man from which all linguistic convention has been arbitrarily banished'' (p. 160). Diderot always marveled at the metaphorical possibilities of gesture language to communicate feelings which could be completely understood. He never tired of referring to the color harpsichord of Father Castel, which simulated music visually by displaying colored flags when the keys were touched. When the harpsichord was shown to Diderot's deaf-mute, he came to the realization that music was a "peculiar manner of communicating thought." Music, gesture, and touch were all viable mediums of communication. Indeed, signs and cries also bulked large in Diderot's mind as methods for communicating, pointing toward the primitivist aestheticism and romanticism of the later eighteenth century.

In praising the unique power of gesture language and silent expression, Diderot moved to formulate a theory which saw artistic creation in terms of a language which could represent the deepest inner emotions synthetically, without resorting to the analysis often imposed upon them by formal or conventional poetics. He saw poetry as the vehicle best able to convey the profound sentiments of an experience because it reflected language at its closest synthesis of thought and feeling. The basic question which Diderot was considering, and a question central to the shift in emphasis away from the mimetic and classical theories of art, was whether the language of poetry—its metaphors in particular—was a natural expression of emotion and the imagination or a willful copying of poetic conventions. How close is the poem to the intent of the poet? Poetry, which Diderot defines in the *Letter* as a "series of hieroglyphs" or as "symbolic," was able to use the inherent potential of both the verbal and plastic arts. In a perfect hieroglyph, sound and meaning are joined. The hieroglyphs could flash upon the imagination of the reader ideas and emotions as a complete picture, very similar to that picture which Diderot had observed as a "moving scene" which the artist's eye saw in an instant. What Diderot is suggesting here is that the act of poetic creation is so unique and delicate that it is perceived only by the creator who must then find a recipient, also a sensitive and perceptive critic or reader, able to participate in the poet's insights which travel into the realm beyond logic and scientific knowledge (Doolittle, 1952, p. 161).[8] Idea and expres-

---

[8]The idea is treated more extensively by Paul H. Meyer (1964, pp. 133–155).

sion are so perfectly joined into a unique expression that it cannot be translated. Diderot's discussion has a good deal in common with T. S. Eliot's (1960) famous definition of the objective correlative:

> The only way of expressing emotion in the form of art is by finding an "objective correlative"; in other words, a set of objects, a situation, a chain of events which shall be the formula of that *particular* emotion; such that when the external facts, which must terminate in sensory experience, are given, the emotion is immediately evoked. (pp. 46–50)

Indeed the *Letter* epitomizes the basic antithesis which Diderot was attempting to define between science and poetry: the artistic, synthetic, unconventional creation as opposed to the scientific, analytical, and conventional one—and the methods or materials of communication used by each. The poet, who in his creative act is able to transcend logic and convention, must be able, nevertheless, to communicate these sentiments. His use of hieroglyphs or symbols to communicate the incommunicable is similar to the gesture language of the deaf-mute who uses gestures and signs to communicate sentiments for which there is no verbal equivalent.

Again in *Rêve de d'Alembert,* Diderot's scheme indicates that there are real distinctions between reason and the imagination; the former combines and uses those things which are dependent upon scientific knowledge, whereas the latter, although based on experience, may combine illusion and fact (Doolittle, 1952, p. 161). Diderot anticipates Coleridge's famous, if ambiguous, distinction between the primary and secondary imagination and fancy.[9]

Diderot's concern with gesture language is not surprising in that it was being discussed throughout the century in relation to the movement of actors in the drama and to the movements in the ballet, and was, in general, thought to be a natural language, the earliest form of human communication. In dance and in the theater during mid-century and later, there were attempts to replace the stylized movements of the dancers and the formalized gestures of actors with a gesture language that was more expressive and was closer to the original sentiments and passions. Diderot tells us that when he went to the Comédie Française, he would stuff his ears with his fingers and imagine that he was deaf in order to assess the gestures of the actors.

It was this general interest in gestural language in France which gave

---

[9]*Biographia Literaria,* Chapter 13.

rise to the development of the sign language devised by the famous Abbé l'Epée. L'Epée was concerned with the complete intellectual development of the deaf-mute, especially his spiritual nature, and he was quick to realize that the mind functions through the use of a language or, as he conceived it, a symbol system. Moreover, he believed that the language did not necessarily have to be French (Stokoe, 1960, pp. 9–10).

However, the language of signs as developed by l'Epée and his followers, such as Sicard, is different from the pure "expressiveness" of Diderot's gesture language in that the sign language of the deaf and dumb is particularly dependent, in l'Epée's case, upon the formalized grammatical structure of the French. Certain distinctions should be made, though, regarding the term "natural language of sign." The term, as Stokoe (1960) has argued, is a false entity. "Any extremely close, non-arbitrary, relation of sign to referent will be in those few areas of activity where pantomime and denoted action are nearly identical, for instance eating" (pp. 10–11). L'Epée realized that, however necessary the natural gestures of the deaf and dumb were for their daily existence, this primitive system of communication could hardly instruct the deaf and dumb in the French language, culture, and religion. He therefore developed a metalanguage called "signes méthodiques," a system of signs with which he could connect the natural language of the deaf with the formalized language of the culture. It was Diderot who had suggested that gesture language and thought patterns were the same, that they moved simultaneously. In fact, he indicated that gestures might be so sublime as to be untranslatable. This would be understandable if gesture language indicated true poetic feeling, but this was not precisely the system that l'Epée formulated. In l'Epée's system, we have both a gesture language, which evolved from the spontaneous gestures of the deaf, and a sign language ("signes méthodiques"), which was developed for the purpose of analysis. L'Epée's language of signs was primarily one of analysis and analogy—a method through which abstract ideas could be communicated (cf. Knowlson, 1965; Lane, 1976; Seigel, 1969).

Diderot's concern in the two Letters is with the mind—its mechanics and its mystery. He seems also to be saying that all men are blind and deaf and dumb, but that they have unique capacities for perception and communication and are able to understand and communicate their individual worlds. However, there is the Swiftian suggestion that each of these worlds can never be truly known outside itself and the consciousness of its own creator with precision and scientific accuracy. The forms of communication used by the blind man are never truly perceived by the men who see, nor of the deaf man by those who hear. Indeed, as the full titles indicate, the *Letters* are addressed to those "who can see" and those "who can hear and speak."

References

Abrams, M. *The mirror and the lamp: Romantic theory and the critical tradition* (2nd ed.). New York: The Norton Library, 1958.

Chomsky, N. *Cartesian linguistics: A chapter in the history of rationalistic thought.* New York: Harper & Row, 1966.

Crocker, L. G. *Diderot: The embattled philosopher* (2nd ed.). New York: The Free Press, 1966.

Doolittle, J. Hieroglyph and emblem in Diderot's *Lettre sur les sourds et muets.* In *Diderot Studies,* II, edited by Otis Fellows and Norman Torrey. Syracuse: Syracuse University Press, 1952.

Eliot, T. S. Hamlet and his problem. In *Selected essays of T. S. Eliot* (new edition). New York: Harcourt Brace & World, 1960).

Grava, A. Diderot and recent philosophical trends. In *Diderot Studies,* IV, edited by Otis Fellows. Geneva: Droz, 1963.

Hunt, H. L. Logic and linguistics: Diderot as *grammairien-philosophe. Modern Language Review, 33* (April, 1938).

Joseph, H. *Diderot's dialogue of language and gesture: Le Neveu de Rameau.* Columbus: Ohio State University Press, 1969.

Knowlson, J. R. The ides of gesture as a universal language in the XVIIth and XVIIIth centuries," *Journal of the History of Ideas, 30,* No. 4 (Oct.—Dec., 1965), 495–508.

Lane, H. *The wild boy of Aveyron.* Cambridge: Harvard University Press, 1976, pp. 207–254.

Meyer, P. H. "The *Lettre sur les sourds et muets* and Diderot's emerging concept of the critic. In *Diderot Studies,* VI, edited by Otis Fellows. Geneva: Droz, 1964.

Seigel, J. P. The enlightenment and a language of signs in France and England. *Journal of the History of Ideas, 36,* No. 1 (Jan.–March, 1969), 96–115.

Stokoe, W. C., Jr. Sign language structure: An outline of the visual communication systems of the American deaf. In *Studies in linguistics* (Occasional Papers 8). Buffalo, New York: University of Buffalo, 1960, pp. 9–10.

Stewart, D. *The works of Dugald Stewart* (Vol. III). Cambridge, Mass., Hilliard & Brown, 1829.

Villey, P. *The world of the blind: A psychological study* (A. Hallard, trans.). London: Duckworth, 1930.

PART III

NINETEENTH CENTURY CONTRIBUTIONS

5

Peter Ostwald and R. W. Rieber

JAMES RUSH AND THE THEORY OF VOICE AND MIND

The leadership of Benjamin Rush as psychiatrist and politician has received considerable attention, particularly during the recent bicentennial celebration (Carlson & Wollock, 1976). Less well known is his role as a father. This chapter focuses on one of Rush's children, his third son, James Rush, who made significant contributions to scientific thought in the mid-nineteenth century.

James Rush, M.D., is best known for his major work *The Philosophy of the Human Voice*, first published in 1827, in Philadelphia. This was a highly original attempt to understand the physical properties of the human voice and how vocalizations are used to express emotions and to communicate ideas. With its emphasis on the actual sounds of speech, Rush's *Philosophy* anticipated some of today's research that uses tape-recordings and other objective methods for obtaining a precise inventory of the behavioral events during social communication.

The Relationship between Benjamin Rush and James Rush

Benjamin Rush held James in very high esteem, and letters to James are filled with expressions of affection, concern about his health, and

Peter Ostwald • Langley Porter Institute, University of California San Francisco, San Francisco, California 94143. *R. W. Rieber* • John Jay College of Criminal Justice, CUNY, and Columbia University, College of Physicians and Surgeons, New York, N.Y. 10019.

admonitions regarding proper spelling, punctuation, and grammar—a topic we shall return to shortly. Benjamin Rush wanted to have sons who might be able to carry on his own work in medicine, psychiatry, and education. A stern and demanding father, he punished his children by forcing them to endure solitude (Hawke, 1971). His first son, John Rush, obtained medical training and joined the navy but became mentally ill after killing his closest friend—a "young man as dear to him as a brother"—in a duel (Butterfield, 1951). Rush's second son, Richard, entered government service and was appointed Secretary of State, Minister to England, Secretary of the Treasury, and Attorney General of the United States (Damrau, 1940). This left James Rush, born in 1787, ten years after the revolution, to be groomed to follow in his father's footsteps. (He actually was the third James in the illustrious Rush family. Benjamin Rush had two close relatives of the same name: his grandfather and an older brother who died following a "nervous breakdown." This event occurred when Benjamin was 14 years old and probably contributed to his later efforts on behalf of the mentally ill.)

Important connections between the scientific work of father and son have been described. For example, Kurtz (1954) presented the view that after graduating from Princeton, James "sat at his father's feet as a medical student at the University of Pennsylvania taking careful notes on the elder Rush's lectures." He then went abroad for more advanced clinical work. Benjamin Rush was eager to have his son renew old acquaintances from his own student days in Edinburgh and London, but James "found that his father's scientific theories were viewed as fantasy". Letters exchanged between 1809 and 1811 "reveal how completely the scientific outlook of the younger man had been warped by his father's dogmatism." At first James tried to defend his father's pathophysiological theories and to debunk the newer medical developments in Edinburgh. He wrote that "the medical world is in chaos here—none of that order and connection which form the uses and beauty of (a system)."

When James Rush reached London, where his sister had become involved in the social life of the metropolis through marriage to a British army officer, a reorientation in his attitudes took place. He studied medicine assiduously, and "whatever time was left over from this heavy schedule, the American physician devoted to the salon life—he became deeply impressed with the cultural benefits of upper-class English life" (Kurtz, 1954). He was particularly impressed by the world of music, art, and the theater. As we shall see later, these were important stimuli for the development of his ideas about vocal communication. Furthermore, following the tragedy of his brother John's madness, his father urged James Rush to visit "madhouses near London, and pry into everything that relates to the management both of the bodies and minds of the patients that are confined in them" (Butterfield, 1951).

After returning to the United States, James took a major share of responsibility in caring for his father's patients and giving his lectures at the University of Pennsylvania. He also inherited most of his father's estate. James became an extremely wealthy man thanks to his marriage to Phoebe Ann Ridgway, daughter of a millionaire Philadelphia merchant, and was able to have the leisure and security he needed for intellectual pursuits. Strongly believing that "scientific truth best prospers in an aristocratic social structure" (Kurtz, 1954), James led a rather detached and solitary existence and was considered somewhat eccentric—"a recluse whose only passion in life seemed to be his studies." He died in 1869, at the age of 82 (Klaf, 1961).

The Philosophy of the Human Voice

James Rush (see Fig. 1) recognized certain differences between his own approach to human problems and that of his illustrious father. James was more introverted, more academic, and less the politician and man of action. Benjamin Rush had been an effective orator with enormous faith in his vocal power and the possessor of a voice that "has been called sweeter than any flute, like droppings from a sanctuary" (Damrau, 1940). James by contrast was not a successful lecturer. But he believed that elocution is central to effective teaching and he started his scientific career by collecting numerous facts and observations about vocal behavior. He intended The Philosophy of the Human Voice to be the opening volume of a much larger effort, devoted to a comprehensive study of the human intellect, which was completed and published as two volumes in 1865. According to Kurtz (1954), James Rush had the distinction of being one of the first men of his generation to decide "that the field of human behavior was a legitimate one for scientific investigation—he chose to work in obscurity, firmly persuaded that his attitude towards mental phenomena was years in advance of his age."

Indeed it was. Philosophy is a strikingly innovative attempt to analyze all the sounds of speech, their physiology of production, and their organization into patterns capable of carrying meaning. A major contribution of the book is the clear distinction it makes between two contrasting

Figure 1.   Portrait of James Rush.

classes of sounds that people communicate with: (1) the "natural or vocal" signs and (2) the "artificial or verbal" signs. Rush was aware that when a person speaks, these audible signs are rarely produced in isolation but are "united in a single act of expression and employed in every manner of compatible combination" (Rush, 1893).

For purposes of analysis, Rush separated the human voice into five attributes[1] which he called "vocality, force, time, abruptness, and pitch."

[1]See Lester L. Hale, "Dr. James Rush" in K. R. Wallace (Ed.), *History of Speech Education in America*. New York: Appleton Century Crofts, 1954, p. 219, for an excellent discussion of Rush and his works.

Using today's scientific terminology (Ostwald, 1973), we would translate these terms as follows:

> vocality—the voice spectrum
> force—vocal intensity
> time—the temporal organization of speech
> abruptness—onset and decay characteristics
> pitch—intonation or melody of speech

Unfortunately, Rush was severely handicapped by the relatively crude state of the art of speech science in his day. He lamented the fact that most available texts were based on the teachings of ancient Greek and Roman authorities. He wanted to correct their errors by doing a naturalistic analysis of Anglo-American speech patterns, aided by direct listening and auditory analysis of sensorimotor components. Rush was strenuously opposed to an idealistic, "metaphysical," and theoretical approach to the study of human behavior, but it was not until 1845, after he had already published three editions of the *Philosophy of the Human Voice,* that he was able to return to Europe, where physiological research in phonetics was under way in France and Germany.

In dealing with the verbal signs, Rush eschewed the alphabetic tradition of dividing speech into five vowels and twenty-one consonants. He described a total of 35 speech sounds, similar to what are called *phonemes* today. Twelve of these he called "tonic" sounds—mostly vowels and diphthongs like /ah/, /ee/, /oo/, etc.; 14 were called "subtonic sounds"—mostly voiced consonants such as /v/, /b/, /z/, etc.; and 9 voiceless consonants, /sh/, /t/, /p/, etc., he called "atonic sounds." In discussing the phenomenon of voice quality, Rush described four ways of speaking: a "natural" voice used in ordinary speech; a "falsetto" voice with breaks and excessively high pitches; "whispering" when the voice is held back; and an "orotund" voice, bombastic and exaggerated, used for oratory.

Quite remarkable for a pre-Darwinian writer are Rush's ideas about bioacoustical continuity. He felt that certain aspects of human speech closely resemble the noise-making of animals. "There is no vowel in the voice of a man that is not heard from some speechless brute, or bird, or insect" he wrote (1893), while at the same time insisting that certain unique properties of human speech separate us as language users from all other forms of life. Only among humans does one observe that "speech is employed to declare the states and purposes of the mind."

Above all it was Rush's wish to show how "the voice must have distinct means or signs" for declaring "our thoughts and passions." He was determined to find precise relationships between inner, psychological states and external, social communication. Toward this goal he postulated a tripartite mental organization in which *thoughts,* or what we today would call the more formal cognitive structures, were supposed to be externalized in the form of vocal signs consisting mostly of simple rising and falling intonations, short intervals, an unobtrusive voice quality, moderate degrees of force, and short syllabic time. *Passions,* or what we would call the affective states, are signaled by the use of greater variability of intonation, rhythm, and vocal force. Into an intermediate or overlapping category, Rush placed what he called "Inter-thoughts," expressed in an "admirative" or "reverential" tone of voice with "orotund vocality, and a moderate, dignified force."

Many chapters of *The Philosophy of the Human Voice* are devoted to extremely detailed descriptions of the speed, flow, and rhythm of speech. Rush used numerous examples from poetry, especially Milton's *Paradise Lost* and also from Shakespeare's plays. Because of a fear that his research might become a "curiosity only, if it does not lead to some application", he also gave rules and instructions designed for improving the art of speaking. His thoroughness makes the book seem prolix and redundant, particularly in later editions, with its many footnotes and editorical comments. Some of these are however quite revealing from a biographical viewpoint. For example, Rush recalls his great admiration for the English tragic actress, Mrs. Siddons, from his student days in England. He obviously felt at home in the theater, and it is of interest that right after completing his *Philosophy,* Rush wrote and published his own version of the play *Hamlet, a Dramatic Prelude in Five Acts"* (1834).

Rush's auditory sensitivity not only enabled him to describe nuances of vocal behavior in extraordinary detail, but also caused him to resent people who make excessive noise. In a footnote that is prophetic of the problem of noise pollution in our own century, he described "the alarming bells of a whole city at once; the jangling clappers of horse carriages, the ceaseless roar of inarticulate trumpets; the screams of boys; the uproar of a thousand brutal throats; and the cautious absence of a 'non-commital' republican police" (1893, p. 283).

Not content just to comment on what he often considered to be a misuse of our "natural" vocal abilities, Rush, as he grew older, wanted to go so far as to reform the English language. His father had frequently commented on the importance of proper spelling, punctuation, and

MELODY OF SPEECH.

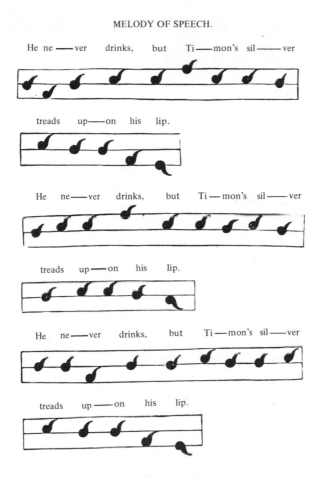

Figure 2.   An example of Rush's use of musical notation to describe the flow and melody of speech.

grammar and criticized his children for their errors in writing. The later editions of James's books introduce a new spelling system that eliminates all double letters and other extraneous symbols. Thus we see "curent," "receve," "thot," and many other oddly spelled words. What is more, Rush liked the idea of a double-comma/,'/to separate embedded clauses and other parts of sentences. He expected the English language to have an "unbounded prospect before it. The unequaled millions of a great continent, into whatever forms of Anarchy, or Despotism, they may be hereafter led—still hold community in the wide and astonishing difusion of one cultivated and identical speech" (Rush, 1893).

One of the more interesting features of *The Philosophy of the Human Voice* is Rush's attempt to utilize musical notation as a way to depict the melody of speech (Fig. 2). In this respect his work resembles that of a contemporaneous English author, William Gardiner, whose book *The Music of Nature* was published in Boston in 1838. It too uses musical notation to describe biological phenomena. Rush fully realized the limitations of this method, which nevertheless is still today applied for certain kinds of research in the field of linguistics (Bolinger, 1972). A much better method for denoting the sounds of speech, one which probably Rush would have adapted for his book had it been available in his day, is the well-known "Visible Speech" technique developed by Bell Telephone Laboratories (Potter, Kopp, & Green, 1966).

James Rush and the Human Intellect

Following the death of his wife in 1857, Rush began work in earnest, work actually begun around 1814, on what was to become his other major accomplishment, the *Brief Outline of an Analysis of the Human Intellect*. He wanted to develop the subject of the mind and integrate it with that of the voice, believing that "when we shall have a clear physical history of the mind as we now have of the voice, the two subjects will form the first and second parts, but not the whole of the physiology of the senses and the brain" (Rush, 1865). Rush used the term "mentivity" to refer to thinking, and he conceived of the mind as basically a physical function of the senses and the brain.

One historian (Roback, 1952) observed that Rush's "red-blooded temperament and mercurical nature" may have led him to emphasize "the motor phase of the nervous system which had been neglected by the early psychologists," thus crediting him with being the true founder of the "behavioristic" school of American psychology, long before J. B. Watson. But there is a great deal more in this book than the term behaviorism would imply. It contains references to free association, personality styles, social psychology, and what today might be called communication theory (Miller, 1967; Ruesch, 1975). Indeed, one can take Rush's "voice" and "intellect" as an attempt to formulate a comprehensive statement about human behavior, as observed with scientific detachment in the nineteenth century. There are definite premonitions of present-day ideas regarding the special functions of verbal information-processing (see Table I).

Table I.   Similarities between James Rush's Formulations and
Those of Communications Theory in Twentieth-Century Psychology

James Rush—nineteenth century (Rush, 1865, 1893)	Twentieth century communications theory (Miller, 1967; Ruesch, 1975)
The notion of a "percipient" and a "Hearer."	The concept of "Sender" and "Receiver."
Explains "how the verbal sign is interwoven with the proper working plan of the mind."	Postulates a mental process of "encoding and decoding" the verbal signs.
"Perceptions are sometimes quiescent or silent in being known only to the mind of the Percipient; at other time Actionary, in declaring his silent thought by words or other conventional signs."	A distinction is made between "inner speech" as a private psychological event and "outer speech" that leads to social action.
"At its origin, in infancy—the mind has silent perceptions before it has signs for them; and silent before it has actionary signs."	Receptive language precedes productive language.
The Hearer hears "what he never heard before (while the Percipient) is the hearer of words formed into a significant train of language,—which when uttered, reacts on the ear of him who uttered it."	The phenomenon of linguistic novelty or creativity, and the notion of auditory feedback.
"Nature may have provided the same impressive and reviving process, for the use of silent perceptions as they occur in dreams; by connecting with them, silent verbal signs, to brighten the pictures on the silent mind."	The relationship between visual fantasy and verbalization.

Rush maintained the belief, throughout his study of the psychology of language and thought, that the mind basically comprises perception and memory (see Table II). His conviction led him further to conclude that the manner in which the mind was capable of expression was a part of the function of the mind itself. In an effort to substantiate this theory, he embarked on a course of careful experimentation and observation of vocal expression to establish the relationship between this expression and its apparent complement, perception.

Mental processes, to Rush, are one in the same with physiological sensation and expression. Speech cannot be isolated or (to use a word

Table II.   James Rush's (1865)
System of the Constituents of the Mind

I. Primary perceptions
  A. Sense of sight
    (form, magnitude, number,
    space, time motion)
  B. Sense of hearing
  C. Sense of touch
  D. Sense of taste
  E. Sense of smell
	V. *Verbal perceptions*
	  A. Formation of perceptive
	    abstraction and relationship
	    of language and thought
	  B. Origin of the formation
	    of verbal signs
	  C. Division of language into
	    parts of speech

II. Memorial Perceptions A,B,C,D,E, (as above)	VI. Varied qualities of perceptions

III. Joint perceptions
  A,B,C,D,E, (as above)
	VII. *Relation of verbal signs to*
	  perceptual qualities

IV. Conclusive Perception
  A,B,C,D,E, (as above)
	VIII. *Disorderly conditions of the*
	  mind, i.e. (insanity)

	IX. General application of the
	  system toward a better
	  understanding and improvement
	  of the individual and society

coined by his father) disassociated from the physiological being or whole personality. In Rush's system, speech is actually the fifth constituent of the mind itself.

Numerous authors of the period wrote textbooks based on Rush's *Philosophy of the Voice* and dedicated the books to him[2] (Barber, 1830; Comstock, 1841; Murdock, & Russell, 1840). Rush was not pleased, however, with attempts by others to abridge his own work, and he refused to undertake the task himself. There were authors, nonetheless, who were more than pleased to abridge their own work in the same field, men such as Thomas Upham.

Rush, Upham, and the American Ideal

Thomas Cogswell Upham was born on January 20, 1799, at Deerfield, New Hampshire. The son of a congressional representative and leading citizen of his state, Upham graduated from Dartmouth College in 1818 and

[2]Rush indicated in the second edition of *Philosophy of the Human Voice* that Barber was the first teacher to use his system. See M. M. Robb, "The elocutionary movement," in K. R. Wallace (Ed.), *History of Speech Education in America*. New York: Appelton Century Crofts, 1954, p. 201, for a list of the outstanding followers of Rush.

went on to attend three years of theological study at Andover Seminary, where his teacher, Professor Moses Stuart, selected him to assist in the instruction of Greek and Hebrew. Upham later became pastor of the Congregational Church at Rochester, New York, which he left in 1824 to assume the professorship of mental and moral philosophy at Bowdoin College in Maine.

In many ways, the work of Thomas C. Upham appears to represent the epitome of Puritan traditions in the field of mental and moral philosophy. He emerges as a principal founder of an American system of psychology, the acceptance of which was virtually guaranteed in nineteenth century America because it reflected the prevailing American social image of that time. As a system, Upham's work contains the essence of the American Dream, even as it exists to this day. Moreover, the image projected through Upham's system lent itself to the four great institutional pillars of society: the church, the school, the family, and the government.

The primary task of the church is to inculcate morality. Sectarian differences, although not of great importance, must be tolerated in the spirit of mutual respect. For Upham, questions of time and the cosmos are partitioned into two subdivisions: historical criticism and science. As long as each of these functions—morality, history, and science—is invested by the church with some sense of sanctity, and as long as the church remains supportive of the state, doctrinal differences are essentially insignificant.

As to the part played by the school, Upham subscribed to the conviction that the child's mind should be institutionalized to the greatest possible degree, so that his life will follow the image prescribed. To this end, education should cultivate all parts of the mind, including reason, affections, and skills. Emotional security, primary discipline, and moral training could all be provided to the preschool child by the family. Recognizing a great compatibility between democracy and the free enterprise system, Upham supported the maintenance of a government based on the interests of agrarian capitalism.

Upham's development of a system of the mind (see Table III) continues to reflect the American image, addressing the three primary constituent parts of the mind—intellect, sensibilities, will—as distinct entities. When it comes to language, however, Upham is reluctant to integrate language among the other constituents. Rush, on the other hand (see Table II), expands upon the number of mind constituents to account for verbal perceptions and their interrelationships among the remaining constituents.

Rush did not enjoy the acceptance so easily attained by Upham. The

Table III.
Upham's system of the Mind (1827–1834)

I. INTELLECT
   1. Intellectual states of external origin
   2. Intellectual states of internal origin
   3. Disordered intellectual action: i.e. (insanity)

II. SENSIBILITIES
   1. Natural or pathomatic
      a. Emotions
      b. Desires
   2. Moral
      a. Emotions of approved and disapproved
      b. Feeling of moral obligation
      c. Disordered sensitive action

III. THE WILL
   1. Nature and relations of the will
   2. Laws of the will
   3. Freedom of the will
   4. Power of the will
   5. Disordered actions of will

LANGUAGE

two men were indeed on opposite ends of the scale. To Upham, the will was the thing to catch the consciousness of the mind, whereas to Rush the will was simply a word, and not an important factor at all.[3] In a comparison of three outstanding American figures—Emerson, Thoreau, and James Rush—Melvin H. Bernstein (1974) makes an interesting observation:

> The three men were marginal orthodox Christians, Rush easily the most irritatingly iconoclastic and abrasive. The three men testify that America as Zion was not feasible in the middle of the 19th century—but for different reasons. America needed more "soul," according to Emerson; more imagination, according to Thoreau; more scientific knowledge, according to Rush. (Vol. II, p. 2)

Three basic assumptions underlay the system of the constituents of the mind according to Rush. First, the mind should be regarded as a physiological operation, as orderly as sensation itself, and as tangible as muscle movement. Rush saw the mind as comprising five constituents, rather the three which Upham assigned to it.

Second, Rush considered thought and language to be inseparable. For instance, Rush believed that in order to fully understand the mind, it

---

[3]By this we mean that it did not play a role as a major constituent in his theory of mind.

was necessary to show the inseparable connection between thought and language, and the reciprocal relationship that these have upon each other.

Third, the demonstrated interdependence of thought and language within the framework of mind as a physiological phenomenon leads to the conclusion that human communication is an integrated mental and physiological response.

The case of Rush's lack of acceptance is not unique. Another nineteenth-century psycholinguist, Alexander Johnson [1786–1867] similarly failed to attain the recognition that his important contributions would seem to demand (Tweney, 1977). The circumstances of both Rush and Johnson raise the question, Why were only certain nineteenth-century theories of language popular and accepted within the scientific community?

The answer seems to be that only those theories of language which were by-products of larger theories of the mind were popular during the nineteenth century. The major concern of the era was for a systematic explanation of how the mind functions. Theories of language were important to nineteenth-century scholars, but such theories depended for their acceptance largely upon their compatibility within the larger framework of an establishment-approved mental and moral philosophy. Many variables determine whether or not a particular theory becomes popular. For example, James Rush produced theories of both mind and language, but he still did not gain popular recognition. The major reason for this was that his basic philosophical approach was incompatible with the establishment and its goals. He also published his work on the mind at a time (the last half of the nineteenth century) when the circumstances of newly emerging, popular theories—those of Darwinism (Darwin and Spencer) and the physiology of mind (Laycock and Carpenter), to name two—were working against him. Upham, on the other hand, had published his system of the three-part division of the mind thirty years before, at a time when popular acceptance depended to a large extent on meeting the criteria of a traditional establishment.

The Place of James Rush in the History of the Behavioral Sciences

When Roback (1952) proclaimed James Rush to be "the most original American psychologist of the nineteenth century," he bemoaned the fact that even the Harvard University Library did not own this man's remarkable books. Fortunately, that situation is now remedied, and excellent facsimile copies of *The Collected Works of James Rush* are now readily available (Bernstein, 1974). The four volumes contain important biographical and scholarly notes by the editor, Melvin H. Bernstein, who mentions that "next to Dr. Benjamin Rush, (Francis) Bacon was James Rush's greatest teacher." Bernstein also provides valuable insights into Rush's work habits, his solitary existence, and the manner in which he seems to have used writing as a way of speaking to himself: "Read aloud, Rush's prose has the rhythm (he spelled it rythm) of an earnest speaker who is determined to indoctrinate the reader."

James Rush certainly must be included among those who "came after" Benjamin Rush (Braceland, 1976) to provide intellectual leadership in the United States. His book about the human voice, though almost forgotten today, had a legitimate place in the teaching of speech and rhetoric before the invention of electronic media to make public elocution easier. For many years the book was used as a text at Harvard, Yale, Columbia, Princeton, and Brown Universities. In spite of his personal eccentricities, which he shared to some extent with his famous father and his psychotic brother, James Rush was a very practical man. He was a product of what Professor Henry F. May (1976) has called the American era of "Didactic Enlightenment." This period followed the "European Enlightenment" in emphasizing anything practical over anything abstract and in preferring "useful" arts—engineering, agriculture, and technology—over "useless" speculation in metaphysics and theology. In that respect, one may forgive Rush's arrogance in claiming that whatever he personally observed to be true must indeed be the TRUTH. The principles of relativity and uncertainty, which hopefully guide scientific thinking today, were not yet available in the nineteenth century. James Rush actually felt quite skeptical about the influence which his work might have in the long run, and his notes express both an undue modesty and an embittered sense of hurt pride and a feeling of neglect. As he said in his *Philosophy* (1893), "there is a kind of hypocritical compliment always paid to originality, with this inconsistent purpose; that mankind are eager to receive what is new, provided it is told in the old way."

References

Barber, J. *Grammar of evolution*. New Haven, 1830.
Bernstein, M. *The collected works of James Rush* (4 vols.). Weston, Mass.: M and S Press, 1974.

Bolinger, D. (Ed.). *Intonation*. Baltimore: Penguin Books, 1972.

Braceland, F. J. Bicentennial address: Benjamin Rush and those who came after him. *American Journal of Psychiatry*, 1976, *133*, 1251.

Butterfield, L. H. (Ed.). *Letters of Benjamin Rush* (2 vols.). Princeton: Princeton University Press, 1951.

Carlson, E. T., & Wollock, J. L. Benjamin Rush on politics and human nature. *Journal of the American Medical Association*, 1976, *236*, 73–77.

Carpenter, W. B. *Principles of mental physiology*. New York: Appleton, 1874.

Comstock, A. *A system of elocution*. Philadelphia, 1841.

Damrau, F. *Pioneers in psychiatry*. New York: Dios Chemical Co., 1940.

Darwin, C. *The descent of man*. New York: Appleton, 1977. (Originally published, 1871.)

Gardiner, W. *The music of nature*. Boston: Wilkins & Carter, 1838.

Hawke, D. F. *Benjamin Rush, revolutionary gadfly*. Indianapolis: Bobbs-Merrill, 1971.

Klaf, F. S. Benjamin Rush's son. *American Journal of Psychiatry*, 1961, *118*, 174–175.

Kurtz, S. G. James Rush, pioneer in American Psychology. *Bulletin of the History of Medicine*, 1954, *28*, 50–59.

Laycock, T. *Mind and brain*. New York: Appleton, 1869.

May, H. F. *The Enlightenment in America*. London: Oxford University Press, 1976.

Miller, G. A. *The psychology of communication*. New York: Basic Books, 1967.

Murdock, J., & Russell, W. *Orthophony or cultivation of the voice*. Boston: Ticknor, 1846.

Ostwald, P. F. *The semiotics of human sound*. The Hague: Mouton, 1973.

Potter, R. K. Kopp G. A., & Green, H. *Visible speech*. New York: Dover, 1966.

Roback, A. A. *History of American psychology*. New York: Library Publishers, 1952.

Ruesch, J. Communication and psychiatry. In A. M. Freedman, H. I. Kaplan, & B. J. Sadock (Eds.), *Comprehensive Textbook of Psychiatry* (2nd ed.) (Vol 1). Baltimore: Williams & Wilkins, 1975, pp. 336–348.

Rush, J. *Brief outline of an analysis of the human intellect* (2 vols.). Philadelphia: Lippincott, 1865.

Rush, J. *The philosophy of the human voice* (7th ed.). Philadelphia: The Library Company, 1893.

Rush, J. *Hamlet, a dramatic prelude in five acts*. Philadelphia: Key & Biddle, 1834.

Spencer, H. *The principles of psychology*. New York: Appleton, 1874.

Tweney, R. D. American psycholinguistics in the nineteenth century. In R. W. Rieber & K. Salzinger (Eds.), *The roots of American Psychology*. N. Y. Academy of Sciences. Annals N281, 1977.

6

Jeffrey Wollock

WILLIAM THORNTON AND THE PRACTICAL APPLICATIONS OF NEW WRITING SYSTEMS

Introduction

The contribution of Dr. William Thornton [1759–1828] to the study of language and cognition has so far received little attention from historians. Thornton is today chiefly remembered as a gifted, self-taught architect who not only designed Library Hall in Philadelphia (presently the library of the American Philosophical Society), but also drew up the original plans for the United States Capitol and other historic buildings in the Washington area. (For Thornton's place in the history of American architecture, cf. Andrews, 1964; Brown, 1896, 1913, 1915; Crenshaw, 1926; Jackson, 1923; Kimball & Bennett 1923; Newcomb, 1928; Peter, 1969; Peterson, 1953; Rusk, 1929, 1935; Tayloe, 1872; Thurman, 1935.)

Besides this, Thornton served for over a quarter of a century as the nation's first superintendent of patents (Evans, 1919), and is also notable for his activities as an early abolitionist, his partnership with John Fitch [1743–1798] in the development of the first functional steamboat in America (Hunt, 1914) and his friendship with many famous figures, such as Franklin, Rittenhouse, Washington, Jefferson, the Madisons, Count Volney, and Baron Alexander von Humboldt.

Jeffrey Wollock • New College, University of Oxford, Oxford, OX1 3BN, England.

In addition to all these accomplishments, Thornton published in 1793 a "treatise on the elements of written language," entitled *Cadmus,* to which he appended an "Essay on the Mode of Teaching the Deaf... to Speak." Some years later, he drew up a vocabulary of the language of the Miami Indians in his own phonetic alphabet. The immediate influence of these works was limited but quite definite, and their significance grows when viewed against the historical background. Thornton was mainly concerned with phonology, phonetic orthography, primary reading instruction, teaching of speech to the deaf, and ethnolinguistics, and his contribution to these areas was more of a practical than of a theoretical nature.

Brief Biography

William Thornton was born on May 20, 1759, of Scottish parents, on the small island of Jost Van Dyke, one of the Virgin Islands, into a Quaker community centered at Tortola. Sent to England at the age of five, he attended school first at Lancaster, then London, and subsequently studied medicine at the University of Edinburgh [1781–84], taking his M.D. at Aberdeen, November 23, 1784. After a tour of the Highlands and a stay at Paris, Thornton returned to Tortola. He first arrived in the United States in 1787, took American citizenship the following year at Wilmington, Delaware, and moved to Philadelphia a short time later. He married Anna Brodeau in 1790 and returned with her to Tortola, but by November, 1792, they were once again in Philadelphia. The following year, Thornton's designs for the U.S. Capitol were approved by George Washington, and he was awarded a building lot in the virtually nonexistent city, which he soon adorned with a house of his own plan. Thornton thus became one of the first householders in Washington, where he remained the rest of his life.

In May, 1802, President Jefferson appointed Thornton clerk in the State Department in charge of patents. During the war with the British in 1814, he saved the patent office from destruction by lecturing to the invading troops on the folly of such an act.

Thornton died at Washington on March 28, 1828, survived by Mrs. Thornton but leaving no descendents (Clark, 1915; Kimball, 1936).

A general idea of the content of Thornton's first published linguistic paper can be gleaned from its full title: *Cadmus, or a Treatise on the*

Elements of Written Language, illustrating, by a philosophical Division of Speech, the Power of each Character, thereby mutually fixing the Orthography and Orthoepy. This is followed by a brief "Essay on the Mode of teaching the Deaf, or Surd and consequently Dumb, to Speak" (Thornton, 1793a, b).

Cadmus was the legendary Phoenician king who first taught the alphabet to the Greeks. In proposing a new phonetic alphabet, Thornton saw himself as an American Cadmus. With a blend of idealism, optimism, and pragmatism so characteristic of the time, he assumed that if a scheme were truly rational on its own terms, it would be only more rational to urge its universal adoption. Thus, Thornton the philosopher must be Thornton the reformer, and he made it clear that he intended not an adjunct or tool but a *replacement* of standard, or as he put it, of "incorrect" orthography. *Cadmus* is, ipso facto, a political as well as a philosophical statement; hence its frequently aggressive tone.

Because the English language is not "properly written," said Thornton, children have great difficulty learning to read,[1] whereas foreigners find it impossible to learn English pronunciation without a teacher.[2] Besides, with hundreds of "savage" languages still unwritten, there would be need of a standardized alphabet capable of exactly recording native pronunciation. A universal literacy taught according to this system would annihilate all nonstandard dialects. Finally, adoption of the new system must necessarily aid the American publishing industry in its competition with the British, since foreigners would certainly prefer to know how to pronounce what they were reading.

Next, Thornton presented his new alphabet (Fig. 1), followed by a physiological description of all the "simple sounds"—roughly, phonemes—of English: twenty-one "vowels" and nine "aspirates." By "vowels", he meant all voiced sounds, distinguishing what we call vowels

---

[1] A memorandum in one of Thornton's notebooks (Library of Congress) refers to a note in an unspecified edition of Madame de Genlis, *Veillées du Château* (1784) "respecting a system of teaching children to read in a very short time," the work called *Quadrille des Enfans, ou Système Nouveau de Lecture,* by an Abbé Berthaud. This book, first published in 1743, had gone into at least seven editions by 1820. There is no indication of whether Thornton ever actually saw the book.

[2] In one of his notebooks, Thornton would later record an anecdote about Montesquieu, who "after long studying the English language in his closet, hazarded articulating a few words of it, to which when he had frequently repeated them to some indulgent native, he received for answer, 'Beg pardon, sir, but I don't understand French'" (*Quarterly Review,* Boston edition, May, 1820, p. 189).

C A D M U S.

The Characters.

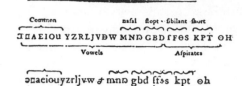

The following characters are particularly recommended.

ƆƱⱯ⅃ꞮOUYZR⅃JVꞵɯ m ɳGɑpſ ſⱭꙅKPTⱣH ·

	Pronounced like,	ɛ					as in herd,
ɔ					ɑ		law
ʊ	-	-	-	-	ɑ	-	-	rat
a	-	-	-	-	ɑ	-	-	rat
e	-	-	-	e	-	-	-	red
i	-	-	-	i	-	-	fit
o	-	-	-	o	-	-	-	fog
u	-	-	-	o	-	-	fool
y	-	-	-	y	-	-	-	ye
z	-	-	-	z	-	-	zeal
r	-	-	-	r	-	-	red
l	-	-	-	l	-	-	let
ꝃ	-	-	-	g	-	-	judge
v	-	-	-	v	-	-	vaſt
ꝺ	-	-	-	th	-	-	that
w	-	-	-	w	-	-	wolf
m	-	-	-	m	-	-	met
n	-	-	-	n	-	-	nap
ŋ	-	-	-	ng	-	-	king
g	-	-	-	g	-	-	get
b	-	-	-	b	-	-	bat
d	-	-	-	d	-	-	dim
ſ	-	-	-	ſh	-	-	ſhip
f	-	-	-	f	-	-	fit
ſ	-	-	-	th	-	-	thin
s	-	-	-	f	-	-	ſet
h	-	-	-	k	-	-	kiſs
p	-	-	-	p	-	-	pen
t	-	-	-	t	-	-	ten
Ᵽ	:	-	:	wh	-	when
h	-	-	-	h	:	-	hat

Figure 1. From Wollock, J. William Thornton, An Eighteenth Century American Psycholinguist: Background and Influence. In R. W. Rieber & K. Salzinger (Eds.), *The Roots of American Psychology: Historical Influences and Implications for the Future*. New York: The New York Academy of Sciences, 1977, p. 266.

as a special group of seven "common vowels," the rest being voiced consonants. His "aspirates" correspond to our voiceless consonants. This is the main body of the treatise, which then concludes with some miscellaneous observations on language, including conjecture about its origin. "The language of man," wrote Thornton, "was originally formed by imitating the objects of nature and beasts to decoy them, and by imitation alone he forms a very extensive scale of sounds." To support this, Thornton made an imaginative comparison of the consonants with the sounds of nature.[3] As for the cause of the variety of human languages, they "differ so much in a few years, by the particular circumstances of the people, that there is no occasion for miracles to explain the varieties."

Thornton dealt briefly with the old dream of a universal language, noting the highly artificial nature of Hebrew, in which every simple idea is represented by a triliteral root, and the shifting of vowels and accents within this root, as well as the addition of prefixes and suffixes, express the various mutations of the simple idea in a highly regular manner. A philosophical language might be constructed with an even greater economy of letters, whose permutations would generate a copious supply of words.

Thornton ended his essay with considerations of a more strictly orthographical kind. He suggested several new signs for the indication of figures of rhetoric, including the inverted marks which signal the start of a question or an exclamation in Spanish (¿... ?   ¡... !), actually used in the text of *Cadmus* with startling effect. Thornton also proposed the study of what he called *agophasis* or *agophonics,* a means of indicating variations in the pitch of a sound, word, or sentence. All these ideas connect Thornton with the contemporary "elocutionary movement," about which there will be more to say further on.

The "Essay on the Mode of Teaching the Deaf" is a plan for practical and specialized application of the ideas set forth in *Cadmus*. Thornton saw that his phonetic alphabet, by visually reinforcing particular patterns of motion and placement of the speech organs, would be a great aid in teaching speech to the deaf.

In the essay, Thornton began by suggesting that the deaf child be taught together with a hearing child of his own age. The teacher would open his mouth and show the formation of each sound with great exaggeration. "The pupil will try to imitate it. He will make no doubt a sound of

---

[3]*Cf.* a similar comparison by Avicenna: K. I. Semaan, ed., *Arabic Phonetics; Ibn Sïna's Risālah on the Points of Articulation of Speech Sounds* (Lahore: Ashraf, 1963), pp. 57–60.

some sort . . . if that sound be contained in the language you mean to teach him, point immediately to the letter which you find is the symbol, and repeat it so often, that he can neither forget it, nor have any idea of the symbol without that sound, nor of the sound without the symbol." He will learn to distinguish between voiced and voiceless sounds by feeling the teacher's throat. If he should at any time hit upon the wrong sound, the teacher should point to the symbol for the sound thus erroneously obtained, and go on as if that had been the one intended. Sounds and symbols already learned should be constantly drilled.

Depending upon the age of the child, different methods of directing the speech organs should be tried; he may perhaps feel the teacher's mouth, or the teacher may form the child's mouth to the correct pattern; a mirror should always be handy. Thornton also discussed the difficulty of lip-reading: that many of the sounds are produced by similar or by invisible articulations. Yet, with assiduous practice, the deaf child will learn to pick up sufficient information from those organs which are visible, to supply those which are not; much as a good stenographer can read transcriptions despite the lack or similarity of many letters.

If Thornton's orthography were to be generally adopted, or at least used in texts for the deaf, the child would simultaneously learn to speak, to understand others, to read, write, and draw. Thornton deplored the lack of a truly "philosophical" pronouncing dictionary and criticized Kenrick (1773) and Sheridan (1780) for indicating many sounds by combinations of letters, or using a single letter for more than one sound. Under his own system, "reading would offer an eternal source of improvement in pronunciation, not only to the deaf, but to all."

Thornton paid lip service (so to speak) to the manual sign method, noting only that the deaf can learn as easily in this way as hearing people do by ear, provided there is constant repetition.

In Thornton's method for teaching vocabulary, one sees a reminiscence of Bishop Wilkins's categorical arrangement of all simple ideas by genus, difference, and species, about which more later. Thornton suggested that the deaf pupils compile books with the names and pictures of familiar objects, beginning with genera and descending to species, as *animals:* mankind, beasts, birds, fishes, reptiles, insects, and amphibians; *beasts:* carnivores, graminivores; *graminivores: horse,* mare, foal; *horned cattle:* bull, cow, calf; *sheep:* ram, ewe, lamb; etc.[4]

---

[4]Systems of this kind may be traced back through such as J. A. Comenius, Petrus Ramus, Tomasso Campanella, Giordano Bruno, and Raymond Lully. See F. Yates, *The Art of Memory* (Chicago University Press, 1966).

The deaf pupil must "leave no name unpronounced, unwritten, or unread"; he must carefully observe the teacher's mouth, and his own in a mirror, must draw a picture of the object, "and if the word be incorrectly spelled, [he must] write it properly besides." The mutual reinforcement of all these methods "will impress the child's mind so strongly," that he will rarely need to look at his book; and he will become proficient at drawing besides. He should be taught the actions and passions by seeing them acted out, at the same time learning their names; for the stock of words must keep pace with the increase of knowledge.

In his conclusions, Thornton affirmed his confidence in the value of this system "from short trials I have made"; and though he admitted the sign method was more easily learned, he believed speech quite feasible, and "so useful upon every occasion, that to attain it is to facilitate the very means of existence... in all the common occurrences of life... speech would be so useful, that it would certainly more than repay the trouble of obtaining it; especially as it would be a mode of facilitating every other acquirement."

Cadmus, as Thornton informs us, was composed in 1792 at Tortola, where few books were available. But he did consult Bishop John Wilkins's [1614–1672] *Essay towards a Real Character and a Philosophical Language* (1668), and appears also to have made use of Thomas Sheridan's [1719–1788] "prosodical grammar" (1789),[5] John Horne Tooke's [1736–1812] *Diversions of Purley* (1786), Dr. Johnson's "Grammar" (appended to his *Dictionary,* London, 1755), and Noah Webster's *Dissertations on the English Language* (1789). Not mentioned in *Cadmus,* but cited in one of Thornton's notebooks, now in the Library of Congress, is a paper "On the Invention of Language", from George Gregory's [1754–1808] *Essays, Historical and Moral* (1785).[6] Thornton also mentioned, and may have known at first hand, the papers (1788) of James Beattie [1735–1803] and the writings (1779) of Benjamin Franklin [1706–1790]. He described as "absurdities" the etymological theories of Lord Monboddo [1714–1799] (1773–1792) and James Harris [1709–1780] (1751) whereas he believed those of James Robertson [1714–1795] (1758, 1783) were at least heading in the right direction (Thornton, 1783).

There is no definite indication as to how Thornton first became interested in speech for the deaf. In a notebook of his tour through the Scottish Highlands, dated 1786, one already finds a phonetic transcription

[5]Prefixed to the second edition of his *Complete Dictionary* (London, 1789).
[6]Published in London and excerpted in the *New Annual Register for the Year 1785* (London, 1786), "Classical and Polite Criticism," pp. 86–94.

of spoken Gaelic, several pages long, though written in the conventional alphabet. It is also particularly worthy of notice that Thomas Braidwood [1714–1806], who achieved great success teaching speech to the deaf in a school which he had founded for that purpose at Edinburgh, was at the height of his fame during the very period when Thornton was studying medicine in that city. Braidwood's work was of general interest to the philosophical community; he is discussed by Lord Monboddo (1773–1792, Vol. 1, p. 179), and the school was visited as early as 1773 by Dr. Johnson (Gordon, 1967–1968). Not long before Thornton completed his studies at Edinburgh, Braidwood moved the school to London; this in particular must have drawn attention to his already well-known accomplishments. Looking at the method he employed, one can see how similar it is to Thornton's. According to a report on "Dumbness" in the *Encyclopaedia Britannica* of 1797:

> When we conversed with Mr. Braidwood concerning the nature and method of teaching this wonderful art, he seemed to be very desirous of communicating and transmitting his discovery to posterity; but observed, from the nature of the thing we believe it to be true, that he could not communicate it so fully in writing as to enable any other person to teach it. The first thing in the method is, to teach the pupil to pronounce the simple sounds of the vowels and consonants. We have even seen him performing this operation; but are unable to give a clear idea of it. He pronounces the sound of *a* slowly, pointing out the figure of the letter at the same time; makes his pupil observe the motions of his mouth and throat; he then puts his finger into the pupil's mouth, depresses or elevates the tongue, and makes him keep the parts in that position; then he lays hold of the outside of the windpipe, and gives it some kind of squeeze, which it is impossible to describe: all the while he is pronouncing *a,* the pupil is anxiously imitating him, but at first seems not to understand what he would have him to do. In this manner he proceeds, till the pupil has learned to pronounce the sounds of the letters. He goes on in the same manner to join a vowel and a consonant, till at length the pupil is enabled both to speak and read. (Vol. 6, pp. 169–170)

When Thornton returned from Tortola to Philadelphia in November, 1792, he lost no time in submitting *Cadmus* to the American Philosophical Society in competition for the Magellanic gold medal. It is recorded in the society minutes for November 28 that the officers and council, David Rittenhouse presiding, ordered the treatise admitted and referred to a committee for examination,[7] who reported on December 21

> that they have perused it, and found it to be a very ingenious and learned Performance, proposing many improvements in the science of communicating

---

[7]See Minutes, December 7, 1792, *Early Proceedings of the American Philosophical Society* (Philadelphia, 1884), p. 209.

ideas by visible signs. They are of the opinion that it is perhaps not to be expected that many of these improvements will suddenly be adopted; it may nevertheless, have the best tendency to introduce gradually, greater perfection in speaking and writing the English language. And that such encouragement as the Society may think proper to give the Author, will be judiciously bestowed.

William Smith,
Sam. Magaw,
John Andrews.[8]

The medal was duly awarded, and in the minutes of February 15 it is announced that Dr. Thornton was permitted "to have printed on his own account the Dissertation entitled *Cadmus,*" the Society reserving the right to print it also in the Transactions,[9] and it was indeed published in both forms (Thornton, 1793a,b). A notice of the work appeared in the *Analytical Review* (1794, *19,* 138), without comment, and there is a brief, unfavorable notice in the *Monthly Review* of 1795.

Historical Background

Attempts at a phonetic spelling for English were nothing new by Thornton's time. As early as 1569 John Hart [d. 1574] had published *An Orthographie,* using a purely phonetic system with symbols for five vowels and twenty-one consonants. The following year, Hart applied this "newe maner of writing" to a *Methode or comfortable beginning for all unlearned, whereby they may be taught to read English, in a very short time, with pleasure* (Danielsson, 1955). The reformed spelling system of William Bullokar, given in *A Book at Large* (1580), used no new symbols; Alexander Gill the elder [1565–1635] proposed a fairly precise system of sound representation in his *Logonomia Anglica* (1619, 2nd ed. 1621); Charles Butler [d. 1647] suggested adoption of a system whereby men should "write altogether according to the sound now generally received", in *The English Grammar* (1633, 2d ed. 1634); and there were others.[10] In none of these early systems, however, were the powers of the symbols explained according to the physiology of sound production; they were simply described according to their sound in specimen words: "b as in

---

[8]Minutes, December 21, 1792, *ibid.,* p. 210. See Also Clark (1915) p. 160.

[9]Minutes, *ibid.,* p. 213.

[10]For a list of spelling reformers, see A. C. Baugh, *A History of the English Language* (New York: Appleton-Century-Crofts, 1935), pp. 485–493; see also Abercrombie (1965, pp. 45–75); cf. S. Harvey, "Observations on Alphabetical Characters," *Memoirs of the Manchester Literary and Philosophical Society,* 4, pt. 1 (1793):135–209; Scragg (1974).

boy," etc. Although Thornton (1793a, p. 262) mentioned Bullokar and Gill, he had not seen their books.

Systematic speech instruction for the deaf also had a long history by this period, going back at least as far as Pedro Ponce de Leon [c. 1520–1584], a Spanish Benedictine monk who taught his pupils to speak not only Spanish and Latin but, in some cases, even Greek and Italian. None of his writings survives, but contemporary accounts suggest that Ponce began instruction with writing and introduced articulation once the pupil was able to write the names of some objects. This would be followed by a process of connecting the sounds to form words and associating these muscular movements with the written characters which the pupil already understood (Hodgson, 1953, p. 83). Of course, the orthographies of Spanish, Italian, Latin, and Greek, are all very much more nearly phonetic than that of English. Another Spaniard, Juan Pablo Bonet [d. 1629], author of a *Reduccion de las letras, y arte para enseñar a ablar los mudos* (published in Madrid, 1620), likewise based his method on the principle that the association of printed letters and sounds would expedite both speaking and reading (Mullett, 1971; Navarro Tomás, 1920; Perez de Urbel, 1973; Werner, 1932, pp. 131–235).

A more direct ancestry of Thornton's *Cadmus* and "Teaching the Deaf" is seen in the activities of a number of founding members of the British Royal Society in the mid-seventeenth century, and certain other philosophers well known to them. It is not surprising that this powerful intellectual movement, which championed atomism and the mechanical philosophy, should have fostered the reduction of language to its *atoms,* or simple ideas and sounds, the fixing of symbolic notations to them, and a careful investigation of the *mechanics* of voice and speech production. The component sounds of the English language and the physiology of their production were carefully described for the first time by Dr. John Wallis in "De Loquela, sive litterarum omnium formatione & genuino sono," prefixed to his *Grammatica Linguae Anglicae* (1653), but without a phonetic alphabet or any proposal of speech for the deaf. In the early 1660s, however, Wallis successfully instructed two deaf mutes,[11] and in 1692 he entered into correspondence with Johann Conrad Amman [1669–1724] the great teacher at Amsterdam. It was through Wallis's efforts that

---

[11]See the letters to Robert Boyle in R. Boyle, *Works* (London, 1772, vol. 6) p. 453; also *Philosophical Transactions of the Royal Society* (July 3, 1670); cf. J. Locke, *A New Method of Making Common-place Books* (London, 1706).

Daniel Foote (see note 25, *infra*) translated Amman's *Surdus Loquens* into English (*The Talking Deaf Man*) in 1694 (Amman, 1965, 1972).

William Holder's [1616–1698] *Elements of Speech, with an Appendix concerning Persons Deaf and Dumb* (1st ed., 1669) presents close parallels with Thornton's proposal. In this work, the sounds of English are elaborately described and classified, and the teaching method is given in a fixed order, in even greater detail than with Thornton. Holder, too, regrets the state of the alphabet, but there is a difference in attitude, perhaps more one of time and place than of personality. Holder writes:

> it is not to be hoped or imagined that the incongruous Alphabets, and Abuses of writing can ever be justled out of their Possession of all libraries and Books, and universal habit and practice of Mankind. This were to imply, that all Books in being should be destroyed and abolished, being first new Printed after such rectified Alphabets; and that all the Age should be prevailed with, to take new pains to unlearn those habits, which have cost them so much labour. (1677/ 1975, pp. 108–109)

But the late eighteenth-century philosopher was convinced that he was building a new world in America. So Thornton (1793a) could write:

> All good authors whose works are too voluminous or expensive, or too abstracted for new editions, would still afford ample matter for the learned and ingenious, and they would be read, with as much ease as the ancient English and French. If they were books of more general use, and worthy of new editions, they would no doubt be republished; if not, the rising generation would be much benefitted by their suppression. (p. 272)

It is just as well, perhaps, that this did not come to pass: the Enlightenment philosophers had rather idiosyncratic opinions about what was and what was not worth reading.

Holder did however see the value of such an alphabet in teaching the deaf. After some tentative remarks as to the best way of representing the vowels, he gives a working alphabet of consonants for teaching the deaf, containing the two Greek symbols for *theta,* θ and ϑ (to represent English voiceless and voiced *th*, respectively) and the letter ŋ (for *ng*), which Albright (1958, p. 12) believes to be Holder's own invention; but no sign for *sh*. Unlike Thornton, Holder considered a phonetic alphabet

> your own *Clew* to guide you; but the Deaf person is not to be troubled with it, because he is also to learn to write and read as others do; and therefore must be taught the common *Alphabet* of that language, which he is to learn, and must use those incongruous compositions, and other Anomalies of vulgar writing; in which you must understand how to manage him, by Reduction of them to the true Alphabet of Nature. (1677/1975, p. 133)

This expression recalls another important work published at Sulzbach by Francis Mercurius Van Helmont [1618–1699] just two years earlier, *Alphabetum Naturale Hebraicum,* or natural Hebrew alphabet (1667). Van Helmont proposed the use of the Hebrew language and alphabet as a medium for teaching the deaf to speak. Strongly influenced by the thaumaturgical teachings of the Kabbala,[12] Van Helmont believed that Hebrew was the primordial language, and that each character of the Hebrew alphabet was an actual diagram of the disposition of the speech organs for the production of the corresponding sound. One need not take this "literally," as it were, to appreciate the mnemonic value of such an approach, especially in conjunction with the use of a mirror: the Hebrew orthography being very nearly phonetic. Van Helmont was in England nearly all the time from October 1670 to 1679,[13] and the book, published only in Latin and German, was noticed in the *Philosophical Transactions* of the Royal Society (Mullett, 1971, p. 139).

Bishop John Wilkins, mentioned above, whose *Essay towards a Real Character* (1668) is cited on the first page of *Cadmus,* was another, perhaps the central, figure of this group. Wilkins's project was the construction of the Universal Language itself. His basic aim was to classify systematically all simple ideas (a concept which would later become the basis of Marc Peter Roget's [1779–1869] *Thesaurus* and Melvil Dewey's [1851–1931] decimal system of library classification), and to invent mutually corresponding visual and vocal symbols by means of which all words might be generated from these simple ideas according to a fixed hierarchical classification.

This project required an analysis of simple sounds, which Wilkins provided in a section entitled "Discourse on the Functions of Sounds in Speech."[14] Here we learn that Wilkins had consulted with both Holder and Francis Lodwick [fl. 1647–1686]; Wallis (1678, p. 17) says that he too had been consulted. Lodwick, for his part, had invented his own phonetic alphabet and universal language.[15]

Wilkins designed an organic alphabet, each character being a stylized diagram of the position of the speech organs. Very likely the idea, minus the Hebrew, had been borrowed from Van Helmont; Abercrombie (1965)

---

[12]See G. Scholem, *Kabbalah* (New York: Signet, 1978), pp. 416–419.
[13]See M. H. Nicolson, ed., *Conway Letters,* (New Haven: Yale University Press, 1930), pp. 309–377.
[14]See Part 3, chapters 10–14, in *Essay Towards a Real Character.*
[15]See Introduction, V. Salmon, ed., *The Works of Francis Lodwick,* (London: Longmans, 1972). For Daniel Foote, see p. 71.

suggests the influence of Lodwick.[16] According to Wilkins's express statement, these characters were not meant for ordinary use, but only as "natural pictures of the letters." Albright (1958) calls it "a remarkable anticipation of Melville Bell's 'Visible Speech,'" invented two centuries later.

The Scot George Dalgarno [1626–1687], who also consulted with Wallis, Wilkins, and others (Wallis, 1678, p. 16), suggested that simple and easy characters would be of value in teaching tone, accent, and emphasis to the deaf (*Didascalocophus, or the Deaf and Dumb Man's Tutor*, 1680) (Mullett, 1971, p. 140).[17]

More immediate antecedents of *Cadmus* can be seen in the earliest pronouncing dictionaries, whose origins are linked to the "Elocutionary Movement" which began in Britain in the mid-eighteenth century and slightly later, for somewhat different reasons, in America. At that period, with increased nationalism spurring the development and standardization of vernacular languages,[18] natural philosophers began to propose new applications of the research done in the previous century. The elocutionists derived their principles, rules, and systems by using the methods of natural philosophy to observe and record actual speech. Out of this they built a program of training in persuasive delivery tailored to exert mass public influence through Parliament, podium, and pulpit.

The elocutionists divided their subject into four broad areas. The first of these, *bodily action*, was entirely ignored by Thornton; *voice management*, the second, he mentioned only briefly in connection with his new punctuation marks; but his description of English sounds would have come under the elocutionists' third heading, *vocal production*, which covers the actual anatomy and physiology of speech; however, Thornton did not deal with speech defects and their treatment, which also come under this heading. The final area of elocution is *orthoepy*, a correct (standard-dialect) pronunciation, which also includes *orthography*, namely, a rational system of conveying this in writing.[19] Although a ra-

---

[16]See "Forgotten Phoneticians," p. 52, in Abercrombie (1965).

[17]On this whole period, see V. Salmon, "Language Planning in 17th-century England," in C. A. Bazell *et al.*, eds., *In Memory of J. R. Firth*, (London; Longmans 1966), pp. 370–397.

[18]For analogous developments in Germany, see I. Weithase, *Anschauungen über das Wesen der Sprechkunst von 1775–1825*, (Berlin: Emil Ebering, 1930).

[19]See C. A. Fritz, "From Sheridan to Rush: The Beginnings of English Elocution," *Quarterly Journal of Speech*, 16 (1930):75–88; W. S. Howell, "Sources of the Elocutionary Movement in England, 1700–1748," *Quarterly Journal of Speech*, 45 (1959):3–18; W. Guthrie, "The Development of Rhetorical Theory in America, 1635–1850," *Speech Monographs*, 18 (1952) *seriatim;* F. W. Haberman, "English Sources of American Elocution,"

tional orthography had already been attempted in the pronouncing dictionaries of William Kenrick (1773) and Thomas Sheridan (1780), Thornton and others believed their methods had not been sufficiently "philosophical." (This would also apply, *mutatis mutandis,* to John Walker's great pronouncing dictionary, although Thornton does not seem to have known of the work, which appeared in 1791, a year before Cadmus.) Furthermore, the United States, unlike Britain, was committed to the idea of mass education, which meant that *reading* would become a public concern as schools were set up to instruct the children of all the people. Finally, as a new and in many ways artificial nation, the United States was thought to be especially in need of a standardized speech to promote unity through uniformity. It is not surprising, then, to discover that *Cadmus* is only one of a number of American orthographic proposals of the time. Others are Benjamin Franklin's "Scheme for a New Alphabet and Reformed Mode of Spelling" (written in 1768 and published in 1779); Noah Webster's "Essay on the Necessity, Advantages and Practicability of Reforming the Mode of Spelling, and of Rendering the Orthography of Words Correspondent to the Pronunciation" (1789); James Ewing's *Columbian Alphabet; being an Attempt to New Model the English Alphabet, in such a Manner as to Mark every Simple Sound by an Appropriate Character . . .* (1798); and Thomas Embree's *Orthography Corrected; or, a Plan Proposed for Improving the English Language by Uniting Orthography with Pronunciation . . .* (1813).

Franklin's alphabet called for six new characters. Wise (1948) has suggested that Franklin "probably still cherished some of his own ideal of a great English-speaking empire, standing astride the ocean; such an empire would need a lithe, active, rejuvenated language, stripped clean of the cumbersome, non-functional, hindering baggage which the spelling habits of centuries had accumulated. What might pass for patriotism toward this dream-empire might have motivated Franklin's revolutionary proposal of a new alphabet." This reminds one immediately of Thornton's own dream of a "United States of North and South America", with the capital to be located at Panama. (His good friend Jefferson had a similar proposal.)

Noah Webster advocated a simplified spelling rather than a phonetic alphabet, which he felt could never find acceptance as a substitute; but

---

in K. R. Wallace, ed., *History of Speech Education in America* (New York:Appleton-Century-Crofts, 1954), pp. 105–126; F. W. Haberman, "John Thelwall: His Life, his School, and his Theory of Education," in R. F. Howes, ed., *Historical Studies of Rhetoric and Rhetoricians* (Ithaca: Cornell University Press, 1961), pp. 189–197.

Webster's new spellings were completely inconsistent.[20] What is most interesting is Webster's philosophy, for, like Thornton, he stressed not only ease of reading and spelling for children and foreigners but also the claim that such a system would render pronunciation as regular as spelling: "A general uniformity throughout the United States... would remove prejudice, and conciliate mutual affection and respect." Also he claimed the shorter spellings would somewhat decrease printing costs, and be

> a capital advantage... it would make a difference between the English orthography and the American... such an event is an object of vast political consequences. For, the alteration, however small, would encourage the publication of books in our own country. It would render it, in some measure, necessary that all books should be printed in America. The English would never copy our orthography for their own use; and consequently the same impressions of books would not answer for both countries.... Besides this, a *national language* is a bond of *national union*. Every engine should be employed to render the people of this country *national;* to call their attachments home to their own country; and to inspire them with pride of national character. However they may boast of Independence, and the freedom of their government, yet their *opinions* are not sufficiently independent; an astonishing respect for the arts and literature of their parent country, and a blind imitation of its manners, are still prevalent among the Americans. Thus an habitual respect for another country... prevents their respecting themselves. (1789, p. 393)

James Ewing's "Columbian" alphabet included a number of inverted letters and diacriticals to mark different powers of vowels. With utmost economy he avoided the invention of new characters by using an inverted *k* for voiceless *th,* inverted *y* for voiced *th,* q for *ng* (having eliminated the former power of q), *c* (no longer needed in its old capacity) for *ch,* and the long *s* (ſ) for *sh.* The work is remarkable also for its complete lack of polemic.

Most elaborate of all was the system of Thomas Embree (1813). It was arrived at, he tells us, over a period of fifteen years (p. 50), during which time he, "with the assistance of another person, tried above fifty different plans..." (p. iii). He offered three alternative alphabets, varying in the degree of precision, complexity, and departure from custom. All his new characters were inversions or italic forms of old ones, with the exception of ŋ. He asked teachers to give the idea a fair trial, and readers in general to

> promote the election of a learned person or two in each state, to meet and compromise the most material local anomalies that exist in the United States of

---

[20]In one short paragraph (*Collections of Essays and Fugitive Writings,* p. 337) he has: mezures, prezerve, skools, yuth, business, haz, whoze, karacter, character, nabourhood.

America, and fix a uniform standard of pronunciation, and let the same be recommended for general use. Perhaps it would not be improper for Congress to undertake it.... And as the reader will have the pronunciation uniformly depicted to his eye, it will be a powerful regulator of speech with the natives; and a means of removing a material cause of local anomalies and diversity of pronunciation, and preventing misunderstandings, and reciprocal ridicule. (pp. 16, 26)

With the exception of Embree's *Orthography Corrected,* which had yet to appear, all these systems were mentioned by Peter S. Duponceau, the dean of American linguists, in his annotations (ca. 1808) to the article "Alphabet" in the American edition of the *New Edinburgh Encyclopaedia,*[21] one of the best-known reference works in America during the first half of the nineteenth century (Walsh, 1968). Duponceau, incidentally, took exception to Thornton's inclusion of *wh* among the simple sounds. Most modern phoneticians would agree with Thornton.

Thornton's Miami Vocabulary and the Beginnings of Ethnolinguistics

Although we have no direct account of the preparation of Thornton's "Miami Vocabulary," the circumstantial evidence leaves an unmistakeable trail. First there is Thornton's own comment in *Cadmus:*

All the world have to lament that not only the circumnavigators of different nations, but even of the same nation, who make vocabularies of the languages they hear, are so little acquainted with the philosophy of speech, as never to write them alike: indeed the same person cannot read in his second voyage, but with difficulty, what he wrote in the preceding one, with a pronunciation intelligible to a native. (p. 265)

The Miami vocabulary, then, was a trial application of the new alphabet toward solving this problem. Its intrinsic value as a vocabulary could not have been great, since it nearly duplicated one taken down by Count Volney [1757–1820] four years earlier. This French traveler and linguist was, in fact, a good friend of Thornton, staying at his home whenever he was in Washington.[22] Volney had finally been able to get a specimen of an

---

[21]See *Whiting & Watson's American Edition of the New Edinburgh Encyclopaedia conducted by David Brewster...* (New York, 1832), vol. 1, pp. 539–540. There were earlier editions published in Philadelphia in 1808 and 1813.

[22]One of these visits took place in May, 1796 (Clark, 1915, pp. 169–170); another in July, 1797 (G. Chinard, *Volney et L'Amérique,* Baltimore: Johns Hopkins, 1923, pp. 87–89). Many letters from Volney to Thornton are extant among the Thornton papers in the Library of Congress.

American Indian language when William Wells [c. 1770–1812] and his father-in-law Michikinakua, or Little Turtle [c. 1752–1812], a chief of the Miamis in Indiana, arrived at Philadelphia in the winter of 1797–98. Wells, who had been captured and adopted by Little Turtle at the age of 13, was fluent in English and Miami. Volney spent nine or ten evenings in January and February, 1798, taking down the vocabulary. It was published in 1803, in a consistent orthography based on French.[23]

After their first trip, Little Turtle and Wells appeared frequently in American cities and even became celebrities of a sort. Thornton took his vocabulary at Washington, January 11, 1802, "in part from Little Turtle, but principally from Capt. Wells."[24] It begins with a table of sounds in Thornton's elegant cursive hand, exactly like that in *Cadmus,* but with the addition of a crossed *h* (ħ) for the guttural *ch* (as in Scots *loch*). The vocabulary contains 288 words, written in ruled columns to the right of the English; a few English words appear without a Miami equivalent. To the left of the English is another column giving most of the words in a slightly different orthography using the conventional alphabet. There is no indication of where this list comes from, but it would seem to be earlier. The first six words of the vocabulary also show equivalents in a "German orthography," perhaps that of Rev. John Heckewelder (Heckewelder & Duponceau, 1819). Another Miami vocabulary, in this same German orthography, can be seen in a MS copybook of Peter Duponceau, labelled "Indian Dialects" (American Philosophical Society Library, 497 Ind.)

Thornton must have originally presented this MS to Thomas Jefferson, since the words "communicated by Mr. Jefferson" (i.e., to the American Philosophical Society) are written on the title page in another hand.[25] His reasons for doing so are clear. First, Jefferson had long been interested in Thornton's linguistic work; in a letter of June 11, 1793, he writes:

> Th: Jefferson, with his compliments to Dr. Thornton returns him many thanks . . . for his dissertation on the elements of language which he had read in manuscript with great satisfaction, but shall do it with more in print. (Clark, 1915, p. 159)

---

[23]See C. F. Chasseboeuf, comte de Volney, *Tableau du Climat et du Sol des Etats-Unis d'Amérique* (Paris, 1803), vol. 2, pp. 427–431, 525–532. According to a 1961 estimate, there were 10 to 100 speakers of Miami, all in Indiana, most over 50 years of age; W. L. Chafe, "Estimates Regarding the Present Speakers of North American Indian Languages," *International Journal of American Linguistics,* 28(3) (Oct. 1961):167.

[24]MS., American Philosophical Society.

[25]A catalogue of MS works on the Indians and their languages, presented to the American Philosophical Society, or deposited in their library, indicates that copies of both Volney's and Thornton's Miami vocabularies were presented by Jefferson.

More to the point, Jefferson spent some 30 years in collecting Indian vocabularies, eventually bringing together a master list of about 250 English words with their equivalents in as many as 50 Indian languages. The idea had been suggested by a similar massive project carried out by Peter S. Pallas at the direction of Catherine the Great of Russia, and published at St. Petersburg in 1787–89.[26] Unfortunately, the bulk of Jefferson's work was lost in 1809, when a thief broke into the trunk, in which it was being carried by boat from Washington to Monticello, and dumped them in the river. A small part of these were recovered and sent to the American Philosophical Society at Philadelphia.[27] Despite this loss, the project had served as a major incentive to the organized study of American Indian languages (Hoijer, 1976, pp. 3–22).

Nor was Jefferson the only ethnologist who admired *Cadmus*. The great naturalist-explorer Baron Alexander von Humboldt [1769–1859] wrote Thornton from Philadelphia, June 20, 1804 (in French):

> At Lancaster I read... your Cadmus... full of new and ingenius ideas. The celebrated Darwin has recently (1804) treated this same subject of letters and sounds in his poem *The Temple of Nature*... but your system is quite a bit simpler than his.[28]
>
> HUMBOLT
>
> (Clark, 1915, p. 170)

Incidentally, Alexander's brother Wilhelm von Humboldt [1767–1835] was to become the leading European authority on American Indian languages.

The erudite Peter S. Duponceau [1760–1844], later President of the American Philosophical Society (1828) was another student of American Indian languages who had read *Cadmus*, according to his annotation in the *Edinburgh Encyclopaedia*. These notes of his were later expanded into a monograph entitled *English Phonology* (1817).[29] Here he makes the

---

[26] *Sravnimel'nye slovar' vsyokh' yazykov' i naryochiĭ*, etc. The vocabularies were given in the Cyrillic alphabet, with a pronunciation guide for foreigners. See F. Adelung, *Catherinens der Grossen Verdienste um die Vergleichende Sprachenkunde* (St. Petersburg, 1815), p. 65.

[27] See Sheehan (1973), p. 55. The American Philosophical Society has about 100 of Jefferson's linguistic MSS; C. Wissler, "The American Indian and the American Philosophical Society," *Proceedings of the American Philosophical Society*, 86(1) (1942):192.

[28] The reference is to Erasmus Darwin, *The Temple of Nature*, additional note XV, "Analysis of Articulate Sounds" (Baltimore: Bonsal & Niles, 1804), pp. 123–129.

[29] *English Phonology, or an Essay towards an Analysis and Description of the Component Sounds of the English Language* (Philadelphia, 1817). An adverse review is printed in *Analectic Magazine* (1819):16–39.

important point that reading, once it has been learned, proceeds by sight and not by sound, and therefore "it is of very little consequence whether the words spoken are or are not accurately represented as to sound, by graphic language." In order to avoid associating the sounds of English with *any* particular orthography, Duponceau coined words for them, such as *aulif, arpeth, airish, oomin*, etc. This would avoid the error, he writes, of

> proceeding from the sign to the thing signified; they are sounds and not letters that I wish to make known. If I succeed, nothing will be so easy afterwards, as to affix signs to them, and an auxiliary table of characters, to be used only as an instrument by which to compare, fix and ascertain the pronunciation of words and as a key to pronouncing dictionaries.... I am very far from wishing to see such an alphabet introduced into common use, to the destruction of our literature, and perhaps, ultimately, the entire corruption of our language. (1817, p. 30)

Following this, Duponceau made certain recommendations for a phonetic alphabet: it should be composed neither of characters in common use nor of entirely new signs; perhaps the lower case Greek with additions from Cyrillic. Here is a strictly scientific view of a phonetic alphabet, poles apart from Thornton's democratic spirit of reform.

When John Pickering [1777–1846], the leading authority of his time on American Indian languages, came to write his *Essay on a Uniform Orthography for the Indian Languages of North America* (Cambridge, Massachusetts, 1820), he closely followed Duponceau's guidelines. His alphabet, employing the Roman alphabet with continental values, was designed for practical use, and was arranged in the common alphabetical order rather than according with the organic formation of the sounds (as Thornton's):

> It never was my plan to give a universal alphabet on strict philosophical principles for the use of the learned, but merely a practical one, to be applied to the Indian languages of North America. (p. 32)

The *Essay* is remarkable in having exerted a major influence, if one may so express it, before it was written. For in 1819, when Rev. Hiram Bingham was about to leave for Hawaii as the first missionary sent by the American Board of Missionaries, he consulted with Pickering about the best mode of writing the language. William Ellis, an English missionary who had "considerable influence in the final determination" of Hawaiian orthography, had also read Pickering (Wise & Hervey, 1952). The work was warmly praised by Thomas Jefferson, William H. Prescott, Charles Sumner, and Duponceau (Pickering, 1887, pp. 318, 321–322).

Prior to publication, Pickering had sent a MS copy to Duponceau for comment. In a letter of July 7, 1820, the latter replied:

> I have given it a cursory perusal, and am upon the whole exceedingly pleased with it. . . . I shall send back your manuscript, and also Volney's late work on the same subject, which Sir William Jones has so ably treated—the manner of writing the Oriental languages with Roman characters. I mean to propose to you . . . to have your Alphabet, with a few explanations, printed singly, and distributed among missionary societies, etc. (Pickering, 1887, p. 287)

And again on July 17:

> I feel much flattered by your approbation of the hints I have taken the liberty to give you. I do not regret not having written upon the subject, as I find you are so fully adequate to it . . . You must take and use my letters and notes as you would a conversation . . . in which ideas are mixed . . . indeed, it would be very difficult in most cases to separate my ideas from your own. (Pickering, 1887, p. 288)

Count Volney had also kept up his interest in orthography and phonetics, and produced *L'Alfabet Européen appliqué aux langues Asiatiques* in 1818. In a preface, Volney explains that he had developed a version of the idea as early as 1795, but that he had not conceived of the possibility of establishing a single system for all languages until his stay in the United States (from 1795 to 1798), at which time he had become acquainted with "the treasures of the British literature in Oriental studies." This flattering remark may be explained by the circumstance that it was addressed to the Royal Asiatick Society of Calcutta; undoubtedly, Volney was thinking of Sir William Jones's "Dissertation on the Orthography of Asiatick Words in Roman Letters"[30] in particular. He did not think it necessary to mention, evidently, that while in America he had been the frequent guest of a Dr. Thornton, who had written at length upon this very subject but a short time previous.

L'Alfabet Européen consists of three parts, the first dealing with definitions and principles of the general system of spoken sounds and the letters designated to represent them; the second reviewing the pronunciation of the principle languages of Europe, among which Volney isolates 19 or 20 vowels and 32 consonants, including 2 aspirates. He thus needs 52 54 characters but selects the Roman alphabet as the basis on which

---

[30] *Transactions of the Asiatick Society,* 1:1–56. Also in *The Works of Sir William Jones,* (London, 1807), vol. 3, pp. 253–318. See also P. J. Marshall, ed., *The British Discovery of Hinduism in the Eighteenth Century* (Cambridge: Cambridge University Press, 1970).

to build. The final section demonstrates the application of his alphabet to Arabic. Here we can begin to see the future International Phonetic Alphabet approaching the end of its long gestation.

Conclusions

As an orthographic reform, *Cadmus* obviously had no more effect than any of the other attempts. It is remarkable, with the unprecedented innovations in all walks of life over the last two centuries to which English-speaking countries have so largely contributed, that our orthography, one of the things most constantly in use, has scarcely changed at all. Certainly there has been no lack of attempts. Our eighteenth-century American reformers point in the same direction as the English John Thelwall and the Scottish Rev. James Gilchrist, who, reacting to the inequities of the industrial revolution, committed themselves to the democratization of society through the democratization of education. They were all the direct forerunners of the many utopian "phonographic" movements which sprang up in the late 1830s, as equally of the opinions expressed by George Bernard Shaw in *Pygmalion* (1912). The best known of these was led by Isaac Pitman, and it had great influence in this country through his brother Benn Pitman. Its chief legacy, of course, is the Pitman phonetic shorthand. But these movements embraced a whole panoply of revolutionary ideas such as vegetarianism, phrenology, pacifism, and communal living (Abercrombie, 1965, pp. 92–107; Haberman, 1954).

In the academic world, the phonetic alphabet was gradually perfected as a necessary tool in the study of language. Pitman played an important part here as well; so did Henry Sweet, with his Broad Romic, which became the basis of the International Phonetic Alphabet adopted in 1888. Its development was delayed no doubt until improved transportation and communication had made an international convention of scholars possible. Certainly its success rested on the fact of its separation from questions of orthographic reform in individual countries.[31]

Later work in linguistics has corroborated Duponceau's idea that the

---

[31]For a detailed review of the history of French and English phonetic studies from mediaeval times to 1889, see F. Techmer, "Beitrag zur Geschichte der Franz. und Engl. Phonetik und Phonographie," *Internationale Zeitschrift für Allgemeine Sprachwissenschaft, 5* (1890), 144–295.

lack of a phonetic, or, more accurately, a phonemic spelling or alphabet is only a small part, and not the most important part, of learning to read. The act of reading consists in recognizing language signals expressed in patterns of graphic shapes, as skilfully as these same signals are recognized when expressed in auditory patterns. No matter what alphabet or spelling is used, this remains the basic difficulty of learning to read. The spelling system of English, though rather complex, does in fact follow a recognizable pattern of phonetic representation. Spelling reformers tend to exaggerate the problem by selecting examples from the many subsystems, or occasional exceptions, ignoring the fact that the great majority of words do adhere to a consistent pattern. If a child learns this pattern, he can certainly sound out words, which are corroborated by context. This stage of reading instruction may take slightly longer in English than in some other languages, but its difficulty for normal children has been grossly exaggerated by recent "scientific" studies. Of course, if children's minds are damaged by too much television viewing, they can never learn to read properly in any language. See the superb study by Mathews (1966).

In 1852, the Pitman-Ellis phonetic alphabet was introduced in 119 public and 5 private schools in Massachusetts, and in Syracuse, New York, in 1858. According to George Farnham, "for a time it was thought that the true method of teaching children to read had been discovered. After a trial of five years, however, it was seen that while pupils learned to read by this method in much less time than usual, and attained a high state of excellence in articulation, their reading was as mechanical as before, and few of them became good spellers. The two systems of analysis, phonic and graphic, had so little in common that permanent confusion was produced in the mind" (Fries, 1963, pp. 240–241; but cf. Mathews, 1966, Chapter 15).

It is in the field of deaf education that Thornton's contribution has been most clearly recognized. The oral method nurtured in the bosom of the Royal Society was further developed by a later Fellow of that Society, Henry Baker, who set up the first real school for the deaf in Britain in the early eighteenth century. The next important teacher was Thomas Braidwood, who began with a single pupil in 1764, and kept a school in Edinburgh until 1783, when he moved it to London; it remained in operation until his death in 1806 at the age of 91 (Best, 1943, p. 381). So many students came to Braidwood from America that eventually John Braidwood, a grandson, was sent to Virginia in 1812 to become the first regular teacher of the oral method in this country. Perhaps "regular" is not the right word, for although his efforts met with considerable success, John Braidwood had an unfortunate passion for gambling and liquor, which interrupted his teaching and landed him in jail more than once. A later associate, Rev. John Kirkpatrick, was the first native-born American to teach the oral method. After a final break with Braidwood in March, 1818, Kirkpatrick carried on alone, but all trace of him is lost after 1819 (Bell, 1900, pp. 489–510).

Meanwhile the Rev. Thomas Gallaudet had traveled to Europe in 1815 to study methods of educating the deaf. From the Braidwoods in London he received no cooperation, whereas the Abbé Sicard in Paris, who used the sign method exclusively, showed great interest and provided all the assistance he could. Hence the sign method became the basis of all American instruction for some time to come, and members of the Braidwood family on both sides of the Atlantic, far from spreading the oral method, were responsible for its disappearance in the United States. This goes far to explain Thornton's lack of influence. His own life does the rest. Thornton was a polymath, and never took the time to promote or refine his method. He was a volcano of ideas: once thrown out, they were on their own.

It was only when Melville Bell, coming directly out of the Pitman-Ellis movement, developed his *visible speech*,[32] and his son Alexander Graham Bell began teaching the deaf by means of visible speech at Boston in 1871, that the oral method was revived here. And once Graham Bell began his careful researches into the history of the art, recognition of Thornton was not long in coming. "To Dr. William Thornton," wrote Bell in 1900, "we are indebted for the first work upon the education of the deaf, actually written and published in America. . . . Thornton saw very clearly that one great obstacle to the acquisition of speech by the deaf lay in the unphonetic character of our spelling. . . . The Volta Bureau has in contemplation the republication of Thornton's works, so as to render them more accessible to students. They certainly have not received that attention from practical teachers of the deaf that their importance demands" (Bell, 1900, pp. 113–115). The *Essay*, at least, was reprinted in a journal in 1917 (Bell, 1917, pp. 225–236).

[32]Visible speech is a graphic system that schematically depicts the actions of the speech organs; it is capable of expressing any sound made by the human voice, even sneezing, snoring, and grunting.

Tabula Rasa

The various strands of Thornton's writings on language—primary reading instruction, social reform, deaf education, and ethnolinguistics— all coalesce in that favorite image of Lockean psychology, the *tabula rasa,* or blank slate.

To the empirical psychologist Locke and his followers, the human mind at birth is a blank slate; but the reforming spirit sees blank slates everywhere. If the child is a blank slate, then by extension so is society, via its children. If society has stages of growth, then a "primitive" society is childlike, another blank slate. Uncultivated nature serves no use: one more blank slate, and likewise the (supposedly) long uncultivated vernacular languages.

The Enlightenment loved imagery; it loved logic even more; the airtight syllogism best of all. So many new philosophical "certainties" rested upon "the conclusion following necessarily from the premises." Considerably less attention was paid to the verisimilitude of the premises. Nor was there much subtlety to the reasoning: the Enlightenment loved simplicity. All x is y; z is x; then z is y. Rarely was such a thought framed as all x is y; z is *to a certain extent, and in a certain sense, x;* then insofar as, and in the sense that z actually is x, it is y. Although this is certainly logical, and has the added advantage of more closely resembling reality, it is not quite as pretty.

The tabula rasa was just such a premise, and the philosopher of the Enlightenment, who loved bold, straight outlines, saw the tabula rasa in many places where it was not, or in other words looked at substance and saw blankness. If he had looked more closely at the slate, he would in most cases have found a coherent message already inscribed upon it. Not simple, but coherent.[33]

The paradoxical figure of the philanthropist has played a central role in American life. The archphilanthropist is always seeking blank slates. Loving mankind, but not very fond of actual people, he is ever enthusiastic to re-create them according to a shining master plan. He forgets one thing: no matter what sweeping changes he may advocate, he cannot create a new society, because he himself is far from a tabula rasa; the

[33] An exception, striking by its very abnormality, is "the experience of certain nineteenth-century Russian priests who discovered a tribe on the islands of the Bering Sea leading a life so nearly in accord with the Gospel of Christ that the missionaries confessed they had better be left alone." See L. U. Hanke, *Aristotle and the American Indian* (Bloomington: Indiana University Press, 1959), p. 26.

message he writes on the slate is but a new version of the message he himself has received from that same society.

Dr. Thornton found orthography an uncultivated wilderness; he wished to make it a formal garden; he wished to make mass education a vehicle for social transformation. For this, all must learn to read; therefore, reading must be made easier. He failed to take account of the fact that the straightforward encounter with difficulty is the most important element in education.

The reduction of the languages of "savages" to writing has been another encounter with a tabula rasa; the domesticating of outlandish, incomprehensible sounds to an exact code of written symbols. The effort in itself has met with considerable success, particularly through the International Phonetic Alphabet, and has been of immense value to science. Still one may well ask of the modern dissectors of linguistic cadavers, how many of them understand anything of the grammatical-metaphysical traditions as understood by the primitive people themselves. The fact is, since the reduction of languages to writing has been so closely connected with religious *and political* missionary efforts, it has more often than not been a prelude, even the gateway, to the disruption and destruction of traditional societies. The modern missionary effort is virtually the classic case of a tabula rasa which is not; and the classic story is that of George Guess, known as Sequoyah, one of the most remarkable phonetician-orthographers of his or any other time.

In 1813, one of our spelling reformers, Thomas Embree, wrote, "such uncivilized nations as now lack the use of letters, as they become peaceable and civilized . . . may be benefitted by having a correct mode of writing first propagated among them. . . . And herein our boasted superiority will be degraded by savage civilization, if we continue in our old habit" (p. iv).

Strangely enough, Embree was soon proved right, for while scholars were pondering the best way to represent the simple sounds of English, Sequoyah, an Indian of the civilized Cherokee tribe, applied himself to the same task with his native language, the only language he ever knew. In the year 1809, in northern Alabama, during the course of a discussion with some other Indians regarding the white man's "talking leaves," Sequoyah expressed the belief that it was neither a divine gift, nor magic, nor imposture, but that the marks on paper stood for words, and that he could invent a way to do the same thing. It took him twelve years, but by 1821 he had a nearly phonetic syllabary of 86 characters. His method had been the same as the elocutionists'. He went to all public gatherings, listening carefully to speeches and conversations. Eventually an English book came his way, and although he could not read it, he set about adapting the letters to his own use, modifying some of them and inventing new forms. What happened next was extraordinary: not a schoolhouse was built and not a teacher was hired, but within a few months the syllabary had spread spontaneously to every corner of the Cherokee country. It generally took a native speaker three or four *days* to learn to read, seldom more than a week. A short time later the tribe had obtained a printing press and type, and started a newspaper.[34]

In the beginning of 1825, John Pickering was at work on a Cherokee grammar, following his own *Essay on Orthography,* with three additional characters. As soon as he heard about Sequoyah's syllabary he gave up the project, despite the fact that 48 pages had already been printed (Pickering, 1887, pp. 334, 337). Nevertheless, the American Board of Missionaries doggedly continued to insist on the Pickering orthography for years to come, despite the opposition of the Indians and even some of the missionaries. As Sheehan (1973) put it: "An apparently workable system of Indian writing encroached on the exclusivity of English as a necessary precondition for civilized life. Many philanthropists, consequently, kept a distinct reserve in their reaction to Sequoyah's invention (p. 139).

And just as worldly piety was beginning its transformation into pious worldliness, and one begins to hear from more and more so-called citizens of the world about the blessings of Western civilization, so the religious missionary was beginning to change into the political missionary. Only thus can we understand Count Volney's astonishing rhapsody (in the preface to his *European Alphabet*):

> It is not sufficient to have projected a universal alphabet, it is necessary to put it to use . . . our best European books, translated by able interpreters, must be transcribed and printed in this form as well. An outmoded prejudice vainly extols Oriental literature: but good taste and reason attest that no fund of solid instruction nor of positive science exists in its productions: here history is but a recitation of fables, poetry but hyperboles, philosophy but sophisms,

---

[34]See J. B. Davis, "The Life and Work of Sequoyah," *Chronicles of Oklahoma,* 8 (1930):159–162; J. K. White, "On the Revival of Printing in the Cherokee Language," *Current Anthropology,* 3 (5) (Dec. 1962):511–514. Sequoyah's syllabary is not perfectly phonemic, particularly with regard to consonant clusters. It is, however, quite well adapted to the language, is still taught in most of the 59 Oklahoma Cherokee-speaking churches, and is known by a large proportion of adults. Total number of Cherokee speakers is well over 10,000. Cf. W. Walker, Review of J. Frederick & A. G. Kilpatrick, *The Shadow of Sequoyah, International Journal of American Linguistics, 33* (1) (1967): 82–84.

medicine but recipes, metaphysics but absurdities; here natural history, physics, chemistry and higher mathematics are scarcely more than names. The spirit of a European can only shrink and waste itself in such a school; it is up to the orientals, Gentlemen, to attend the school of the modern West. The day when Europeans shall translate their ideas into the Asian languages with facility, they shall acquire all over this region a decided superiority over the natives in every walk of life: the latter, astonished to hear their languages spoken more purely, read more fluently, written and understood more quickly by strangers than by themselves, will want to know the mechanical instrument of this singular phenomenon: they will end by discussing, by studying our new European alphabet; the older generation will reject it; the younger will adopt it; it will create a healthy schism, and from that moment a great and fortunate intellectual revolution will commence for Asia, a revolution alone capable of regenerating her. (1818, pp. xiv–xvi)

For all the difference between an American farmer and an Indian Brahmin, this does not seem so far from Thornton's idea: "If the orthography of the language were to be corrected, the pronunciation of the scholar would, by reading alone, be perfectly attained by the peasant and the foreigner; destroying thus, *in the most effectual manner,* all vulgar and local dialects" (1793a, p. 279, his emphasis). These architects of rational, mass society seem to have been intent on the idea of plundering people of their most basic property right, the right to their own languages and cultures.[35]

It is certain that orthography has great political and psychological overtones. Can the history of Russian expansion into Asia be separated from the expansion of the Cyrillic alphabet (already begun, one recalls, by Catherine the Great), in which such languages as Kara-Kalpak (Turkic language; Arabic script until 1928) or Buryat (a Mongol language; old Mongolian vertical script until 1929) are now written? In the late 1920s the Soviets actually converted the orthographies of all their Asian languages to Roman characters; they had a change of heart in the late 1930s and converted them again, this time to Cyrillic (Gilyarevsky & Grivnin, 1970). Before that time it had been possible for an educated Tadjik, for instance, to correspond with an Afghan or a Persian in a mutually intelligible literary language, despite the great differences in their everyday speech.[36] The

---

[35]This is by no means to suggest that folk and street dialects should be taught in their own written forms; a standard written language is necessary as a common resource. Dialects ought to be left to themselves, however.

[36]See J. Castagné, "Le mouvement de latinisation dans les républiques soviétiques musulmanes et les pays viosins", *Revue des Etudes Islamiques,* 2 (1928):559–595. Cf. R. Austerlitz, Review of E. G. Lewis, *Multilingualism in the Soviet Union* (The Hague, 1972), *Russian Review,* 33 (3) (July, 1974):350: "Even ch. 3, the best one in the book, is marred

same story of Western expansionism and intellectual shallowness lies
behind these seemingly minor changes. Nothing could more effectively
cut a culture off from its own history and traditions, while at the same
time rendering it defenseless against propaganda and more intellectual-
sounding verbiage published in the new alphabet. All this Count Volney
well understood.[37]

From the evangelistic point of view, moreover, the effort to teach the
deaf was a mission no less than, and in precisely the same sense as, the
bringing of the Bible to the heathen and the illiterate. Hence the epithet

---

by glaring inaccuracies, such as on pp. 56–57, where it is said that 'about fifty minority
languages' acquired alphabets only after 1917 or after 1930. Many of the languages listed
did in fact have alphabets before the revolution, a not unimportant point if one wishes to
draw conclusions from it."

[37] On these issues, consult: J. Acevedo, "¿Habrá pueblos africanos que hayan perdido su
alfabeto?" *Cultura Universitaria* (Caracas), 82 (1963): 120–123; G. H. Bantock, *The
Implications of Literacy* (Leicester, 1966); A. K. Coomaraswamy, *The Bugbear of Literacy* (Bedfont, Mdsx., 1979); D. Diringer, *The Alphabet; a Key to the History of
Mankind,* 3rd ed. (London: Hutchinson, 1968); J. R. Francisco, "The New Function
of Ancient Philippine Scripts," *Philippine Social Sciences and Humanities Review,*
28 (Dec. 1963): 416–423; J. Goody, ed., *Literacy in Traditional Societies* (Cambridge
University Press, 1968); *idem, Domestication of the Savage Mind* (Cambridge University Press, 1978); T. Harrisson, ed., *Borneo Writing and Related Matters* (Kuching:
Sarawak Museum, 1966); K. Hau, "Evidence of the Use of Pre-Portuguese Written
characters by the Bini?" *Bulletin de l'Institut Française d'Afrique Noir,* Ser. B, 21
(Jan.–Apr. 1959): 109–154; *idem,* "Oberi Okaime Script (Nigeria)," *ibid.,* 23 (Jan.–Apr.
1961): 291–308; *idem,* "The Ancient Writing of Southern Nigeria," *ibid.,* 29 (Jan.–Jun.
1967): 150–190; *idem,* "Pre-Islamic Writing in West Africa," *ibid.,* 35 (Jan. 1973): 1–45; S.
B. Heath, *Telling Tongues* (Mexico) (New York: Columbia University Press, 1972); S. I.
A. Kotei, "The West African Autochthonous Alphabets," *Ghana Social Science Journal,*
2 (1972): 98–110; A. B. Lord, *The Singer of Tales* (Cambridge: Harvard University Press,
1964); T. Monod, "Sur un nouvel alphabet ouest-Africain," *Trabalhos de Antropología e
Etnología,* 17 (1959): 35–42; J. A. Notopoulos, "Mnemosyne in Oral Literature," *Transactions and Proceedings of the American Philological Association,* 69 (1938): 476 ff.; F. D.
Nzonzila, "Auf der Spur einer kongolesischen Schrift," *Afrika Heute,* 13–14 (1 Aug.
1968): 200–203; W. J. Pichl, "L'Ecriture bassa au Libéria," *Bulletin de l'Institut Fonda-
mental d'Afrique Noir,* Ser. B, 28 (Jan.–Mar. 1966): 481–484; W. A. Smalley *et al.,*
Orthography Studies (London: United Bible Society; Amsterdam: North Holland, 1964),
esp. pp. 1 ff., 35–37, 71, etc.; T. Stern and F. M. Voegelin, eds., "Three Pwo Karen
Scripts: A Study of Alphabet Formation," *Anthropological Linguistics,* 10 (Jan. 1968):
1–34; E. M. Todd, "Ojibwa Syllabic Writing and its Implications for a Standard Ojibwa
Alphabet," *Anthropological Linguistics,* 14 (Dec. 1972): 357–360; C. Velder, "Thailands
Tua Tham; die Lao-Thau Schrift der Nord- und Nordost-Provinzen," *Anthropos,* 58
(1963): 829–838; W. Walker, "Notes on Native Writing Systems and the Design of Native
Literary Programs," *Anthropological Linguistics,* 11 (May 1969): 148–166 (Cherokee and
Cree); C. E. Filstrup, "Romanizing Oriental Languages," *College and Research Libraries*
(in preparation).

applied to Gallaudet: "missionary to the deaf." Add the Constitution and the newspaper to the Scriptures, and you have Thornton's position: as Romans 10:17 says, "faith cometh by hearing, and hearing by the word of God." But, in fact, the teaching of the deaf *really does* correspond, at least as far as speech is concerned, to the model of the tabula rasa; for speech really is a faculty of man, even if being a white man is not a faculty of a Cherokee. The deaf child's acquisition of speech—imperfect though it may be—can help to put him in better contact with the culture to which he already belongs. But even here Utopian aims have had to be modified, and the oral method, in this country at least, is generally supplemented with instruction in signing.

References

Abercrombie, D. *Studies in phonetics and linguistics.* London: Oxford University Press, 1965, pp. 45–75, 92–107.

Albright, R. W. *The international phonetic alphabet: Its backgrounds and development.* Bloomington: Indiana University Press, 1958.

Amman, J. C. *A dissertation on speech* (C. Baker, trans., R. W. Rieber, intro.). Amsterdam: North Holland, 1965.

Amman, J. C. *The talking deaf man.* Menston, England: Scolar Press, 1972.

Andrews, W. *Architecture, Ambition and Americans.* New York: Free Press of Glencoe, 1964.

Beattie, J. *The theory of language. In two parts. Part I: Of the origin and general nature of speech. Part II: Of universal grammar . . . A new edition, enlarged and corrected.* London: A Strahan, 1788.

Bell, A. G. Historical notes concerning the teaching of speech to the deaf. *Volta Review,* 1900, *2,* 113–115; 489–510.

Bell, M. H. G. Dr. William Thornton and his essay on teaching the deaf. *Columbia Historical Society Records,* 1917, *20,* 225–236.

Best, H. *Deafness and the deaf.* New York: Macmillan, 1943.

Brown, G. Dr. William Thornton, architect. *Architectural Record,* July–Sept., 1896.

Brown, G. Letters from Thomas Jefferson and William Thornton, architect, relating to the University of Virginia. *American Institute of Architects Journal, 1* (Jan.) 1913, 21–27.

Brown, G. *The Octagon, Dr. William Thornton, architect.* Washington, D.C.: American Institute of Architects, 1915.

Clark, A. C. Dr. and Mrs. William Thornton. *Columbia Historical Society Records,* 1915, *18,* 144–208.

Crenshaw, M. M. Stately Woodlawn mansion. *Antiquarian,* 1926, 7 (Sept.) 41–44.

Danielsson, B. (Ed.). *John Hart's works.* Stockholm: Almquist & Wiksell, 1955.

Embree, T. *Orthography corrected; or, a plan proposed for improving the English language by uniting orthography with pronunciation.* Philadelphia: D. Heartt, 1813.

Encyclopaedia Britannica (3rd ed.) (Vol. 6). Edinburgh: A. Bell & C. Macfarquhar, 1797.

Evans, G. W. The birth and growth of the patent office. *Columbia Historical Society Records,* 1919, *22,* 105–124.

150 JEFFREY WOLLOCK

Ewing, J. *Columbian alphabet; being an attempt to new model the English alphabet, in such manner as to mark every simple sound by an appropriate character.* Trenton, N.J.: Mathias Day, 1798.

Franklin, B. *Political, miscellaneous and philosophical pieces.* London, 1779.

Fries, C. C. *Linguistics and reading.* New York: Holt, Rinehart & Winston, 1963.

Gilyarevsky, R. S., & Grivnin, V. S. *Languages identification guide.* Moscow: Nauka, Central department of Oriental Literature, 1970.

Gordon, A. Thomas Braidwood. In L. Stephen & S. Lee (Eds.), *Dictionary of National Biography* (Vol. II). Oxford: Oxford University Press, 1967–1968, pp. 1107–1108.

Harris, J. *Hermes; or, a philosophical inquiry concerning language and universal grammar.* London, 1751.

Heckewelder, J., & Duponceau, P. S. Correspondence. *Transactions of the Historical and Literary Commission of the American Philosophical Society,* 1819, *1,* 351–448.

Hodgson, K. W. *The deaf and their problems.* London: Watts & Co., 1953.

Hoijer, H. History of American Indian linguistics. In T. A. Sebeok, (Ed.), *Native languages of the Americas* (Vol. 1). New York: Plenum, 1976.

Holder, W. *Elements of speech, with an appendix concerning persons deaf and dumb.* (Reprinted with an Introduction by R. W. Rieber & J. Wollock, Eds.). New York: AMS Press, 1975. (Facsimile of 2d ed., 1677.)

Hunt, G. H. W. Thornton and J. Fitch. *Nation,* 1914, *98* (May 21), 602–603.

Jackson, C. Tudor place. *Columbia Historical Society Records,* 1932, *25,* 68–86.

Kenrick, W. *A new dictionary of the English language.* London, 1773.

Kimball, F. William Thornton. In D. Malone (Ed.), *Dictionary of American Biography* (Vol. XVIII). New York: Charles Scribner's Sons, 1936, pp. 504–507.

Kimball, S. F., & Bennett, W. William Thornton and his design for the national capitol. *Art Studies,* 1923, *1,* 76–92.

Mathews, M. M. *Teaching to read, historically considered.* Chicago: University of Chicago Press, 1966.

Monboddo, J. *Origin and progress of language.* Edinburgh, 1773–1792.

Mullett, C. F. "An arte to make the dumbe to speake, the deafe to heare": a seventeenth-century goal. *Journal of the History of Medicine and Allied Sciences,* 1971, *26,* 123–149.

Navarro Tomás, T. Doctrina fonética de Juan Pablo Bonet. *Revista de Filología Española,* 1920, 7, 150–177.

Newcomb, R. Dr. W. Thornton, early American amateur architect. *Architect,* 1928, *9* (Feb.) 559–563.

Perez de Urbel, D. J. *Fray Pedro Ponce de León y el origen del arte de enseñar a hablar a los mudos.* Madrid, 1973.

Peter, A. *Tudor Place: designed by Dr. William Thornton....* Georgetown, 1969.

Peterson, C. E. Library hall. In *Historic Philadelphia.* Philadelphia: American Philosophical Society, Philadelphia, 1953.

Pickering, M. O. *The life of John Pickering.* Boston: 1887.

Robertson, J. *Grammatica linguae Hebraeae, cum notis et variis questionibus philologicis.* Edinburgh, 1758.

Robertson, J. *Grammatica linguae Hebraeae, cum notis et variis questionibus philologicis* (2nd ed., considerably altered). Edinburgh, 1783.

Rusk, W. S. *W. Thornton, B. H. Latrobe, T. U. Walter and the classical influence in their works.* Unpublished doctoral dissertation, Johns Hopkins University, Baltimore, 1929.

Rusk, W. S. W. Thornton, architect. *Pennsylvania History,* 1935, *2,* 86–98.

Scragg, D. G. *A history of English spelling.* New York: Barnes & Noble, 1974.

Sheehan, B. W. *Seeds of extinction: Jeffersonian philanthropy and the American Indian*. Chapel Hill: University of North Carolina Press, 1973.

Sheridan, T. *A complete dictionary of the English language*. London, 1780.

Tayloe, B. O. *In Memoriam Benjamin Ogle Tayloe*. Washington, D.C., 1872.

Thornton, W. *Cadmus*. Philadelphia: R. Aitken & Son, 1793. (a)

Thornton, W. Cadmus. *Transactions of the American Philsophical Society*, 1793, *3*, 262–319. (b)

Thurman, F. L. Little known and unfrequented haunts of Washington. *Virginia Magazine of History*, 1935, *43*, 139–143.

Tooke, J. H. Ἔπεα πτεροεντα, *or, the diversions of Purley*. London: J. Johnson, 1786.

Volney, C. F. Chasseboeuf comte de. *L'Alfabet Européen applique aux langues Asiatiques*. Paris: Didot, 1818.

Wallis, J. *A defence of the Royal Society*. London, 1678.

Walsh, S. P. *Anglo-American general encyclopedias: A historical bibliography*. New York: R. R. Bowker, 1968.

Webster, N. *Dissertations on the English language*. Boston: I. Thomas & Co., 1789.

Werner, H. *Geschichte des Taubstummenproblems bis ins 17. Jahrhundert*. Jena: Gustav Fischer, 1932.

Wise, C. M. Benjamin Franklin as a phonetician. *Speech Monographs*, 1948, *15* (1), 111.

Wise, C. M., & Hervey, W. The evolution of Hawaiian orthography. *Quarterly Journal of Speech*, 1952, 38 (Oct.), 314–315.

7

Michael J. Clark

JEAN ITARD: A MEMOIR ON STUTTERING

A Biographical Note on Jean Itard

Jean-Marie-Gaspard Itard[1] was born at Oraison in Provence in April, 1774, and was educated at Riez and Marseilles (latterly by the Oratorians) during the closing years of the ancien régime in France. His parents, who were comfortably well-off, had originally intended him for a

[1]Details of Itard's life and work, with some bibliographical information, may be found in Bousquet (1840), Morel (1845), in Hoefer (1858, Vol. 26, pp. 102–103), and in Michaud and Desplaces (1858, Vol. 20, pp. 417–419). Useful twentieth-century accounts include Saint-Yves (1914, pp. 24–32), Castex (1920), G. Humphrey's Introduction in Itard (1932, pp. v–xviii), Porcher (1938–1940), Malson's "A Note on Jean Itard" in Malson and Itard (1972, pp. 83–88), and Lane (1976, especially pp. 51–53, 153, and note to p. 51 on p. 325). This list, however, is only a very brief selection of all the available accounts. Of the earliest full accounts, Morel's is generally more precise and circumstantial than Bousquet's, even though both Morel and Bousquet were among Itard's friends and sometime colleagues. Subsequent accounts have differed significantly from each other, especially in their respective implicit or explicit chronologies of Itard's career up to 1806 to 1807, according to whether they derive primarily from Morel's or from Bousquet's account. Thus, the accounts of Castex, Porcher, and Lane are largely based on that of Morel; those given in Hoefer's *Nouvelle Biographie*, and in Michaud and Desplaces's *Biographie Universelle*, and those by Saint-Yves, Humphrey, and Malson, on that of Bousquet. This account is based primarily on those of Morel and Lane, with some additional information from those of Bousquet, Humphrey, and Malson. Morel's account is that most favored by Lane, the most recent investigator of manuscript sources on Itard's life and work. See Lane's comments on these problems in Lane (1976, note to p. 51 on p. 325.)

Michael J. Clark • Linacre College, Oxford, England.

career in banking and commerce in Marseilles, but the upheavals of the French Revolution were to give an altogether different direction to his career. During the siege of Toulon in 1793, at the height of the Revolution, Itard, despite having had no previous medical training or experience whatever, became attached to the military hospital at Soliers as a surgeon, through the influence of a clerical uncle, in order to procure his exemption from active military service. However, Itard soon discovered a genuine vocation for his new career, and after serving as a military surgeon with the Army of Italy at Toulon from 1795 to 1796, he removed to Paris at the end of 1796 to continue his medical studies as an assistant surgeon to the Baron De Larrey at the military hospital of Val-de-Grâce. During this period, Itard came under the influence of the great clinician and psychiatrist Philippe Pinel[2]; and throughout his professional career, Itard was to retain his mentor's strong belief in expectant medicine and the power of the *vis medicatrix naturae* and to distrust heroic therapeutics and the explanatory pretensions of pathological anatomy (Bousquet, 1840, p. 18; Morel 1845, p. 90).

In 1799, once again more or less by chance, came the second decisive change of direction in Itard's career—his appointment as physician to the Institution Nationale des Sourds-Muets in Paris, at the instance of its director the Abbé Sicard. Although his appointment at the Sourds-Muets commenced in December, 1800, Itard retained his post at Val-de-Grâce until 1804, when he declined the opportunity of foreign service with the French armies in favor of sole commitment to the Sourds-Muets.[3] By this time, he had become absorbed in the educational experiments with Victor, the so-called Wild Boy of Aveyron, for which he became

---

[2]See Bousquet (1840, pp. 2–3) and Lane (1976, pp. 74–78). For a brief account of Pinel's views in the general context of early nineteenth-century Parisian clinical medicine, see Ackerknecht (1967, especially pp. 8, 47–51, 72–73, and 168–169).

At least during the early years of his medical career, Itard was also strongly influenced in the formation of his educational ideas by the sensationalist philosophy of the abbé de Condillac [1714–1780] and of his disciples, the Idéologues, which was to provide much of the inspiration for his attempts to educate and socialize Victor, the "Wild Boy" of Aveyron between 1801 and 1806 (see below). For Condillac and the Idéologues, see Rosen (1946) and Ackerknecht (1967, pp. 3–12, 48). For Condillac's influence on Itard, see Bousquet (1840, p. 6), Saint-Yves (1914, pp. 25–26), Boyd (1914, pp. 67, 72), and Lane (1976, pp. 53–54, 73–82, 91–95).

[3]See Morel (1845, p. 86) and Lane (1976, pp. 53 and 133). Bousquet (1840, pp. 2–3) implies that Itard had already severed his connection with Val-de-Grâce by the time that he was appointed to the Sourds-Muets. See Lane (1976, note to p. 51 on p. 325) for these chronological problems.

internationally renowned, and for which he is chiefly remembered today by the lay public. These experiments, which lasted from 1801 to 1806, were recorded in the famous and much-debated *Rapports* which Itard submitted to the Ministry of the Interior in 1801 and 1806, and which were to comprise the basis for his repeated attempts during the following two decades to devise some means of teaching deaf-mutes to speak normally (Itard, 1894).[4] Although Itard was eventually obliged to admit defeat in his efforts to teach Victor to speak, and to accept that Pinel had been correct in his diagnosis of irremediable mental deficiency (which Itard had previously rejected),[5] nevertheless, the quality of his work ensured his lasting reputation as an authority on the special education of the mentally subnormal. In this capacity, Itard was to number the great psychiatrist and special educator Edouard Séguin among his pupils and disciples.[6]

However, Itard's principal concern, and his life's work, remained the treatment and education of the deaf and dumb; and his contributions in other fields (such as speech disorders) stand in an essentially ancillary relation to his principal concern with deaf-mutism, in which field he quickly acquired an unrivaled experience. During the first three decades of the nineteenth century, in addition to his reports on the Wild Boy of Aveyron, Itard published several papers on mutism, deafness, and the diseases of the ear, culminating in his *Traité des Maladies de l'oreille et de l'audition* (1821a), regarded by his contemporaries as the definitive work in an hitherto obscure area of medicine, and by posterity as marking the beginnings of modern otology.[7] In 1807 and 1808, he read two papers on the treatment of deafness and of mutism in deaf-mutes to the Société of the Paris Faculty of Medicine (Itard, 1808); in 1824, he read a paper on mutism to the Académie Royale de Médecine (of which he had become a member in 1821) (Itard, 1828); and in 1828, he submitted three further

---

[4]For Itard's reports to the Ministry of the Interior on the progress of his educational experiments with Victor and for his later work as an educator of the deaf and dumb, see Itard (1894, 1932), Bousquet (1840, pp. 3–8), Morel (1845, pp. 86–89), Saint-Yves (1914, pp. 25–31), Boyd (1914, pp. 64–87), Malson and Itard (1972), and Lane (1976, pp. 99–170).
[5]For Itard's disagreement with Pinel's diagnosis of Victor's condition, see Lane (1976, pp. 55–69, 99, 172–176).
[6]For Itard's influence on Séguin, see Saint-Yves (1914, pp. 58–67) and Lane (1976, pp. 258, 261–266, 268–279, and the references cited therein).
[7]Itard's work as a founder of modern otology is referred to briefly in Stevenson and Guthrie (1949, pp. 59 and 72) and at greater length in Mantel (1965). For contemporary evaluations of Itard's contribution to otology, see Bousquet (1840, pp. 8–13) and Morel (1845, pp. 89–91).

memoirs to the Académie on the treatment of deafness in deaf-mutes, and on the possibility of teaching those deaf-mutes not entirely devoid of the sense of hearing to speak (Husson, 1833).[8] In addition, he was one of the principal contributors to the French version of J. C. Hoffbauer's *La Médecine Légale relative aux Aliénés et aux Sourds-Muets* in 1827 (Itard, 1827), as well as the inventor of the Acoumeter, the "sonde d'Itard," and improved hearing aids for the differential diagnosis and treatment of different degrees of deafness.[9] Thus, Itard was already becoming established as an authority on speechlessness, particularly in the context of deaf-mutism, when he turned his attention to disorders of speech, and, in particular, to stuttering. In addition to his 1819 article on the subject, Itard was also primarily responsible for the report presented to the Académie de Médecine in 1830 on the plan of treatment of stuttering, submitted to the judgment of the Académie in that year by Colombat, in which Itard collaborated with three other leading Parisian physicians—Marc, Hervez de Chégoin, and his close friend and fellow-pupil of Pinel, the psychiatrist J.-E.-D. Esquirol (Colombat, 1831).[10] Itard also published a considerable number of other memoirs, articles, and reports, notably a thesis on pneumothorax (Itard, 1803), and an article on hydropsy for the *Dictionnaire des Sciences Médicales* (Itard, 1818); but, although acknowledged by his contemporaries as one of the leading medical stylists of the day, his publications were somewhat curtailed by the extreme difficulties he experienced in composition (Bousquet, 1840, p. 18; Lane, 1976, p. 257). His last years were marred by a long, painful, and ultimately fatal illness, which drove him into semi-retirement while still at the peak of his professional career. Much of this period was spent in gathering materials for a second, revised and enlarged edition of the *Traité des Maladies de*

[8]See Itard (1808, 1828). Itard's later memoirs are discussed in Husson (1833). See also Itard (1821b). Itard submitted three further (unpublished) memoirs on the same subject to the administrators of the Sourds-Muets in 1824, 1825, and 1826, which have recently been rediscovered. See Lane (1976, p. 207, note to p. 207 on p. 327, and his select bibliography of Itard's works on pp. 304–306). These aspects of Itard's work are discussed in some detail in Bousquet (1840, pp. 13–15), Morel (1845, pp. 90–91), Boyd (1914, pp. 81–86), and Lane (1976, pp. 185–204).

[9]See Morel (1845, pp. 90, 91) and Lane (1976, note to p. 185 on p. 334). Itard also made extensive use of surgical operations, notably the perforation of the eardrum and the catheterization of the Eustachian tube, in order to facilitate injections into the inner ear. See Bousquet (1840, pp. 11–12), Morel (1845, p. 90), and Lane (1976, note to p. 185 on p. 334).

[10]This report was reprinted by Colombat (1831) himself. See also the accounts of Itard's report given in Rullier (1833, pp. 167–169, 171) and in the *Revue Médicale Française et Etrangère,* 1830, *4,* 530–533.

l'oreille, which was still unfinished on his death, but completed and published posthumously under the aegis of the Académie de Médecine in 1842 (Itard, 1842), in accordance with a provision made by Itard in his will (Bousquet, 1840, pp. 16–17; Morel, 1845, pp. 98). Although apparently vivacious and sociable in his youth, in later years Itard became retiring, taciturn, and even solitary in his habits, especially during the later phases of his terminal illness (Bousquet, 1840, p. 18; Morel, 1845, pp. 93–94; Lane, 1976, pp. 257–258). He never married, and seldom went out even in professional society, despite having built up a large and lucrative practice in the middle years of his career which included many of the elite of Parisian society. His leisure pursuits (notably gardening, wood and metalwork, and collecting furniture, paintings and objets d'art) were mainly solitary pursuits (Morel, 1845, p. 94; Lane, 1976, p. 257), and his medical and educational interests always commanded the greater part of his attention and energies. In particular, although forced by ill-health to curtail his professional activities in the service of the Sourds-Muets, he retained a lively concern for the mental and physical welfare of its inmates. On his death in July, 1838, he left an endowment of F8,000 to the Institution, to realize his long-cherished ambition to provide a special advanced reading class (*classe d'instruction complémentaire*), and stock worth F1,000 to the Académie de Médecine, to found a triennial prize for the best published work on the practice of medecine or on therapeutics.[11]

Introduction—Itard's Mémoire sur Le Bégaiement

Itard's *Mémoire sur le Bégaiement* (A Memoir on Stuttering) was cited repeatedly by both French and British writers on speech disorders in the nineteenth century as among the earliest authoritative modern medical sources on stuttering, and was often accorded the same significance in this field as was his *Traité des Maladies de l'oreille* in that of otology. Not only the clinical picture of the phenomena of stuttering (psychological as well as physiological), but also the evaluation of previous medical work, and even some of the therapeutic measures given in Itard's *Mémoire* (though not its account of the etiology of stuttering) were substantially to be reproduced in several other contemporary and subsequent discussions

[11]For the terms of Itard's will, see Morel (1845, pp. 95–99) and Lane (1976, pp. 240–241, 258–261).

of stuttering (Rullier, 1821a, pp. 342–348, 350–353; 1833, pp. 147–148, 152–157, 160–161; Magendie, 1830, pp. 63–65, 67). In his historical review of stuttering theories written for the *Dictionnaire Encyclopédique des Sciences Médicales* (1868) the French physician A. Guillaume, although placing Itard's work in what he called the "*périod de tâtonnements*" (period of vague guesswork or "pre-history") of stuttering theory, wrote that:

> *ce travail* [Itard's *Mémoire*] *tranche nettement par son importance avec toutes les productions antérieures. Nous avons dû nous y arrêter comme au point de départ des publications subséquentes, desormais plus suivies*

> this work stands out clearly from all previous writings by virtue of its significance. It should be acknowledged as the starting-point for the more systematic works which have succeeded it [my translation].[12]

Similarly, for the British anthropologist and writer on speech disorders James Hunt (1861), "the modern literature of Psellism may be said to have commenced with Itard."[13] Clearly, any interpretation of medical views on stuttering in the early nineteenth century must take careful account of a work which exercised such an apparent influence on subsequent developments in the theory of speech disorders. However, any attempt to assess the historical significance of Itard's contribution faces several complex problems of interpretation, of which only the most immediately apparent will be referred to here. Accordingly, the remainder of this section is devoted to a discussion of three such salient problems arising from Itard's *Mémoire:* first, the terminological problems which beset any historical account of early nineteenth-century views on speech pathology; second, the difficulties involved in understanding Itard's conception of

---

[12]See Guillaume (1868, p. 697). Guillaume divided the history of stuttering theory and treatments into four periods: first, that of vague guesswork (*périod de tâtonnements*), extending roughly from Demosthenes and antique medicine to circa 1825; second, that of muscular, respiratory, and vocal exercises (*périod gymnastique*), from circa 1825 to 1841; third, the brief wave of enthusiasm for surgical treatments of stuttering (*périod chirurgicale*) in 1841; and fourth, that of a modified return to muscular, etc., exercises (*retour à la gymnastique*), from 1842 to the time of writing. In this view, Itard's concern with stuttering spanned the end of the first and the beginning of the second period—i.e., it comprised a link between the "prehistory" of stuttering theory and treatment, and the beginnings of more "scientific" approaches (although Guillaume considered that stuttering theory was still in a kind of scientific infancy in his own time). See pages 695 and 732 *passim,* and 695 to 726 *in extenso* for his detailed historical review.

[13]Hunt (1861, p. 71). Hunt used "psellism" as a general term for impediments of speech. See page 120, footnote. For Hunt's more detailed remarks on Itard's works, see pages 71–74 *passim,* and 115.

stuttering as a functional disorder; and third, those problems arising from his account of the causation of stuttering.

Terminological Problems Involved in Defining and Translating the Term "Bégaiement"

In addition to the familiar problems likely to be encountered in any work of translation, the frequent absence of any precise definitions or standard usages of diagnostic terms from works on speech pathology and therapeutics until most recent times presents the historical commentator on such a work as Itard's *Mémoire* with very serious difficulties.[14] Thus much confusion arose in nineteenth-century British works on speech disorders from the existence and more or less indiscriminate use of the two terms *stammering* and *stuttering,* neither of which had any precise definition or uniform diagnostic usage, sometimes to denote the same disorder of speech, but on other occasions to denote different disorders, according to criteria which varied from one author to another.[15] This definitional problem does not arise in exactly the same way in early nineteenth-century French medical writings on speech disorders, where normally only the single term *bégaiement* is used to denote the disorder we now refer to as "stuttering." But at the time of Itard's work, the word *bégaiement* often implied much else besides "stuttering" in a narrow sense—it was used not so much to describe a specific disorder as to signify a loosely-associated, ill-defined *group of disorders,* of which the condition we now describe as stuttering was regarded as merely the principal representative or type.[16] Thus, Auguste Savary (1812), writing in the

[14]This does not necessarily imply that such terms did not originally have quite precise meanings. See footnote 42, below, and the references cited therein. Jeffrey Wollock and Denyse Rockey are at present working on the clarification of diagnostic terminology in works on speech disorders from antiquity to the early modern period.

[15]See Hunt (1861, pp. 12–24, especially pp. 12–14 and 17–20), for a discussion of the various different meanings ascribed to these terms in British works on speech disorders in the first half of the nineteenth century.

[16]See, for example, the section on stuttering (*le bégaiement*) in Richerand (1802, p. 338) (reprinted and translated almost verbatim in later French and English editions throughout the next two decades). See also Beaugrand (1843, p. 121). This habit of using the term *bégaiement* in a generic rather than a specific sense persisted even as late as the 1890s, when Arthur Chervin, noting that the word was used to refer to infantile nonfluencies and to any kind of hesitation of speech in adults, as well as to stuttering, observed that "*Il n'y a pas de mot plus élastique*" (no word can have so many different meanings). See Chervin (1898, p. 10).

Dictionnaire des Sciences Médicales, did not distinguish stuttering either from infantile normal nonfluencies (later to be known as *balbutiement*), or from similar disorders of speech arising from definite organic lesions[17]; whereas François Magendie (1830), writing in the *Dictionnaire de Médecine et de Chirurgie Pratiques,* although drawing a distinction between stuttering proper and occasional symptomatic stuttering caused by organic lesions of the nervous system, did not distinguish stuttering proper from normal nonfluencies of childhood.[18] Savary (1812) defined stuttering as

> *difficulté de parler, ou plutôt vice de la prononciation, qui consiste à répéter plusieurs fois de suite la même syllabe. (p. 69)*

> an impediment of speech, or rather defect of pronunciation, which consists in repeating the same syllable several times over [my translation].

and Magendie (1830) as

> *difficulté plus ou moins grande dans la parole, hésitation, répétition saccadée, suspension pénible et même empêchement complet de la faculté d'articuler, soit toutes les syllabes, soit certaines syllabes en particulier. (p. 63)*

> a more or less pronounced impediment of speech, a hesitation, gasping repetition, painful suspension or even a complete prevention of the power of speech, either in the case of every syllable or of some particular syllables [my translation].

but both of these definitions refer essentially to a group of phenomena, rather than to any single, clearly-defined clinical picture with a definite pathological basis, and neither of them can be said to give clear and unambiguous guidelines to differential diagnosis. Rullier (1821a, b), writing in the *Dictionnaire de Médecine,* seems to have been the first French medical writer to have distinguished clearly both infantile nonfluencies (*balbutiement*) and occasional, temporary stutters, occurring in adulthood as the result of some definite physical or psychological cause (*balbutiement essentiel*), from stuttering proper (*bégaiement*).[19] As will be apparent from the text of his *Mémoire,* Itard was well aware of the dangers of differential-diagnostic confusion, and went to some lengths to

---

[17]See Savary (1812, pp. 69–70). Under "Balbutiement," the *Dictionnaire* simply notes: "Voyez BÉGAIEMENT."

[18]See Magendie (1830, p. 65). Under "Balbutiement," the *Dictionnaire de Médecine* similarly notes: "Voyez BÉGAIEMENT."

[19]See also Rullier (1833, pp. 147, 152). Rullier also distinguished these various disorders from that of speaking too quickly and confusedly to complete each articulate sound properly (*bredouillement*). See Rullier (1821c).

distinguish the primary, functional disorder with which he was principally concerned from other, normally short-lived, secondary conditions whose symptoms bore a superficial resemblance to those of stuttering, and from infantile nonfluencies.[20] However, he disdained any overelaborate system of subdivisions of stuttering, and did not use any definite terminology to distinguish between the different types of condition to which he was referring[21]; and the subsequent complaint of Guillaume (1868, p. 697) that Itard had merely perpetuated long-established differential-diagnostic errors by including defects of pronunciation arising from apoplexy and other cerebral diseases, or from tumors of the tongue, in his category of *bégaiements accidentels* ("occasional, temporary stutters") was not without some justification. In his *Mémoire,* Itard clearly *intended* the term *bégaiement* to refer primarily to the condition which would today be described as stuttering; but he did not care to define it in such a way as to make this usage specific to one particular condition, rather than generic to a loosely defined group of conditions of which stuttering was merely the most typical. Indeed, at times Itard's use of the term *bégaiement* might more correctly be rendered by the now almost obsolete term *psellism* (Fr. *psellisme*), which was often used by nineteenth-century British writers on speech disorders as a generic term for all kinds of defect of speech, arising from whatever cause.[22]

Itard's Conception of Stuttering as a "Functional" Disorder

Itard's insistence that stuttering be interpreted as a "functional" disorder, existing in its own right independently of any discernible organic lesion, is historically one of the most interesting features of his paper.[23] Yet, despite the importance which the concept has subsequently assumed in stuttering theory, it may be argued that, on closer observation, Itard's view gives rise to at least as many difficulties of interpretation as it seems to resolve. At the time when Itard was writing, the modern concept of the possibility of disorders of part-functions existing even in the absence of

[20]See ¶ 2, 3, 5, 6 of the text of this translation below.
[21]See ¶ 3 of the text.
[22]See, for example, Hunt (1861, p. 120, footnote) where he explains his use of the word *psellism* "as a generic term for impediments of speech in general."
[23]Itard's *Mémoire* is the first modern medical work definitely to describe stuttering as a "functional" disorder. The first appearance of this concept in British works on speech disorders seems to have been in McCormac (1828), a work through which many of Itard's views on stuttering were introduced to British readers.

any discernible organic lesion had not yet been clearly formulated and was only just beginning to win tentative acceptance in general medicine and medical psychology. This was more particularly the case with regard to complex behavioral functions, such as speech.[24] During this period, phrenology seems to have been one of the most important—perhaps *the* most important—influences on the emergence of the modern concepts of function, and of disorders of function, both in general medicine and psychology; and for much of Itard's career after 1807 (when Gall first came to live in Paris), the physiological and psychological doctrines of Gall and Spurzheim were to be among the most frequent (and fiercest) subjects of controversy in Parisian medical circles.[25] As two of the most well-known Parisian physicians in the first three decades of the nineteenth century, sharing specialist interests in the deaf and dumb and the mentally subnormal, Itard and Gall would almost certainly have had at least *some* acquaintance with each other during this period.[26] However, I have been unable to discover any evidence (at least, in his published works) to suggest that Itard was in any way influenced by phrenological ideas in his conception of stuttering as a functional disorder, or, indeed, in any other aspect of his medical work. Itard's account of stuttering as a disorder of the vocal and articulatory functions of the peripheral speech apparatus makes no reference either to the cerebral or "mental" correlates of the coordinated muscular movements involved in normal speech, or to any phrenological "organs" functionally involved in speech acts; and his remarks on the psychological factors involved in precipitating or exacerbating fits of stuttering show no trace of the influence of any phrenological views. Indeed, whereas phrenological accounts of stuttering as a functional disorder attempted to give a physiological-psychological explanation of its causation, Itard does not really attempt to give any such explanation at all, in spite of his observations on the role of social-psychological factors in inducing bouts of stuttering. The phrenological

[24]The history of the emergence of the modern concepts of "function" in physiology and psychology, and of "functional disorder" in medicine, has yet to be written. Some materials toward such a history may be found in Dallenbach (1915), Hunter and MacAlpine (1963, pp. 711–720, 812–818), and Young (1970, especially pp. 16–31, 246–248, 249–251).

[25]For the influence of phrenology on early nineteenth-century Parisian medicine and physiology, see Temkin (1947, especially pp. 289–299), Ackerknecht (1967, pp. 66–67, 170, 172, 197, 199), and Young (1970, pp. 54–100).

[26]Gall had been a consultant physician to the Viennese equivalent of the Sourds-Muets before being forced to leave the Habsburg domains in 1801. He and Spurzheim were among the numerous physicians who made personal examinations of Victor. See Lane (1976, p. 171).

concept of "function" encompassed both the "mental" and "physical" activity of the organism in specific modes of behavior (such as articulate speech) together in a single framework of ideas.[27] Hence the eminent Scottish physician and phrenologist Andrew Combe (1826/1977) explained stuttering as a failure of coordination or synchronization between the activity of the brain and that of the peripheral speech organs, brought about by what he described as

> a conflict or absence of co-operation among the active faculties[of the mind], necessarily giving rise to a *plurality,* instead of to a *unity,* of nervous impulses, and of simultaneous muscular combinations. (p. 147)

which in his view comprised the essential "functional" disorder manifested in stuttering (or stammering, in Combe's usage).[28] Although agreeing with Itard that stuttering was not due to any gross malformation of the organs of speech but was the *immediate* result of debility in the muscles governing the movements of the tongue and lips, Combe nevertheless rejected Itard's view that this muscular debility constituted the *primary* disorder of function in such cases. The origin of the disorder, he insisted, was to be found in the disordered psychological functioning of the brain; and all the peripheral manifestations of muscular debility, failure of coordination, spasmodic movements, etc., depended upon this initial centric cause, and might, indeed, be exhibited by other motor organs than those of speech, upon the action of the same cause.[29] By contrast, Itard's explanation of stuttering makes no reference either to the psychological "functions" of the brain, or to the behavioral functioning of the organism as a whole, and concerns itself solely with the more purely physiological (i.e., motor) part-functions of the peripheral speech apparatus. His conception of function seems to have been narrowly physiological; and (as his contemporaries pointed out, e.g., Rullier, 1833), his conception of stuttering as a functional disorder can scarcely be distinguished from de Sauvages's view of the condition as comprising one of the *dyskinesiae,* or disorders of voluntary motion (de Sauvages, 1768).[30] For Itard, as for de Sauvages, stuttering appears to have remained simply a disorder of the motor functions of the vocal and articulatory organs, and not a disorder of

---

[27]For the phrenological concept of "function," see Young (1970, pp. 11–23, 29).

[28]For Combe's explanation of stuttering, see Combe (1826/1977, especially p. 147) and Rieber and Wollock (1977, p. 13–14).

[29]Combe (1826/1977 pp. 146–147, 151–152).

[30]Rullier (1833, pp. 156–157). For de Sauvages and his nosological class of *dyskinesiae,* see footnotes 61–63 to the text of the translation, below, and the references cited herein.

the larger function of articulate speech belonging to the organism as a whole.[31]

Itard never attempts seriously to define exactly what he means when he describes stuttering as a "functional" disorder. He merely states that it *is* so, without any prior discussion, bluntly and immediately. His real purpose in using the term seems not to have been to give any detailed or theoretically sophisticated account of the origins and causation of stuttering, but rather simply to serve as a convenient term for the *kind* of disorder he believed stuttering to be from the practical standpoint of its most effectual mode of treatment, rather than from that of its etiology. This comparative indifference towards more abstract theoretical concerns, and strong emphasis on the primacy of the diagnostic and therapeutic functions of medicine, is a hallmark of this as of several other of Itard's medical works.[32]

Itard's Explanation of the Causation of Stuttering

From what has already been said of his conception of stuttering as a functional disorder, it will be apparent that Itard gives no very clear-cut explanation in his *Mémoire* of how stuttering is caused; and it was this aspect of his work which most attracted the critical attention of his contemporaries (Rullier, 1821a, 1833; Combe, 1826/1977; Magendie, 1830). On the one hand, Itard cites a variety of social-psychological factors (such as embarassment, nervousness at having to appear in company, anxiety at the prospect of giving offence, etc.) which tend to bring on fits of stuttering, or to worsen already established attacks, and also notes some other factors of the same kind (such as freedom from critical observation, or the company of a small circle of friends or relations) which tend to ameliorate

[31]Jeffrey Wollock has suggested that certain features of Itard's account of the nature and causes of stuttering, especially his apparent neglect of centric participation in even so complex a behavioral function as articulate speech, and his failure to explain precisely how physiological and psychological factors relate to each other in the causation of stuttering, may be susceptible to a vitalist interpretation. This would not be inconsistent with certain other of Itard's reported medical observations (see, for example, Bousquet, 1840, pp. 15–18), but I have not been able to discover any strong positive evidence that Itard was particularly influenced by the strong vitalist tradition in contemporary French medicine, although there are certain other important considerations (notably Itard's enthusiasm for the doctrines of Condillac, the Idéologues, and Pinel) which would not appear to support such an hypothesis. However, this possibility deserves further serious consideration.

[32]See, for example, Bousquet (1840, pp. 9, 12–13, 16, 17) and Morel (1845, pp. 89–90).

the condition.[33] On the other hand, he also discusses the proximate causation of stuttering in more narrowly physiological terms as the immediate outcome of muscular debility of the peripheral speech apparatus, and relates the fluctuating severity of the disorder to the physiological stages in the life-cycle of the individual.[34] Nowhere, however, does he give any clear account of precisely how these physiological and psychological factors interact to produce the phenomena of stuttering. At first, Itard seems to be suggesting that the social-psychological factors described as tending to induce bouts of stuttering react upon the natural susceptibility of the vocal and articulatory organs to emotional influences, resulting in the muscular debility which constitutes the proximate cause of stuttering. Later, however, he seems to imply that the muscular debility exists independently of the psychological factors, and speaks of such cases as stuttering from birth, or sudden attacks of stuttering following apoplexy or some other cerebral affection, in which psychological factors can scarcely be relevant. Neither of these two suggested modes of explanation is complete in itself or sufficient to account for all the phenomena of stuttering noted by Itard; nor are they integrated into any overall interpretation combining both physiological and psychological aspects of causation. Itard thus makes no attempt to give a physiological-psychological explanation for the susceptibility of the organs of speech (or, indeed, of any other bodily organs) to emotional influences; nor does he attempt to explain why this susceptibility should vary so remarkably in degree, and even in kind, from one individual to another. Nor is it clear from his account why such psychological factors as embarassment, anxiety, etc., should induce muscular debility, rather than increased innervation and capacity for functional action, in the organs of speech. While Itard's contemporaries (e.g., Rullier, 1821a, 1833; Magendie, 1830) largely agreed with his rejection of the older view that stuttering was the outcome of some organic lesion or malformation of the speech apparatus,[35] they could not accept his view that muscular debility comprised the essential condition as well as the proximate cause in stuttering. Thus Rullier (1821a, pp. 347–348; 1833, pp. 156–157) was to insist that the muscular debility hypothesis could not be reconciled either with the admitted facil-

---

[33]See ¶ 6 of the text of the translation, below.
[34]See ¶ 5, 8, 9 of the text of the translation, below.
[35]See ¶ 2 of the text of the translation, below; and, for example, Rullier (1821a, pp. 346–347; 1833, pp. 155–156), and Magendie (1830, p. 65.)

ity with which stutterers moved their tongues and lips, or with the convulsive spasmodic character presented by bouts of stuttering proper, while Magendie (1830, p. 67) was to argue that Itard's explanation in terms of some pathological modification of the original muscular power of contractility was merely a pseudoexplanation, since it was the power of contractility itself that required to be explained. And both Rullier (1821a, pp. 348, 349; 1833, pp. 152–153) and Andrew Combe (1826/1977, p. 151) were to point out that the muscular debility hypothesis failed to account for the phenomena of spontaneous remission of stuttering in old age (when ordinary muscular debility tends rather to increase than decrease), and to argue that, even where the functional action of the vocal organs was impaired in speech by spasmodic immobility and convulsive gasps, this was secondarily consequent upon some disorder of centric functioning or failure of coordination between the activity of the brain and that of the peripheral speech organs, and did not itself constitute the primary disorder.[36] Significantly, Itard's observations on the role of social-psychological factors in precipitating and reinforcing bouts of stuttering were noted but not developed further.[37] Contemporaries were more concerned to find some physiological explanation of speech disorders than they were to investigate the social-psychological contexts in which such disorders developed.

In his discussion of the phenomena of stuttering, Itard has many perceptive and valuable occasional observations to offer, especially with regard to the role of social-psychological factors in reinforcing the characteristic anxiety of confirmed stutterers; but, taken together, these observations do not amount to a coherent explanation of what *causes* stuttering. Indeed, Itard's review of the various organic lesions which he insists do *not* cause stuttering is far more readily intelligible than his attempt to explain what does.[38] However, it may be argued that he was certainly no more inadequate in this respect than some of his contemporary critics, in an era when etiological theories of stuttering were still almost wholly conjecture.[39] The primary purpose of Itard's observations in this regard

[36]See Rullier (1821a, p. 349; 1833, p. 157) and Combe (1826/1977, pp. 146–147, 151–152).
[37]See, for example, Rullier (1821a, pp. 343–345, 349–350; 1833, pp. 152–154, 157–158) and Magendie (1830, pp. 63–64).
[38]Cf. ¶ 2 and 6–9 of the text of the translation, below.
[39]See, for example, Magendie's comments on Rullier's theory (Magendie, 1830, pp. 65–67) and Rullier's comments on Magendie's theory (Rullier, 1833, pp. 158–159). N. B. also Rullier's observation of 1833 that, as we do not yet understand the physiology of normal speech production, we cannot claim to possess any definite knowledge of speech pathol-

seems rather to elaborate his account of what *happens* in stuttering, in such a way as to enable physicians to deal more effectively with it as therapists; and in the longer term it was for this, rather than for any more speculative views, that Itard's contribution was to be remembered.[40]

A Memoir on Stuttering (Le Bégaiement)[41]

(Greek, *psellismos* or *traulismos;* Latin, *balbuties, haesitatio linguae*)[42]

¶ 1. Stuttering is a functional disorder[43] which, being numbered among our physical disabilities, on the very fringes of medicine, has never yet seriously commanded the attention of medical men. The rich corpus of antique medicine is quite barren on this subject. Hippocrates, Aristotle, and Galen have nothing worth mentioning to say about it[44]; and their

---

ogy; and that, as yet, "*une obscurité couvre encore le mode précis d'action isolite et désordonnée* [of the voluntary and involuntary muscles of the peripheral speech organs] ... *chez les bègues*" (the precise mode of pathological action of the voluntary etc.... speech organs in stutterers is still obscure). See Rullier (1833, pp. 149–150).

[40] See Guillaume (1868, p. 697) and Gutzmann (1893, p. 283).

[41] See Jean Itard, *Mémoire Sur Le Bégaiement* (A Memoir on Stuttering) originally published in the *Journal Universel des Sciences Médicales*, 1817, 7, 129–144. The translation and historical commentary that follows was prepared by Michael Clark. See also pages 159–161, "Terminological Problems," for a discussion of some of the definitional problems involved in translating the word *bégaiement*.

[42] Much the same considerations apply to these Greek and Latin words, which were commonly regarded by nineteenth-century writers as synonymous with stuttering, but which seem to have been used to describe a great variety of imperfections of speech in classical literature. See Rieber and Wollock (1977, pp. 3–5) and Jeffrey Wollock's translation and discussion of Hieronymus Mercurialis's interpretation of the classical medical literature in his *De Morbis Puerorum Tractatus*... (Treatises on the Diseases of Children) (Mercurialis, 1584/1977, pp. 127–133). *Ischnophonia* was the more correct Aristotelian term for the disorder today denoted by the term *stuttering*. For Aristotle's distinctions between these various terms, see Rockey and Johnstone (1979).

[43] See pages 161–164, "Itard's Conception of Stuttering," for a discussion of the historical and interpretative problems arising from Itard's use of the term "functional" in this context.

[44] Itard was probably referring principally to Hippocrates, *Aphorisms* 6. 32, and *2 Epidemics* 5 and 6; Aristotle, *Problems* 11. 30, 38; and Galen, commentaries on *Aphorisms* 6. 32, and *De Locis Affectis,* 6. For nineteenth-century discussions of what were then regarded as the principal classical medical sources on stuttering, see, for example, Hunt (1861, pp. 57–60, 62–64, and Guillaume (1868, p. 696). See also Rieber and Wollock (1977, pp. 3–5), Mercurialis, 1584/1977, pp. 127–135), and Rockey and Johnstone (1979). More recent scholarship, however, would suggest that Itard, like many other nineteenth-century medical writers on speech disorders, was very probably misled by long standing textual corruptions and mistranslations not only into misconstruing the classical terminology of speech

silence with regard to its treatment seems to indicate that they regarded it as absolutely incurable. This is all the more surprising, since this disability must have been felt much more acutely among peoples whose forms of government were so closely bound up with the art of public speaking, and for whom oratory opened the way to the highest honors and positions in the state. It is also worth noting that those who were afflicted by similar misfortunes were far more accustomed to take counsel with themselves than they were to seek medical advise—as Plutarch's account of how Demosthenes perfected his pronunciation shows.[45] Sometimes they had recourse to the gods. Thus we read in Herodotus that Battus, the leader of a colony of Theraeans, consulted the Delphic oracle about his stuttering, and that the oracle advised him to remove his household to the deserts of Libya.[46]

¶ 2. Our own treatment of stuttering has scarcely advanced beyond that recommended by the oracle some two thousand years ago.[47] Some pathological-anatomical observations collected by modern authors, far from shedding any light upon this condition, have actually led us away from its proper mode of treatment, by persuading us to regard stuttering as the outcome of some organic lesion or other—as, for example, the two quite adventitious furrows which, according to Sanctorius,[48] are found incised along the roof of the mouth; or the division of the uvula, as reported by Delius[49] (*Act. Nat. Curios,* T.8)[50]; or some malformation of the

---

disorders, and hence into seriously misinterpreting and underestimating the value of the classical sources, but also into neglecting or overlooking several other sources (e.g., Aristotle, *De Audibilibus,* 804b. 27, ff. "*Ischnophonos,*" and Galen, commentary to *1 Epidemics* 2. 78) which would today be regarded as essential for understanding classical medical views on stuttering. I owe most of this information to Jeffrey Wollock, who is working on a comprehensive analysis of the classical terminology of speech disorders.

[45] See Plutarch (trans. Perrin, 1919), Vol. VII (Life of Demosthenes), pp. 24–27.

[46] See Herodotus (trans. Godley, 1963), Vol. II, Bk. IV, pp. 354–359.

[47] See McCormac (1828), p. v.

[48] Santori Santorio (Lat. Sanctorius), Italian physician, born at Capo d'Istria, 1561; professor of physic at Padua from 1611, and inventor of various medical instruments; died Venice, 1636. Details of his life and work may be found in the *Dictionary of Scientific Biography* (C. B. Boyer *et al.,* Eds.) 1975, Vol. XII, pp. 101–104. Itard is referring to Sanctorius (1631), Lib. 3, Cap. 9, pp. 181–184. I owe this reference to Jeffrey Wollock.

[49] Heinrich Friedrich Delius, German physician, surgeon, and anatomist, was born in Wernigerode (Saxony), 1720; professor of medicine at Erlangen from 1749, and a prolific medical writer; died in Erlangen, 1791. Details of his life and work may be found in the *Allgemeine Deutsche Biographie,* 1877, Vol. v, pp. 40–41.

[50] *Acta Physico-Medica Academiae Caesarae Leopoldino—Franciscanae Naturae Curiosorum* (T.8), Nuremberg, 1748, T.8, pp. 378–379.

hyoid bone, if Hahn[51] is to be believed (*Commerc. Litter,* for 1736)[52]. Morgagni[53] has devoted several paragraphs of his *Letters* X, XI, and LI[54] to the etiology of stuttering—but not precisely of that condition which concerns us here. He is concerned only with those speech impediments which are among the commonest after-effects of apoplexy, or which frequently precede the sudden attacks characteristics of this disease.[55] Similarly, Dehaën[56] gives us five or six case histories of symptoms of stuttering caused by congestion of the lungs, in particular from the formation of some abscess, and accompanied by symptoms of hemiplegia arising from the same cause. Unfortunately these observations, left among this distinguished practitioner's *Unedited Minor Works*[57], are very incomplete and altogether badly presented. However, there is one feature of these cases worth noting—namely, that in three instances the expectoration of the pus was followed by the disappearance of both the stuttering and the hemiplegia.

¶ 3. Menjot,[58] Fick,[59] and Bergen,[60] who published treatises on stut-

---

[51]Johann Gottfried Hahn, German physician [1694–1753]. Details of his life and work may be found in the *Allgemeine Deutsche Biographie,* 1879, Vol. X, pp. 362–363.

[52]*Commercium Literarium ad rei medicae et scientiae naturalis incrementum institutum.* Nuremberg, 1731–1745: T. for 1736, pp. 241–242.

[53]Giambattista (or Giovanni Battista) Morgagni, Italian physician and pathological anatomist, born in Forli (Romagna), 1682; professor of physic at Padua from 1711, and member of most of the principal learned and scientific societies and Academies of mid-eighteenth-century Europe; regarded as the father of modern pathological anatomy; died in Padua, 1771. Details of his life and work may be found in the *Dictionary of Scientific Biography,* 1974, Vol. IX, pp. 510–512.

[54]Itard is referring to Morgagni (1761), T.1, Lib. 1, Ep. X, Art. 11, p. 78; Ep. XI, Art. 2, p. 82; Ep. XIV, Art. 38, pp. 121–122; T. 2, Lib. IV, Ep. L1, Art. 35, p. 292. These references may be consulted in translation in Morgagni (1761/1960), Vol. 1, Bk. 1, Letter X, Art. 11, pp. 218–219; Letter XI, Art. 2, p. 231; Letter XIV, Art. 38, pp. 351–354; Vol. III, Bk. IV, Letter L1, Art. 35, p. 108.

[55]For Morgagni's comments on the views of Sanctorius, Delius, and Hahn, and his own theory of stuttering in cases other than those associated with apoplexy, see Morgagni (1761/1977). See also Rieber and Wollock (1977, pp. 8–9).

[56]Anthony De Haën (or Van Haën), Dutch physician, was born in The Hague, 1704; practiced at The Hague and Vienna; professor of medicine at Vienna from 1754, and successor to Baron Von Swieten as first physician to the Empress Maria Theresa; died in Vienna, 1776. Details of his life and work may be found in *A New General Biographical Dictionary* (see Rose, 1845, Vol. VIII, pp. 170–171).

[57]Itard is apparently referring to De Haën [1777–1779], but I have been unable to trace the passages referred to.

[58]Antoine Menjot, French physician, was born in Paris, 1636; personal physician to Louis XIV; died in Versailles, 1696. Details of his life and work may be found in the *Biographie Universelle* (Michaud and Desplaces, Vol. 27, pp. 648). Itard is referring to Menjot (1674).

[59]Jean-Jacques Fick (or Fickins), German physician, anatomist, and botanist, was born in

tering, multiplied its subdivisions, and confused it with several other speech defects, without indicating any rational method of cure. Much the same may be said of Sauvages[61] (who followed Menjot, in his *Nosology*).[62] However, it must be admitted that he had a shrewd insight into the essential nature of this disorder, when he chose to regard it as an infirmity, and placed it accordingly in the class of *dyskinesias,* or disorders of voluntary movements. In view of this, it is all the more surprising that he also felt able to include under the same heading lallation, mogilalism, iotacism and other defects of pronunciation arising from quite different causes.[63]

¶ 4. Such is the present state of medical science in this matter. I shall now offer some further conclusions based on my own reflections and experience.

¶ 5. Stuttering, as everyone knows, is a hesitation of the vocal organs which results in the labored pronunciation and breathless repetition of certain sounds and syllables which require some more or less decided action of the vocal and articulatory organs.[64] This defect in pronunciation is not usually noticed in young children until, having reached the age when speech normally becomes precise and fluent, instead they continue to show hesitation and experience difficulties in articulation. But with

---

Jena, 1662; physician to the Count de Mansfeld from 1691, and to the Duke of Weimar from 1696; professor of medicine at Jena from 1715, and later also of botany, anatomy, surgery and theoretical medicine; died in Jena, 1730. Details of his life and work may be found in the *Biographie Universelle* (Michaud and Desplaces, 1856, Vol. 14, pp. 93). Itard is referring to Fick (1725).

[60]Charles Augustus de Bergen, German physician, anatomist, and botanist, was born in Frankfurt-on-Oder, 1704; professor of anatomy and botany at Frankfurt from 1738, and of therapeutics and pathology from 1744; died in Frankfurt, 1760. Details of his life and work may be found in Rose (1842, Vol. IV, p. 117) and in à Beckett (1836, Vol. I, p. 419). Itard is referring to de Bergen (1756).

[61]Francois Boissier de Sauvages, French physician and medical writer, was born in Alais (Languedoc) 1706; professor of botany and medicine at Montpellier; author of one of the most influential nosological works of the eighteenth century, the *Nosologia Methodica* (first published in 1752); died in Montpellier, 1767. Details of his life and work may be found in Rose (1847, Vol. XI, p. 467).

[62]Itard is referring to de Sauvages (1768, Vol. 1, pp. 780–783).

[63]For a brief survey of de Sauvages's classification of speech disorders, see Rieber and Wollock (1977, p. 8). For a comparative view of various eighteenth- and early nineteenth-century nosological systems, including that of de Sauvages, with their respective classifications of speech disorders, see Hooper (1820, pp. 602–615, especially pp. 603–606); cf. McCormac (1828, p. 64).

[64]See pages 159–161, "Terminological Problems" and footnotes 16–19, above for comparison with other early nineteenth-century French medical definitions of stuttering.

only a little close attention, it is possible to discern it even in infancy, and
to distinguish the imperfect articulations and half-formed words characteristic of infant speech from the imperfect repetitions of a single syllable
which constitute stuttering.[65] However, whether through misapprehen-
sion of the true nature of the disorder, or through hope of its eventual
disappearance, no serious notice is taken of it until about the age of 7 or 8,
when, far from dying down, the disability becomes more pronounced due
to the child's growing anxiety, and grows progressively worse until beyond the age of puberty. But, as middle age draws on, it usually subsides
markedly, and often disappears with the approach of old age. Sometimes
an acute illness disperses it for good. Timaeus[66] (*Casus Medicinales*)[67]
recounts the case of a child who stuttered until the age of eleven, when he
recovered unimpeded speech after a fever lasting for a fortnight.
Strangely enough, stuttering is almost unknown among women; indeed, if
I were to judge solely on the basis of my own experience, in which I have
never met with any such case, I should be inclined to regard them as
entirely free from this calamity.[68]

¶ 6. In order to determine what causes stuttering,[69] it is enough to
reflect for a moment upon the principal clinical phenomena which accompany it. In particular, we may remark on the special peculiarity which
distinguishes this from other speech defects—namely, its being subject to
those variations of degree, depending on the prevailing state of the feelings, which comprise the principal characteristic of states of nervous
exhaustion. We may further remark that, of all our bodily organs, there is
none whose functioning is more closely dependent on emotional states
than the vocal and articulatory organs; and that, consequently, they must

[65]This is an especially remarkable observation when we consider how problematical modern
authorities still find this distinction. See Bloodstein (1969, p. 234).
[66]Balthasar Timaeus Von Güldenklee, German physician, was born in Fraustadt, 1600;
physician to the Duke of Brandenburg during the Thirty Years' War; later in medical
service with the Swedish army, and Court Physician to the Queen of Sweden from 1648; an
authority on the plague; died in Colberg, 1667. Details of his life and work may be found in
the *Allgemeine Deutsche Biographie*, 1894, Vol. XXXVIII, p. 352.
[67]See *Casus Medicinales praxi triginta sex annorum observati . . .* , Leipzig, 1667, Lib. I,
Casus XXXVI, p. 70.
[68]This was one of the most frequently remarked phenomena of stuttering in nineteenth-
century French medical writings on the subject. See, for example, Rullier (1821a, p. 345;
1833, p. 153), Magendie (1830, pp. 63–64), and Guillaume (1868, p. 694). Cf. McCormac
(1828, p. 40).
[69]See pages 161–167, above, for some of the problems involved in Itard's account of the
causation of stuttering.

be affected spasmodically by even the slightest degree of mental agitation. This is precisely what happens in stuttering. Those who are subject to it feel more uncomfortable on social occasions, before large bodies of people, in moments of bad temper, even in moments of elation. Within their own family circles, or in the calm of solitude, they speak much more fluently. The impediment decreases further, and may even disappear, if speech takes a different form from conversation, such as oratory or singing. In the Year XI,[70] I was consulted by a stutterer who told me that he ceased to stutter in company toward evening, if, once it had got dark, the lights were left unlit, so that his interlocutors could not look at him while he was speaking. In his youth, his parents had sought to profit from this observation by trying to blindfold him, but without success.[71]

¶ 7. In most cases, the tongue's hesitancy in speech is particularly noticeable in the articulation of the consonants K, T, G, L; but when (for one of the reasons I have just mentioned) the spasm in the vocal organs becomes aggravated, the difficulty in articulation extends to many more consonants. Those consonants which are sounded with the lips and the tongue, and the nasal consonants, are repeated in much the same way, and even those sounds which only require a simple exhalation of breath are, as it were, choked in the larynx. The convulsive spasm, having overtaken all the vocal and articulatory muscles, extends also to some of the facial muscles, causing them to twitch in the most painful manner.

¶ 8. In some cases, even the respiratory muscles, especially those governing the intake of breath, are intermittently involved in these spasmodic movements, producing a great many aspirated sounds which introduce or punctuate even the easiest words to pronounce in a peculiarly unpleasant way. Catullus is undoubtedly alluding to this form of stuttering, in an epigram against a certain Arrius:

> *Chommoda*[72] *dicebat, si quando commoda vellet*
> *Dicere, et hinsidias insidias*[73]

---

[70]The French Republican Calendar, which supplanted the Gregorian Calendar in France between 1793 and 1807, was reckoned from the proclamation of the first French Republic on September 22, 1792, which was counted as the first day of the Year I. Each year ran with slight adjustments from that date to about the same date in the following year according to the old calendar. Hence Itard is referring to a case occurring during the period from the end of September, 1802, to the end of September, 1803, in his early years as physician to the Sourds-Muets, when he was engaged in his educational experiments with Victor, the ''Wild Boy'' of Aveyron.

[71]Cf. Rullier (1821a, p. 345; 1833, pp. 153–154) and McCormac (1828, p. 44).

[72]The quoted footnote that follows appears in the original text: ''The study of defects of

It is impossible not to recognize a spasmodic affection in these phenomena of stuttering, an affection arising from a deficiency in the motor powers of the tongue and larynx.[74] But this inadequacy is not at all apparent in the more pronounced and extended movements of these muscles. I have undertaken detailed experiments on the movements made by a stutterer's tongue, in order to ascertain whether its perceptible movements were less free, extended, or vigorous than (for example) those of my own tongue; and I have found no difference between them. Only in its most delicate, imperceptible movements does this organ lack the strength, or rather, the assurance necessary to perform them exactly. A phenomenon occurs here, which can be seen more clearly in the cases of other motor organs whose functions may more easily be observed. The finger muscles, for example, may retain that vigorous power of contractility which makes for what is commonly called a strong arm, yet at the same time exhibit the hesitancy and trembling characteristic of enfeebled organs, in those slight movements of contraction and release required in such delicate operations as handwriting.

¶ 9. However, when stuttering occurs abruptly after apoplexy or a prostrating fever, during the premonitions of some cerebral affection, all the movements of the tongue are visibly enfeebled. If (in order to form a more exact judgment) the tongue is held out for a few seconds, it can be seen shaking and trembling, and subject to involuntary movements which tend to displace it from the desired position, which can only be recovered falteringly. It may further be observed, in such cases, that the actions of chewing and swallowing are performed more slowly, and only with great effort. Moreover, the completely debilitated aspect characteristic of sudden attacks of stuttering which clearly result from some kind of paralysis points to the real nature of stuttering from birth (*bégaiement congénial*);

---

pronunciation in the works of the ancients can of itself give us some insight into the way in which they articulated sounds, or rather, into the difference between their pronunciation and ours. Thus we can see, from the first of these two lines of verse, that the Romans sounded their *H*'s even when they came between a *C* and a vowel, whereas according to our way of pronouncing, they remain silent, since we pronounce the first syllables of *chorus* and *coram* alike.''

[73]''Arrius, if he wanted to say 'winnings,' used to say '*wh*innings,' and for ambush, '*h*ambush'; (and thought he had spoken marvellous well, whenever he said 'hambush' with as much emphasis as possible).'' For the full translation, see Catullus (1962, Poem LXXIV, pp. 160–163).

[74]In fact, as will become apparent later, Itard believed that spasms occurred in the larynx only very infrequently. See ¶ 17, below.

and I do not think there can be any doubt that they are both results of the same proximate cause, only slightly modified in each case—namely, muscular debility. But is this debility essential to the condition? More specifically: Is it an original affection of the muscles governing articulate speech, or only a secondary consequence of some other lesion? I believe that, in the case of stuttering from birth, it is primary; whereas when it comes on suddenly, or gradually over the years, it seems to be the result of some cerebral affection, or of some organic lesion of the vocal and articulatory organs, such as tumors growing at the base of the tongue or along the course of the great hypoglossal nerve (Rivière).[75]

¶ 10. Can stuttering be cured? I have no doubt that it can be; and what I shall have to say about its treatment will give credence to this belief. Many people who are afflicted by this defect, being painfully aware of the many embarassments it creates and of the need to escape from them, have succeeded in doing so by stubborn efforts, especially when assisted by advancing age, which tends to reduce the problem, whether by stifling the fear of giving offense which causes the anxiety, or by strengthening the muscles employed in the utterance and articulation of sounds. One of the presidents of the Convention,[76] famed for his heroic sang-froid, and for his commanding eloquence amidst the most appalling scenes, had struggled against this impediment in his speech so effectively that eventually he had succeeded in overcoming it. I myself know of several other equally encouraging instances. We may be even more confident of its disappearance when stuttering occurs in a child who has learned to speak later than usual, whether from general infirmity or fol-

[75]Lazarus Rivière, French physician, was born in Montpellier, 1589; professor of medicine at Montpellier; died in Montpellier, 1655. Details of his life and work may be found in Rose (1842, Vol. XI, pp. 355–356). Itard is referring to his *Praxeos Medicae*, Lib. V, Cap. II and Cap. IV, in Rivière (1669, T. II, pp. 281–282).

[76]The National Convention comprised the unicameral legislature of the first French Republic, from September 1792 to October 1795, and for much of this period also constituted the executive of the Republic through its various Committees, especially those of Public Safety and General Security. Itard is referring to the Comte François-Antoine de Boissy d'Anglas [1756–1826], President of the Convention from 16 Germinal to 1 Floréal, Year III, and one of the principal architects of the Constitution of the Year III. According to Villenave, *"Un léger bégaiement nuisait d'ailleurs à son accentuation oratoire; et de mauvais plaisants l'appelaient, avant les temps de l'empire, l'orateur Babébibobu; ils avaient aussi donné cette épithète burlesque à sa Constitution de l'an 3."* (His oratorical delivery was further impaired by a slight stutter; and, before the days of the Empire, wits used to call him the orator Babébibobu; they also gave this comic title to his Constitution of the Year III.) See Michaud and Desplaces (1854, Vol. 4, p. 605). I owe much of this information to Jeffrey Wollock.

lowing repeated or protracted attacks of intestinal worms. In such cases, the advent of puberty is strongly conducive to recovery, as it fortifies the general constitution and, in particular, gives greater strength to the vocal and articulatory organs. However, whenever the impediment is considerable, the advent of puberty alone is not sufficient to disperse the malady, and then it becomes necessary to have recourse to the therapeutic measures which I shall now set forth.

¶ 11. The appropriate means for correcting stuttering vary according to its duration and severity. If we are dealing with a child whose stuttering is part of an overall volubility of language, with a generally incoherent and imperfect articulation, then it is best to try somehow to curtail the flow of speech. The child should be made to spell out each word, to read aloud and with deliberation, forcing him frequently to reiterate those syllables which he finds most difficult to pronounce. However, this method is not as valuable as another, which I have twice availed myself of with complete success—that is, to entrust the child to the sole care of a foreign governess, who, only being able to speak her own language,[77] forces her charge to learn it slowly and to give up the tongue into which he has been too hastily initiated for a few years. Once I coupled this advice with a counsel of complete abstention from speech for one year,[78] as continual hesitations, and involuntary and tiresome repetitions, forced me to conclude that the organs of speech had been prematurely taxed with a function as yet beyond their powers.

¶ 12. These methods have little effect when the patient has passed adolescence. At this period, the study of elocution will be of great benefit. The patient should begin with that form of declamation furthest removed from ordinary conversational tones, which requires slower, more exact movements of the tongue, and a raised and sustained tone of voice, such as that which tragedy or preaching calls for. He should then pass on to more familiar forms, and finally to reading aloud from plays, whenever possible performing these exercises before large audiences.

¶ 13. In every case, it is above all important to separate out that which is fundamental and permanent in the defect, from that which arises

[77]Although relatively little attention was given to this suggestion of Itard's by later French medical writers on stuttering, several nineteenth-century British writers were to recommend learning a foreign language in this way, or foreign travel, as therapeutic measures—in some instances, apparently under the influence of Itard. See, for example, Bartlett (1839, pp. 66–69).

[78]This regime was subsequently favored by the later nineteenth-century German speech therapists Katenkamp and Wyneken. See Kussmaul (1878, p. 840, footnote 1).

secondarily from self-consciousness and anxiety at the prospect of having to speak in company or in public, if the stuttering is to be cured properly. For, if stuttering were a constant affection (which it scarcely ever is), or only slightly variable, it would be sufficient, in order to banish the defect, simply to give the organs of speech frequent practice in the articulation of difficult sounds. These exercises, so effective in the cases we are presently discussing, are not without some benefit in every case; and I cannot recommend them too strongly. But in order to proceed systematically, it is necessary to have a thorough understanding of phonetics—of simple, as well as articulate, sounds. The works of Wallis[79], Amann[80], and the abbé De L'Epée[81] should be consulted carefully on this matter; and for this reason, I refrain from discussing it in this article.[82] I shall only add one important piece of advice to the precepts laid down by these authors, which none of them seems to have thought of; namely, that in order to habituate the tongue to the articulation of sounds, it is not sufficient

[79]John Wallis, English theologian, grammarian, and mathematician, was born in Ashford (Kent), 1616; Fellow of Queen's College, Cambridge during the Civil War, and later of Exeter College, Oxford; Savilian Professor of Geometry at Oxford from 1659; one of the co-founders of the Royal Society of London, in the 1650s and 60s; chaplain to Charles II; died in Oxford 1703. Wallis devised a method for teaching deaf-mutes to speak, described in his *De Loquela*, a tract appended to his *Grammatica Linguae Anglicanae* (Wallis, 1652). In 1661 and 1662, he taught two young deaf-mutes, Daniel Whaley and Alexander Popham, to speak, presenting the former to the Royal Society in May, 1662, and reporting on his instruction of the latter in the *Philosophical Transactions* for July, 1670. This lead to a heated controversy between Wallis and a Dr. William Holder, whose part in previously instructing Popham, Wallis had persistently failed to acknowledge. Details of Wallis's life and work may be found in the *Dictionary of Scientific Biography* (1976, Vol. XIV, pp. 146–155).

[80]Johann Conrad Amann, Swiss physician and specialist in the medical treatment and eduction of the deaf and dumb, was born in Schaffhausen in 1669; he practiced medicine at Amsterdam and Haarlem toward the end of the seventeenth century; he died in 1724. Details of his life and work may be found in Rose (1840, Vol. I, p. 399). See also Hunt (1861, pp. 68–70). Itard is referring to Amann (1692, 1700).

[81]Charles-Michel, abbé De L'Epée (or De Lépée), French philanthropist and pioneer educator of the deaf and dumb, was born in Versailles, 1712; author of several works on elocution and the use of sign language in the education of the deaf and dumb, principally his *Institution des Sourds et Muets* (De L'Epée, 1776); he died in Paris, 1789. De L'Epée was the founder of the special school which subsequently became the Institution (or Etablissement) Nationale des Sourds-Muets, where Itard served as house physician from 1800 almost until his death in 1838. Details of De L'Epée's life and work may be found in Michaud and Desplaces (1855, Vol. 12, pp. 507–510).

[82]Nineteenth-century British writers on speech disorders similarly placed great emphasis on the use of phonetics in therapy, but their work, unlike that of Itard or of later French and German authors, made comparatively little use of the work of educators of the deaf and dumb.

merely to study the mechanism of articulation, and then to subject it accordingly to repeated exercises, but that it is also necessary to practice articulating these same sounds in every possible combination. Every syllable which is pronounced without hesitation, when preceded by some other which leaves the tongue in a favorable position to surmount the difficulty, will be less easily pronounced when it follows one which does not confer this advantage, or if it forms the beginning of a word or a phrase; so that certain consonants will be stuttered more often, or more markedly, if they are connected with certain vowels rather than with others. Thus stutterers usually pronounce the letter *C* with greater difficulty when it is followed by an *A* than by an *O*.

¶ 14. But when the stuttering tends to get worse, and the impediment affects a great many syllables, and even simple sounds, merely making the articulation of sounds more exact and fluent is quite insufficient. The strength of the vocal organs must be built up by mechanical means, if their susceptibility to spasms is to be eradicated. The articulatory muscles must be developed, just as the strength and flexibility of the locomotor muscles are built up by means of strenuous exercises such as dancing or fencing. In order to give the muscles of the tongue and lips some analogous exercise, I contrive to render their movements more difficult, and more laborious, by placing certain impediments inside the mouth, and then forcing the patient to speak, cry out, sing, whistle, etc., at frequent intervals, in spite of the great discomfort caused.[83] At first, it is impossible; but after a few days, by dint of strenuous efforts, the muscles succeed in

[83]Itard was later to give a fuller explanation both of his own and of other contemporary plans of treatment in his report on Colombat's method presented to the Académie Royale de Médecine in November, 1830: "*Tout moyen employé utilement consiste, en définitive, en une sorte d'entrave ou de modérateur, opposé aux mouvemens tumultueux ou embarassés des agens de la parole, modérateur tantôt physique ou matériel... tantôt intellectuel ou moral.*" (Every useful method, in short, consists of some kind of physical or psychological impediment or restraint placed upon the confused or hesitant movements of the organs of speech). Under the conjoint influence of these direct and indirect means of constraint, he maintained, speech took place under new and more favorable psycho-physiological conditions—in particular, under the therapeutic influence of a new series of correct associations established between certain voluntary movements (such as accompanying rhythmical movements or deep breaths), and certain deliberately chosen positions of the tongue. (Quoted in Rullier, 1833, p. 171. See also the account of Itard's report in the *Revue Médicale Française et Etrangère* 1830, *4*, 531; and Gutzmann, 1893, 314). This was the explanation usually given by Itard's contemporaries for the success of such devices as Demosthenes' pebbles, or Colombat's *bride-langue*, as well as of Itard's *fourchette* itself. See, for example, Rullier (1833, p. 171) and Lee (1841, pp. 37–38). Cf. however, Beaugrand (1843, p. 124) for a somewhat different though closely related view.

overcoming this constraint and recover their original powers of movement, with much greater assurance even than before. To bring about this beneficial effect, I employ one of the simplest of instruments. It is a kind of little platinum or gold fork,[84] which stands up from the concave center of a flat rounded base made from the same metal, whose convex surface fits into the cavity formed by the alveolar arch of the lower jaw. The little fork which this metallic arc supports is about an inch long. Placed horizontally in relation to the *froenum linguae,* it takes this membrane in its bifurcation and supports itself by the ends of its two prongs, each of which terminates in a flat button about the size of a bean, upon the underside of the tongue, in the reentrant angle which it forms where it joins the lower lining of the mouth.

¶ 15. Scarcely is this instrument in place before (as I have previously indicated) the voice can be heard, confused and hesitant, very like that which is characteristic of congenital erosion or cleavage of the palate, yet (and this is the remarkable thing) entirely free from stuttering. The most difficult syllables are articulated painfully, but without repetition, and this improvement is maintained even when the organs of speech, having grown accustomed to the instrument's presence, regain their freedom of movement and pronounce distinctly articulated sounds. However, if this mechanical aid is removed too hastily, the stuttering will reappear as before. It is, therefore, necessary to persevere with this device for a long time, and to abstain rigorously from speech whenever it has to be removed (which is not always necessary) in order to eat or sleep. I cannot say precisely how long this treatment may be necessary, since I can only cite two instances of cure by this method. The subject in the first instance was a young man of twenty. He continued to use this kind of bit for a year and a half, and in the end was so little inconvenienced by it, that in the last months he no longer used to remove it even to eat. The patience with which he bore the discomfort of this apparatus was inspired by a motive which, at his age, makes anything seem worth undertaking and persevering in—namely, the hope of winning the favor of a young woman with whom he had fallen deeply in love, and whose coldness he blamed on his

[84]Itard's fork was later to be described by Guillaume as "*le point de départ des instruments de cette nature inventés depuis lors*" (the starting-point for all the instruments of this kind invented subsequently) (1868, p. 697), and may be regarded as the progenitor of all modern intraoral stuttering devices. For recent surveys of stuttering devices, see Katz (1977) and Wingate (1976, pp. 279–285). Itard's description of his fork and its use was frequently reproduced or discussed in both French and British writings on stuttering during the first half of the nineteenth century. See, for example, Rullier (1821a, pp. 352–353; 1833, p. 161), Guillaume (1868, p. 697), McCormac (1828, p. 78–79), and Lee (1841, p. 29).

accursed stuttering. In fact, his was one of the severest cases of this affliction, tending to engulf the muscles of the mouth, nose, and eyelids in convulsive twitches, which made speech as painful an ordeal for him as it was unpleasant for his interlocutors. Success was complete. When he informed me of this news, he did not say whether or not it had been followed by another, even more ardently desired, success.

¶ 16. The subject of my second observation was a child of eleven, who could not have the same reasons for perseverance. He endured the inconvenience of this device only with great impatience and used to take it out of his mouth every time he could escape from the observation of his parents and his tutor. However, when the child was sent back to me after eight months, his stuttering was much reduced, and although I have had no further news of him, I am almost certain that a few months more will have completed the cure. At the time of writing, a young man of just over thirty, called by his birth to take his seat in the House of Peers[85], has submitted to the same mode of treatment with a constancy and strength of will inspired by the noblest motives. An improvement, already perceptible after a few weeks, gives me grounds for believing that I shall not have undertaken to redress this natural imperfection in vain. The instrument I have had made for this young man is much more advanced than those which I had previously employed. I am indebted to the ingenious craftsmanship of M. Pernet the dentist[86] for this device. Replacement prongs, of various lengths and angles of divergence, allow the pressure of the muscles of the tongue to be built up and the points of support to be varied. I have supplemented the effects of this mechanical device with tonic throat-washes, made up with an alcoholic tincture of cinchona, of cantharides, and asarabacca.[87]

¶ 17. There are few cases of stuttering in which this last therapeutic

---

[85]The House of Peers (Chambre des Pairs) was the upper house of the bicameral legislature established in France under the Bourbon Restoration, according to the Chartes granted by Louis XVIII in 1814 and 1815. It included representatives of both the old pre-Revolutionary nobility and of the new nobility created by Napoleon during the Empire.

[86]This dentist would appear to be the L.-H.-P. Pernet listed in Vol. X, p. 963 of the *Index Catalogue of the Library of the Surgeon-General's Office, United States Army (lst Series)* (1972 reprint), as the author of a Paris medical thesis, *Sur les cas qui nécessitent la bronchotomie* (1813), and described by Lachaise, writing in 1845, as an "officier de santé-dentiste" of Paris, who had for the previous thirty years enjoyed the reputation of being one of the most skillful dentists of the city, well known for his care and ingenuity in the design and manufacture of false teeth and other dental appliances. See Lachaise (1845, pp. 515–516).

[87]These were all medical drugs in common use in the early nineteenth century. Cinchona (or chinchona) was a tonic medication prepared from the bark of the chinchona shrub, native

measure may not usefully be employed. However, exception must be made of that kind of stuttering (albeit very uncommon) in which the organs of voice, even more than those of articulate speech, appear to be the seat of the spasmodic hesitation which suddenly arrests the flow of speech. This may be observed when the sounds appear, as it were, to be trapped in the larynx, and can be confirmed if the same difficulty makes itself felt in trying to pronounce a long series of vowel sounds in rapid succession. In such cases, more benefit will be derived from the study of vocal music, especially from the vocal exercise which consists in singing sustained tones. These hygienic methods may be supplemented by locally applied tonic medications. Moxa[88] on the walls of the larynx and around the hyoid bone can have the most beneficial effects. I prescribed it on one occasion for a case of stuttering of this kind. But the advice alarmed the patient and was not taken. In prescribing this kind of stimulus, I based my advice on the beneficial effects I have often obtained from its use in cases of chronic aphonia, idiopathic mutism, and other lesions of the voice and of speech, which will form the subject of a further article.[89]

---

to the Peruvian Andes, which was largely replaced in general medical use by quinine (another derivative from the bark of the chinchona) from about the mid-1820s. Cantharides (or Spanish Fly, *Cantharis vesicatoria*) was used either as an external blistering agent, or as an internal diuretic and stimulant to the genito-urinary system. Asarabacca was a purgative and emetic prepared from the hazelwort (*Asarum Europaeum*). For a view of their contemporary medical use in France, see the *Dictionnaire des Sciences Médicales* (1820, Vol. 46, pp. 399–541, under "Quinquina" for cinchona; *ibid.*, 1813, Vol. 4, pp. 10–22, for cantharides; and *ibid.*, 1812, Vol. 2, pp. 337–339, under "Asaret" for Asarabacca.

[88]Moxa was prepared from the downy covering of the dried leaves of the mugwort (*Artemisia Moxa*), usually in the form of small cones to be burnt slowly on the skin (a process known as moxibustion) as a counter-irritant, especially in the local treatment of gout. Later in the nineteenth century the word came to be used for any substance like moxa (such as cotton) which was used to blister the skin by combustion in local treatments. Itard's enthusiasm for the use of moxa may derive from his experiences as an assistant surgeon to the future Baron Dominique-Jean De Larrey, the famous military surgeon, during his internship at the military hospital of Val-de-Grâce in Paris in 1796. De Larrey was the author of a treatise on the therapeutic use of moxa (de Larrey, 1822). Further details of De Larrey's life and work may be found in Michaud and Desplaces (1855, Vol. 23, pp. 277–283). For a view of contemporary medical use of moxa in France, see the *Dictionnaire des Sciences Médicales* (1819, Vol. 34, pp. 459–492).

The apprehension felt by Itard's patient is hardly surprising, in view of the drastic and necessarily painful character of the proposed treatment. Only Rullier seems to have followed Itard in recommending the use of moxa as a possible treatment for stuttering. See Rullier (1821, p. 352) and Guillaume (1868, p. 697).

[89]For Itard's later work on mutism, see Itard (1821b; 1828), and note 8 above.

Acknowledgments

My thanks are especially due to Denyse Rockey, formerly of Linacre College, Oxford, and to Jeffrey Wollock, of New College, Oxford, for their unstinted advice and encouragement in the preparation of this translation—in particular, for enlightening me on certain theoretical and historical problems arising from the text of Itard's *Mémoire;* for helping me to locate some of Itard's more obscure references; and for supplying me with many of the comparative and explanatory references cited in the footnotes. The remaining errors and omissions are entirely my own. My thanks are also due to Professor Harlan Lane, of Northeastern University, and to the editor, for helpful comments and suggestions.

References

à Beckett, W., Jr. *A universal biography* (3 Vols.). London: Isaac, Tuckey, and Co., 1836.

Ackerknecht, E. H. *Medicine at the Paris hospital, 1794–1848.* Baltimore: the Johns Hopkins University Press, 1967.

Allgemeine Deutsche Biographie (T. 56). Leipzig, 1875–1912.

Amann, J. C. *Surdus loquens.* Amsterdam, 1692.

Amann, J. C. *Dissertatio de loquela.* Amsterdam, 1700.

Bartlett, T. *Stammering practically considered; with the treatment in detail.* London: Sherwood, Gilbert, and Piper, 1839.

Beaugrand, E. Bégaiement. In the *Encyclopédie du dix-neuvième siècle, ou répertoire universelle des sciences, des lettres, et des arts* (T. 26). Paris: Bureau de l'Encyclopédie du Dix-Neuvième Siècle, 1838–1853. 1843 (T.5), pp. 121–125.

Biographie Universelle (Michaud), Ancienne et Modérne... ('*B.U.*') (T.45) ed. L. G. Michaud, E. Desplaces. Paris: Desplaces. *Nouvelle Édition,* 1843–1865.

Bloodstein, O. *A handbook on stuttering.* Chicago: National Easter Seal Company for Crippled Children and Adults, 1969.

Bousquet, J. B. Eloge Historique de M. Itard. *Mémoires de l'Académie Royale de Médecine,* 1840, *8* (Pt. 1), 1–18.

Boyd, W. *From Locke to Montessori: A critical account of the Montessori point of view.* London: George Harrap, 1914.

Boyer, C. B., *et al.* (Eds.) *Dictionary of scientific biography* (T. 14). New York: Charles Scribner's Sons, 1970–1976.

Castex, A. *Jean Itard (1774–1838): Notes sur sa vie et son oeuvre.* Paris: Baillière, 1920.

Catullus. The poems of Gaius Valerius Catullus. In *Catullus, Tibullus and Pervigilium Veneris* (F. W. Cornish, Trans.) (Loeb Classical Library). London: Heinemann, 1962.

Chervin, A. *Les légendes de l'histoire: Démosthène était-il bègue?* Tours: Paul Bourrez, 1898.

Colombat, M. *Du Bégaiement et de tous les autres vices de la parole, traités par des nouvelles méthodes... précédé d'un rapport fait à l'Académie de Médecine par M. M. Itard, Marc, Esquirol et Hervez de Chégoin.* Paris: Mansut Fils, 1831.

Combe, A. Review of A. F. Voisin. *Du bégaiement, ses causes, ses différents degrés, influence des passions, des sexes, des âges, etc. sur ce vice de prononciation.* Paris:

Croullebois, 1821. Reprinted from the *Phrenological Journal*, 1826, *4* (25), in *Journal of Communication Disorders*, 1977, *10*, 146–152.

Dallenbach, K. The history and derivation of the word "Function" as a systematic term in psychology. *American Journal of Psychology*, 1915, *36*, 473–484.

de Bergen, C. D. *Dissertatio de balbutientibus*. Frankfurt, 1756.

Dehaën, A. *Orpuscula omnia medico—physica in unum nunc primum collecta* (T.6). Naples: Porcelli, 1777–1779.

De L'Épée, Abbé C.-M. *Institution des sourds et muets par la voie des signes méthodiques* (T.2). Paris: 1776.

De Sauvages, F. B. *Nosologia methodica sistens morborum classes juxta sydenhami mentem et botanicorum ordinem*. Amsterdam, 1768.

Dictionnaire des sciences médicales (T.60). Paris: Crapart and Pancoucke, 1812–1822.

Fick, J. J. *De balbis*. Jena, 1725.

Guillaume, A. Bégaiement. In the *Dictionnaire encyclopédique des sciences médicales* (T.100). Paris: Asselin, de Labé, Masson et Fils, 1864–1889. 1868 (T.8), pp. 694–755.

Gutzmann, H. *Vorlesungen uber die Störungen der Sprache und ihre Heilung*. Berlin: Kornfeld, 1893.

Herodotus. *The histories* (A. D. Godley, Trans.) (Loeb Classical Library). London: Heinemann, 1963.

Hopper, R. *Lexicon-medicum: or medical dictionary* (4th ed.). London: Longman, 1820.

Hunt, J. *Stammering and stuttering, their nature and treatment*. London: Longman, Green, 1861.

Hunter, R. & MacAlpine, I. *Three hundred years of psychiatry 1535–1860*. London: Oxford University Press, 1963.

Husson, H. M. De l'éducation physiologique du sens auditif chez les sourds-muets; question soumise par le gouvernement au jugement de l'Académie. Rapport par M. Husson. *Mémoires de l'Académie Royale de Médecine*, 1833, *2* (Pt. 2), 178–196.

Itard, J.-M.-G. *Dissertation sur le pneumothorax, ou des congestions gazeuses qui se forment dans la poitrine*. Paris, 1803.

Itard, J.-M.-G. Extrait de deux mémoires présentés à la Société de l'École de Médicine de Paris.... Mémoire sur les moyens de rendre l'ouïe aux sourds-muets.... Mémoire sur les moyens de rendre la parole aux sourds-muets. *Bulletin de l'École de Médecine de Paris*, 1808, *1*, 72–79.

Itard, J.-M.-G. Hydropisie. In the *Dictionnaire des Sciences Médicales*. Paris: Crapart and Pancoucke, 1818, Vol. 22, pp. 361–456.

Itard, J.-M.-G. *Traité des maladies de l'oreille et de l'audition*. Paris: Méquignon-Marvis, 1821. (a)

Itard, J.-M.-G. Rapport fait à MM. les administrateurs de l'Institution des Sourds-Muets, sur ceux d'entre les élèves qui, étant doués de quelque degré d'audition, seraient susceptibles d'apprendre à parler et à entendre. *Journal Universel des Sciences Médicales*, 1821, *22*, 5–17. (b)

Itard, J.-M.-G. Notes. In J. C. Hoffbauer *La médecine légale relative aux aliénés et aux sourds-muets* (A. M. Chambeyron, Trans.). Paris: Ballière, 1827, pp. 176–230.

Itard, J.-M.-G. Mémoire sur le mutisme produit par la lesion des fonctions intellectuelles. *Mémoires de l'Académie Royale de Médecine*, 1828, *1*, Section de Médecine, 3–18.

Itard, J.-M.-G. *Traité des maladies de l'oreille et de l'audition... considérablement augmentée et publiée par les soins de l'Académie Royale de Médecine*. Paris: Méquignon-Marvis Fils, 1842.

Itard, J.-M.-G. *Rapports et mémoires sur le sauvage de l'Aveyron, l'idiotie et la surdimutité....* Avec une appréciation de ces rapports par Delasiauve. Préface par

Bourneville.... Eloge d'Itard par Bousquet (D. M. Bourneville, Ed.). Paris: Alcan, 1894.

Itard, J.-M.-G. The wild boy of Aveyron [*Rapports et mémoires sur le sauvage de l'Aveyron*] (G. Humphrey & M. Humphrey, Trans.). New York, London: Century Psychology Series, 1932.

Katz, M. Survey of patented anti-stuttering devices. *Journal of Communication Disorders,* 1977, *10,* 181–206.

Kussmaul, A. The Disturbances of speech. In H. von Ziemssen (Ed.), *Cyclopaedia of the practice of medicine* (20 vol's.) 1878, *XIV,* 581–875. London: Sampson, Low, Marston, Low, and Searle, 1875–1880.

Lachaise, C. (pseud, C. Sachaile [de la Barre]). *Les médecins de Paris jugés par leur oeuvres, ou statistique scientifique et morale des médecins de Paris ...* Paris: for the author, 1845.

Lane, H. *The wild boy of Aveyron.* Cambridge, Mass.: Harvard University Press, 1976.

Larrey, Baron D.-J. de (Trans. and ed.), & Dunglison, R. *On the use of the moxa as a therapeutical agent.* London: Underwoods, 1822.

Lee, E. *On stammering and squinting, and on the methods for their removal.* London: Churchill, 1841.

Magendie, F. *Bégaiement.* In the *Dictionnaire de médecine et de chirurgie pratiques,* (T.15), 1830, *4,* 63–82. Paris: Baillière, 1829–1836.

Malson, L. and Itard, J.-M.-G., tr. Fawcett, E., Ayrton, P. and White, J. Lucien Malson: *Wolf Children* and Jean Itard: *The Wild Boy of Aveyron.* London. New Left Books, 1972.

Mantel, I. *L'otologie à Paris aux début du 19ᵉ siècle.* Zurich: Juris-Verlag, 1965.

McCormac, H. *A treatise on the cause and care of hesitation of speech, or stammering.* London: Longman and Co., 1828.

Menjot, A. *Dissertatio pathologica de mutitate et balbutie.* Paris, 1674.

Mercurialis, H. ed. Groscesius, J., tr. Wollock, J. *De morbis puerorum tractatus ...* [treatises on the diseases of children], Lib. 2, Cap. 6, 57–59; Cap. 8. 59–63. Basle, 1584. *Journal of Communication Disorders* 1977, *10,* 127–133.

Morel, E. Notice Biographique sur le docteur Itard. *Annales de l'Éducation des Sourds-Muets et des Aveugles,* 1845, *2,* no. 2, 84–99.

Morgagni, G. B. *De sedibus et causis morborum per anatomen indagatis ...* (T.2). Venice: 1761.

Morgagni, G. B., tr. Alexander, B. *The seats and causes of diseases investigated by anatomy ...* (3 Vols.). London: Millar, Cadell, Johnson and Payne, 1769. Facsimile edn., introd. by P. Klemperer, New York: Hafner, 1960 [Morgagni, 1761, tr. Alexander, 1769, reprinted 1960].

Morgagni, G. B., tr. Alexander, B. Reprint of Vol. I, Bk. I, Letter XIV, Art. 38. *Journal of Communication Disorders,* 1977, *10,* 142–145. [Morgagni, 1761, tr. Alexander, 1769, reprinted 1977]

Nouvelle Biographie Générale ... ('*N.B.G.*') (T.46), ed. F. Hoefer. Paris: Firmin Didot frères, 1845–1866.

Plutarch, tr. Perrin, B. *Lives ...* (Loeb Classical Library). London: Heinemann, 1919.

Porcher, A. Itard. *Revue Générale de l'Enseignement des Sourds-Muets,* 1938–1939, *9,* 113–124; *10,* 129–132; 1939–1940, *11,* 1–6.

Richerand, A. *Nouveaux élémens de physiologie* (2nd ed.) Paris: Crapart, Caille and Ravier, 1802.

Rieber, R. W., & Wollock, J. The historical roots of the theory and therapy of stuttering. *Journal of Communication Disorders,* 1977, *10,* 13–24.

Rivière, L. *Lazari Riverii. . . . Opera medica universa.* Frankfurt, 1669.

Rockey, D., & Johnstone, P. Mediaeval arabic views on speech disorders: Al-Razi (865–925 A.D.). *Journal of Communication Disorders,* 1979, *12,* 229–243.

Rose, H. J. (Ed.). *A new general biographical dictionary* (12 vols.). London: Fellowes, Rivington, 1840–1847.

Rosen, G. The philosophy of ideology and the emergence of modern medicine in France. *Bulletin of the History of Medicine,* 1946, *20,* 328–339.

Rullier, F. Bégaiement. In the *Dictionnaire de médecine* (T.21). Paris: Béchet, jeune, 1821–1828. 1821, T.3, pp. 341–353. (a)

Rullier, F. Balbutiement. In the *Dictionnaire de médecine.* Paris: Béchet, jeune, 1821–1828. 1821, T.3, pp. 245–247. (b)

Rullier, F. Bredouillement. In the *Dictionnaire de médecine.* Paris: Béchet, jeune, 1821–1828. 1821, T.3, pp. 509–510. (c)

Rullier, F. Bégaiement. In the *Dictionnaire de médecine, ou répértoire générale des sciences médicales* (T.30). Paris: Béchet, jeune, 1832–1845. 1833, T.5, pp. 147–172.

Saint-Yves, I. *Aperçu historique sur les travaux concernant l'éducation médico-pédagogique. Itard (1775–1838). Séguin (1812–1880). Bourneville, (1840–1906).* Lyon: Rey, 1914.

Sanctorius, S. *Methodi vitandorum errorum omnium qui in arte medica contingunt.* Geneva, 1631.

Savary, A. C. Bégaiement. In the *Dictionnaire des sciences médicales.* Paris: Crapart and Pancoucke, 1812–1822. 1812, T.3, pp. 69–70.

Stevenson, R. S., & Guthrie, D. *A history of otolaryngology.* Edinburgh: Livingstones, 1949.

Temkin, O. Gall and the phrenological movement. *Bulletin of the History of Medicine,* 1947, *21,* 275–321.

Wallis, J. *Tractatus de loquela.* In *Grammatica linguae Anglicanae* Oxford, 1652.

Wingate, M. E. *Stuttering theory and treatment.* New York: Irvington, 1976.

Young, R. M. *Mind, brain, and adaptation in the nineteenth century.* Oxford: Clarendon Press, 1970.

PART IV

TWENTIETH CENTURY CONTRIBUTIONS

8

W. Keith Percival

HERMANN PAUL'S VIEW OF THE NATURE OF LANGUAGE

The subject matter of Hermann Paul's *Prinzipien der Sprachgeschichte* (1880) seems straightforward enough: the general methodological principles to be observed in the historical study of language. However, Paul wrote with an underlying polemical intent, and it is perhaps not too easy for the modern reader to appreciate this fact. His criticisms were directed at the theory and operating practice of his immediate predecessors, and reflected the views of a group of scholars, all born in the 1840s, who were jocularly referred to as *Junggrammatiker,* a term which has generally been rendered in English by the word *neogrammarians.* The most famous members of this group were August Leskien [1840–1916], Berthold Delbrück [1842–1922], Herman Osthoff [1846–1909], Karl Brugmann [1848–1919], and Hermann Paul himself [1846–1921].

What these men stood for can best be approached indirectly by looking first at the theories they disapproved of most strongly, namely, the ideas of the immediately preceding generation of scholars, as epitomized, for example, in the *Compendium der vergleichenden Grammatik* [Compendium of comparative grammar] by August Schleicher (1821–1868), which first appeared in two volumes in 1861 and 1862. Comparative grammar, as understood by Scheicher, aimed at reconstructing the grammatical system of the putative parent language of the Indo-European

W. Keith Percival • Department of Linguistics, University of Kansas, Lawrence, Kansas 66044.

languages by comparing their respective grammars. Basic to this enterprise was the belief that the only way to show that languages are related,
that is to say, are divergent continuations of one and the same parent
language, is to demonstrate that they share the same grammatical system.
In the early part of the nineteenth century, Franz Bopp [1791–1867] had
demonstrated in this way that Latin, Greek, Gothic (the oldest attested
Germanic language), the Slavic and Baltic languages, Old Persian, and
Sanskrit (the ancient liturgical language of the Hindus) were related languages in this sense, and had founded the new discipline of comparative
philology.

The grammatical systems of such a group of related languages are
sufficiently similar to make it possible for the grammatical system of the
parent language to be reconstructed. By the mid-nineteenth century these
reconstructions had become so precise that Scheicher introduced the
practice of citing reconstructed forms of the parent language alongside
attested forms from the historically recorded languages. In this way, the
analyst could make perfectly clear, in each instance, what specific inferences he was making about the phonetic shape of a particular word,
root, or suffix in the parent language. For example, alongside Greek *hip-
pos,* Latin *equus,* Sanskrit *aśvas,* all with the meaning "horse,"
Schleicher quoted *akvas* as the form he reconstructed for the parent
language. This was to be interpreted as a claim to the effect that Greek *i*
and Latin *e* were phonetic modifications of the earlier vowel *a,* that
Greek *pp,* Latin *qu,* Sanskrit *śv* had developed from an original sequence
kv, and so forth. Schleicher did not, however, insist that his reconstructed
forms had ever really existed; he regarded them as no more than theoretical constructs.

But the linguists of the first half of the nineteenth century were not
content to establish the phonetic shapes of particular words in the reconstructed parent language, they were also interested in reconstructing the
morphological system of that language. What linguists mean by
morphological system is the set of suffixes (or endings) which occur in
nouns and verbs, and whose function it is to indicate abstract notions. For
example, in all the older Indo-European languages, verbs contain suffixes
which indicate person, number, and tense. Thus Latin *amā-verō* means
"I shall have loved," whereas *amā-bunt* means "they will love," and so
forth.

What the linguists of the early and mid-nineteenth century wanted to
do was to discover the origin of these suffixes. They observed, for in-

stance, that the ending of the first person singular in Greek and Sanskrit is typically -*mi,* a form which is very similar to the first person singular pronoun, namely, Latin *mē, mihi;* Greek *eme,* Sanskrit *mā-m.* From facts of this kind, they hypothesized that all the personal endings of the verb were atrophied personal pronouns. Some idea of the interesting speculations which scholars in that period produced may be obtained from Table I, which displays the forms of the present indicative of the verb "to be" in Greek, Latin, and Sanskrit, along with Scheicher's reconstructions for the Indo-European parent language.

What Schleicher assumed was that, in the parent language, each of the words cited consisted of a verbal root and an inflectional suffix, and that the inflectional suffixes had, at a still earlier period, been pronominal roots. He claimed, for instance, that the suffix of the second person singular -*si* was a phonetically weakened form of the fuller -*sa,* and that it had originally been identical with the second person singular pronoun (cf. Sanskrit *tva-m,* Latin *tū,* Gothic *thu*), that the suffix of the third person singular -*ti* (weakened from -*ta*) had been a demonstrative pronoun, and so forth. Moreover, he also assumed that each of the plural suffixes had

Table I.   *The Verb "to be" in the Indo-European Languages*[a]

	Attested forms in historically recorded languages			Schleicher's reconstruction	
				Proto-Indo-European forms	Shape of suffix in earlier root-stage
	Greek[b]	Latin	Sanskrit		
I am	eimi (emmi)	sum	asmi	as-mi	ma
you are	ei (essi)	es	asi	as-si	sa (earlier tva)
he is	esti	est	asti	as-ti	ta
we are	esmen	sumus	smas	as-masi	ma + sa
you are	este	estis	stha	as-tasi	ta + sa
they are	eisi (enti)	sunt	santi	as-anti	an + ta

[a] Based on Schleicher (1876), p. 708.
[b] Forms in parentheses are from dialects other than Attic.

originally been made up of two such pronominal roots: -*masi* "we" from *ma* "I" and *sa* "you" (singular), and -*anti* "they" from *ta* preceded by *an*, another demonstrative pronoun. Finally, Schleicher suggested, rather tentatively, that these pronominal roots were originally on a par semantically with regular roots. Thus, he hypothesized that the *ma* which eventually yielded the first person singular suffix -*mi* had once been a root with the meaning "human being, think, measure" (cf. Sanskrit *ma-nu* "human being," *mā-mi* "I measure," Greek *metron* "an instrument for measuring"). As Schleicher put the matter himself: "What could 'I' originally have been but 'human being'? We clearly cannot ascribe the abstract notion of 'I' to the parent language" (Schleicher, 1876, p. 626).

Schleicher, therefore, divided the prehistoric development of the protolanguage into two periods. In the first, language consisted entirely of unanalyzable roots, each expressing a concrete concept. In the second period, the period of grammatical formation, many of these roots lost their independence and came to express accessory concepts, giving rise in this way to inflectional and derivational suffixes. By the end of the second period the grammatical structure of Indo-European, as reconstructed by comparative linguists, had assumed final shape. In the historical period, the parent language then diverged into a number of separate languages, and the original grammatical system degenerated. This process of decay had many manifestations, the most important of which was *sound-change,* or *phonetic decay,* as it was often called in Schleicher's day. The reason phonetic change was considered a degenerative process was that it rendered unanalyzable what had previously been analyzable. Thus, the form *as-si* "you are" of the parent language is easily analyzed into the root *as* "be" and the inflectional suffix -*si* "you," but the corresponding Greek form *ei* is not analyzable at all.

Although Schleicher assumed that linguistic change was a gradual and continuous process, he considered the successive stages of linguistic development to be *qualitatively* different from one another, in much the same way as the larva, chrysalis, and butterfly are qualitatively different stages in the life cycle of a certain insect. Indeed, like many of his contemporaries and immediate predecessors, Schleicher emphasized the extent to which the history of language does not resemble the history of human contrivances such as art, literature, and religion, but is more akin to the evolution of biological species or the changes which the earth's crust has undergone over the ages. Linguistics, he claimed, was a natural science like biology and geology, not one of the traditional historical disciplines such as classical philology. Therefore, its main purpose was to elucidate the grammatical forms of historically recorded languages by restoring them to the phonetic shapes they had when they were analyzable. Etymological reconstruction was the principal goal of the comparative linguists of the mid-nineteenth century.

If we turn to the linguistics of the latter part of the century, we are struck by a number of radical shifts of emphasis. First and foremost, linguists now began to look upon their discipline as one of the social sciences (*Kulturwissenschaften*), not one of the natural sciences (*Naturwissenschaften*). The opening sentence of Paul's *Prinzipien der Sprachgeschichte* is symptomatic of this shift of orientation: "Like any product of human culture language is an object of historical investigation..." (Paul, 1880, p. 1). Accordingly, language was no longer regarded as a physical organism but as a form of human behavior, more specifically, as overt speech activity and the accompanying covert psychological events. The roots and suffixes with which comparative linguists had operated hitherto began to lose their reality and were regarded instead as convenient abstractions; linguists aimed now at studying the relations obtaining among the actual observable linguistic elements (words, sentences) which speakers use to make themselves understood. Moreover, the development of language from one period to the next came to be regarded as a shifting among these myriad relations. How was such a complicated set of phenomena amenable to scientific study? What was needed was a general theory to provide an understanding of the nature of language and the processes of linguistic change.

Regarding the nature of language itself, Hermann Paul insisted on approaching the problem from a psychological point of view, and for this purpose he resorted to the psychological theories of Johann Friedrich Herbart [1776–1841]. Accordingly, he considered that, although the speech act itself is a psychological and acoustic phenomenon, the underlying psychological processes are what make it what it is, that is, more than a mere physical event. He proceeded to analyze these processes in terms of three kinds of elements, namely, sounds, words, and sentences—in other words, the units of traditional grammar. He regarded a speech sound as the pairing of a motor sensation (*Bewegungsgefühl*) with an auditory impression (*Tonempfindung*). Words, he claimed, are stored in the unconscious in groups of two types, namely, material groups (*stoffliche Gruppen*), which involve likeness in meaning, for example, *go, goes, going, gone, went;* and formal groups (*formale Gruppen*), whose members have the same grammatical function, for example, *cats, tables, children, men.* The two types of groups intersect since the same words necessarily figure in both formal and material groups. For instance, *house* belongs in the same material group as *houses,* and in the same formal group as *box.*

The speaker stores in his unconscious all the words he has ever heard or spoken, where they are arranged in the groups to which they belong. When he utters a sentence, he does not need to reproduce each word from memory, since the systematic character of the unconscious arrays of forms means that he can produce any form afresh on the basis of the regular relations which obtain among them. Thus, a speaker about to utter the word *boxes* may either reproduce the form from memory or create it on the analogy *house : houses = box : boxes,* where the last form can be supplied by "solving the proportion." In this instance, the process of analogical creation produces a form which is already in ordinary use. But sometimes we obtain in this way novel forms, like the child's *foots,* instead of the customary *feet,* on the analogy of *roots*; or neologisms such as *peacenik.* However, since all native speakers of a language have substantially the same internalized set of analogies, they can understand novel forms just as easily as they can produce them.

In the case of sentences, very few are reproduced *in toto* from memory. Most sentences are created afresh when the relevant occasion arises, on the basis of the analogies abstracted from previously heard or uttered sentences. Syntax, therefore, in contrast to morphology, is the area in which speech behavior is predominantly creative. Paul emphasized, however, that new lexical items and new grammatical features are constantly being created. This attitude toward linguistic creativity contrasts with that held by linguists of the mid-nineteenth century, who believed that, after the original creative stage of linguistic development, nothing new was added, and that everything which does not deviate from previous usage is simply reproduced from memory. In this regard, Paul claimed to be doing no more than following to its logical conclusion the principle, enunciated earlier in the century by Wilhelm von Humboldt (see Humboldt, 1836, pp. LVII–LVIII; 1907, pp. 45–47), that speech is a continuous process of creation (Paul, 1880, pp. 68–69).

The reason languages change is because each speaker forms his own set of formal and material groups on the basis of the particular sentences he has heard and produced, and at no time in his life is a state of complete equilibrium in the various groupings reached. Since the speech of the individual is in a constant state of development, the speech of a whole community, which is, after all, only a vast network of interacting individuals, necessarily also changes as these individual variations accumulate in a consistent direction.

The conventional grammatical description of a language as it is spoken at a particular time is merely a set of rough generalizations about the average state of the groupings in the minds of the speakers at that time. If another description is made of the language a few generations later, these generalizations will come out looking different, and the changes which have taken place will be duly reflected in the new description. However, it is a fundamental mistake, in Paul's view, to regard a compilation of the differences between the two descriptions as an adequate account of the changes which have taken place meanwhile. The study of the history of language involves more than cataloging the differences between grammars of successive chronological periods. Unlike the comparative linguist of the earlier generation, the historian of language is concerned primarily with understanding the changes taking place in language. The grammarian's description of a language, on the other hand, does not get at the underlying psychological groupings operative in speech behavior; it merely assembles and formulates generalizations about everyday usage, and in this way it falls short of being truly scientific. As soon as the investigator aims at injecting an explanatory element into the study of language, he inevitably becomes historically oriented. Hence, according to Paul, linguistics must use a historical approach if it is to be both scientific and psychologically valid.

At the same time, this strong emphasis on the processes of historical development led linguists to reject the more speculative side of comparative work, and to emphasize the living languages and their recorded history. Not that linguists of the new generation ceased to be interested in the reconstruction of protolanguages; Karl Brugmann and Berthold Delbrück, for example, summed up what was known at the end of the century about proto-Indo-European in a monumental work, modestly entitled *Grundriss der vergleichenden Grammatik der indogermanischen Sprachen* [Outline of the comparative grammar of the Indo-European languages (1886–1892)]. More typical of the future development of linguistics, however, were such scholars as August Leskien, who worked on the Slavic and Baltic languages, Eduard Sievers, who worked on general phonetics and Germanic, and Hermann Paul himself, who devoted most of his life to a historical grammar of Modern German. It is also worth pointing out in this connection that the two founders of modern descriptive linguistics, the Swiss Ferdinand de Saussure [1857–1913] and the Pole Jan Baudouin de Courtenay [1845–1929], both received an important part of their training in Germany in the sixties and seventies among scholars of the new generation.

The two most important motive forces active in the development of language, according to the neogrammarian view, are *phonetic change* and *analogical formation*. Paul and his colleagues insisted that sound-change is regular; they laid down as an immutable principle that phonetic change affects a particular sound-type in a clearly defined set of phonetic contexts, and that every token of that sound-type so situated undergoes the change with iron necessity. Where there are apparent exceptions to the operation of sound-changes, they result from *subsequent* interfering factors of certain well-defined varieties. This means that it is not possible for a sound-change to be blocked in certain words because the affected sound is too significant to undergo alteration, as some of the linguists of the older generation had asserted. Nor is it possible for a sound change to worm its way gradually through the vocabulary, as Hugo Schuchardt, a contemporary critic of the neogrammarians, suggested.

However, in defending the principle of the regularity of sound-change from criticism, the neogrammarians had eventually to admit that it could not be demonstrated to be true on *empirical* grounds. They fell back, therefore, on theoretical and methodological arguments. They reasoned on theoretical grounds, for example, that a sound change cannot be selective in its operation since it is carried out unconsciously. The physiological process of sound-production, they believed, has a certain random quality to it; it is, in some sense, a hit-or-miss operation. The summation of random variations in a consistent direction leads to an overall shift in the associated motor sensations and acoustic impressions, and a sound change is nothing but such a gradual shift. The members of a speech community, naturally, keep in step with each other while the change is taking place. This is so because the acoustic impression a speaker associates with a sound is a product of the way he has heard the sound pronounced by his fellow speakers and by himself. Consistency is guaranteed, therefore, by the mere fact of constant interaction. On methodological grounds, the neogrammarians argued that to postulate a sound change that is less than completely regular would be tantamount to admitting that language is not subject to the laws of causality, and hence not amenable to scientific investigation.

The second major type of linguistic change recognized by Paul and the other neogrammarians was *analogical formation,* the creation of novel grammatical forms on the basis of already existing analogies. When in English the plural of *cow* changed from *kine* to *cows,* this was not due to sound-change, but to the fact that a new plural was formed on the regular analogy. Analogical change is, therefore, one of the factors responsible for apparent exceptions to sound-changes. To the older generation of linguists it seemed as if the neogrammarians invoked the principle of analogy whenever they needed to explain away an exception which might be used as a counterexample to disprove the principle of regular sound change. It also scandalized these older scholars to be told that a process such as analogical change, which they had often referred to disparagingly as *false* analogy, occurred in venerable languages like Greek and Sanskrit, which they thought had been spoken at a time when men still had a more highly developed "sense of language" (*Sprachsinn*) than they had in later centuries.

It should be borne in mind, however, that, although Paul considered sound-change and analogical formation to be the two most important developmental factors in the history of language, a considerable part of the *Prinzipien* (from the second edition on) was devoted to other topics, for example, semantic change (Chapter 4), syntactic theory (Chapter 6), syntactic change (Chapter 7), word-coinage and onomatopoeia (Chapter 9), changes in the membership of material and formal groups (Chapters 10, 11, and 13), grammatical categories and their relation to psychological categories (Chapter 15), word-classes (Chapter 20), the problem of the origin of inflection and word-formation (Chapter 19), and so forth. In many of these areas, too, Paul adopted theoretical positions which involved him in controversy both with scholars of the older generation and with his contemporaries. For example, his ideas about syntactic theory and semantic change came in for rough treatment at the hands of Wilhelm Wundt, the founder of experimental psychology in Germany. Wundt's notions of syntax and semantic change were, naturally enough, based on his own psychological doctrine, not on the Herbartian principles to which Paul subscribed. Moreover, Paul's contention that word-creation was still going on in modern languages set him at loggerheads with the comparative linguists of the previous generation, one of whom had once asserted that no new root had ever been invented since the end of the root-stage of linguistic development, and that therefore "we may be said to handle the very words which issued from the mouth of the son of God, when he gave names to 'all cattle, and to the fowl of the air, and to every beast of the field' " (Müller, 1880, p. 29).

The essential property of Paul's system, then, is a firm belief that the processes at work in both speech behavior and linguistic change have always been and still are due to causes and forces which operate continuously and with absolute uniformity. Such a belief is logically incompatible with the notion that languages pass through a series of developmental stages of the kind hypothesized by the linguists of the early and middle nineteenth century. Moreover, much of the attractiveness which morphological reconstruction had was precisely that it enabled the analyst to penetrate to a stage of linguistic development significantly different from the one accessible to normal observation. When the parent language was declared to be a language like any spoken at the present time, the whole research strategy of historical linguistics underwent a shift away from the concentration on origins and in the direction of a painstaking study of the ubiquitous phenomenon of linguistic change.

It is interesting to note that no linguists of Hermann Paul's generation actually attempted to justify this uniformitarianism on empirical grounds. But it may be doubted whether such a demonstration is feasible. Be that as it may, this belief has been basic to all subsequent work in linguistics up to the present day. In a real sense, the general view of language and linguistic change which underlies Paul's *Prinzipien* is as topical now as it was a hundred years ago.

References

Humboldt, W. von. *Über die Verschiedenheit des menschlichen Sprachbaues und ihren Einfluss auf die geistige Entwickelung des Menschengeschlechts*. Berlin: Druckerei der Königlichen Akademie der Wissenschaften, 1836.

Humboldt, W. von. *Gesammelte Schriften, herausgegeben von A. Leitzmann*. Siebenter Band, erste Hälfte: Einleitung zum Kawiwerk. Berlin: B. Behr, 1907.

Müller, F. M. *Lectures on the science of language*. (New ed.). (Vol. 1). London: Longmans, Green, 1880.

Paul, H. *Prinzipien der Sprachgeschichte*. Halle: Max Niemeyer, 1880. (Subsequent editions 1886, 1898, 1909, 1920.)

Schleicher, A. *Compendium der vergleichenden Grammatik der indogermanischen Sprachen*. Weimar: Hermann Böhlau, 1876. (First edition, 1861–1862.)

9

John J. Sullivan

NOAM CHOMSKY AND CARTESIAN LINGUISTICS*

The Controversy Over Cartesian Linguistics

The central doctrine of Cartesian linguistics is that the general features of grammatical structure are common to all languages and reflect certain fundamental properties of the mind. It is this assumption which led the philosophical grammarians to concentrate on *grammaire générale* rather than *grammaire particulière* ... the study of universal conditions that prescribe the form of any human language is "*grammaire générale.*" Such universal conditions are not learned; rather they provide the organizing principles that make language learning possible, that must exist if data are to lead to knowledge. By attributing such principles to the mind as an innate property, it becomes possible to account for the quite obvious fact that the speaker of a language knows a great deal that he has not learned. (Chomsky, 1966, pp. 59–60)

Professor Chomsky has significantly set back the history of linguistics. ... I do not see that anything at all useful can be salvaged from Chomsky's version of the history. That version is fundamentally false from beginning to end. (Aarsleff, 1970, pp. 583)

I prefer to think that Chomsky's rendering of continental European rationalism is "fundamentally true." (Verhaar, 1971, p. 10)

*This is a revision of my article "On Cartesian Linguistics" which was first published in Volume 191 of the *Annals* of the New York Academy of Sciences titled "The Roots of American Psychology: Historical Influences and Implications for the Future" in 1977, pp. 287–305.

John J. Sullivan • New York University, New York, New York 10003; University of Utah, Salt Lake City, Utah 84112.

> If historically there had been a Cartesian linguistics, with minor excep-
> tions, it probably would have been something similar to what Chomsky pro-
> poses. (Sullivan, 1977, p. 287)

Both Descartes and Chomsky share a magnificent set of talents, one of
which is the capacity for strong statements of opinions counter to contemporary scientific and philosophical paradigms. The result is that both
had a talent for being embroiled in controversies. Throughout his life
Descartes was dogged with controversies (see Appendix) and thirteen
years after his death the Congrégation de l'Index (on November 20, 1663)
condemned his *Meditations*. Similarly, Chomsky has a flair for polemics,
and his *Cartesian Linguistics* has precipitated a mild controversy about
the facts and interpretations of seventeenth-century philosophy, linguistics, and by implication, cognitive psychology in the general rationalistic
and empiricistic traditions. The opening quotations indicate the basic
Chomsky interpretation of Cartesian linguistics, a strong negative reaction by Hans Aarsleff, a moderating comment by Father John W. M.
Verhaar, and my general evaluation of the issues involved.

In this chapter I shall try to indicate the sense in which Cartesian
linguistics is in the rationalistic tradition. This will require a minor qualification of Chomsky's interpretations of Descartes's theory of mind. I shall
also try to show that to account in general for linguistics, Descartes, in
rejecting as central a radical empiricistic doctrine and a middle position
Aristotelian epistemology, took a Platonic alternative which he later qual-
ified.

Chomsky's Disclaimers

Cartesian Linguistics is a Whig[1] history. Chomsky's general dis-
claimer is as follows:

> I will limit myself here to something less ambitious [than a history of
> linguistics], namely, a preliminary and fragmentary sketch of some of the

---

[1] "Whig" history is a term applied by the distinguished British historian H. Butterfield to
refer to the type of history written by the Whig historians of the early nineteenth century.
These historians were progressive, Protestant, concerned with the development of individual liberty, and tended to write history as exhibiting progress toward these tendencies.
Their versions of history were preambles to their particular contemporary views. Thus, the
phrase "Whig history" is used to refer to that type of history written in terms of present
perspectives instead of the perspectives of the actors of the particular historical period
under examination.

leading ideas of Cartesian linguistics with no explicit analysis of its relation to current work that seeks to clarify and develop these ideas....

Questions of current interest will, however, determine the general form of this sketch; that is, I will make no attempt to characterize Cartesian linguistics as it saw itself, but rather will concentrate on the development of ideas that have reemerged, quite independently, in current work....

This will be something of a composite portrait. There is no single individual who can be shown, on textual grounds, to have held all the views that will be sketched. (1966, p. 2)

He further notes that (a) some of the Cartesian linguistics are rooted in earlier work, (b) that several of the active contributions to the linguistic tradition would have considered themselves antagonistic to the Cartesian doctrine, and (c) that Descartes said little about language, and his few remarks are subject to various interpretations. Chomsky remarks further:

Still, it seems to me that there is, in the period under review here, a coherent and fruitful development of a body of ideas and conclusions regarding the nature of language in association with a certain theory of mind and that this development can be regarded as an outgrowth of the Cartesian revolution. (1966, pp. 2–3)

Method of Procedure

Two levels of analysis in the controversy over Cartesian linguistics and Cartesian philosophy in general, may be distinguished: discussions of outer and inner dialectics. The outer dialectics are sociocultural level conflicts which are the context of the inner or intellectual-philosophical dialectics. An old adage applied to this type of analysis is that the outer dialectic without the inner dialectic has no fruit, the inner dialectic without the outer dialectic has no root.

The discussion of the Cartesian inner dialectics is an illustration of the notion of a method of structural history.[2] This method is simply a structural analysis as propaedeutic to the history of science and philosophy followed by a search for relevant documents.

[2]"Structural" history is a type of history which consists of an analysis of the structure of ideas of a particular person or a succession of persons. The phrase was used by Gustav Bergmann in his *Philosophy of Science* to distinguish the type of writing he did as compared with the description of the social milieu and the examination and comparisons of texts. In structural history, the relations and orders of ideas are stressed. A classical example of the type would be a comparison of Plato's and Freud's theories of mind. After such a structural analysis of similarities and differences, the historians may then examine Freud's library, diaries, and correspondence to estimate the influence of Plato on Freud.

The methodological justification of this type of history is that the historian needs a clear sense of the intellectual issues involved in the history of philosophy or science so that, while pursuing his scholarly researches, he will be sensitized to relevant data on crucial theoretical problems.[3] This prescription applied to Cartesian linguistics results in a general assay of Descartes's theory of mind and its implications for a theory of the creative use of language. With these considerations in mind, a close reading of his works, particularly his correspondence, follows. The stress on the correspondence is because, as Chomsky notes, Descartes did not explicitly devote much attention to the problems of language. Most of the comments he made about language were in the context of discussions of other issues and were thus secondary points. Fortunately, I was able to find a letter which I judge to be excellent evidence for my structural analysis of Descartes's theory of mind (third period) as it could be applied to a theory of language.

Although the procedure of doing an analysis and then looking for a relevant passage, finding one, and then interpreting it as evidence for the worth of the analysis looks circular, in fact, it is not. The original evidence for the structural analysis is not the letter which is then used as evidence for the analysis. Rather, the structural analysis is based on historically presented ontological assumptions rooted in classical Greek philosophy which were modified by seventeenth-century thinkers. These ontological positions constituted the philosophical matrix out of which developed the inner dialectics of the seventeenth century. The letter which I shall produce has the character of confirmatory evidence for the structural analysis and is not the source of the analysis. The pragmatic justification of such historical method is best made by showing the method in use and displaying its outcomes.

The outer dialectic can be considered metaphysico-religious, whereas the inner dialectic is strictly metaphysico-scientific and involves specifics of the theory of mind, method, and theory of knowledge. By contrast, the outer dialectic with its broad philosophico-religious scope

---

[3]A difficulty with structural history is that the positions generated by the analyses might reflect contemporary views rather than the views of the historical issues as seen by the participants. A possible solution to this problem is to conduct the structural analysis in terms of the issues as they were presented to the participants. In the case of the Cartesian philosophy, the issues in religion, metaphysics, and experimental philosophy (science) were related to the classical philosophical positions of Democritean-Epicurean materialism, Aristotelianism, and Platonism.

involves three species of rationalism: religious rationalism, metaphysical rationalism, and scientific rationalism.[4] All these doctrines distinguish between an empirical phenomenalism and a metaphysical realism. In the inner dialectic, we distinguish a concept rationalism of Descartes and a judgment rationalism of Kant.[5]

The Outer Dialectic

René Discartes entered the Jesuit College of La Flèche in 1906 at the age of 10. The college had been founded two years previously by the Jesuit order of the Catholic church. The religious wars of the preceding period had ruined the hope of a united Christianity. As part of a Counter-Reformation reaction, the Church decided to establish a college at La Flèche to help restore the authority of "la scholastique péripatéticienne."[6] At that time the curriculum consisted of the first six years in the humanities and the last three in philosophy. The three-year philosophical curriculum consisted of three parts. (a) morals and logic, (b) mathematics and physics, and (c) metaphysics. During the last three years, it was then the custom of students to remain with one instructor.

[4]"Rationalism" is a term which does not have a precise referent as either an epistemological doctrine or as an intellectual movement. In this sense it is like the term "romanticism" in literature or "existentialism" in contemporary philosophy. In the French intellectual tradition, a distinction has been made between rationalism in religion, in metaphysics, and in science. This type of scheme obviously follows Comte's notion of the development of western intellectual tradition. One of the characteristics of Descartes is that his Platonic doubts about the evidence of the senses was not carried over into doubts about the efficacy of reasoning in detecting the structure of reality. His major accomplishment is that he proposed a highly developed metaphysical doctrine which was consistent in religion, philosophy, and science.

[5]In philosophy, a distinction is sometimes made between the rationalism of Descartes, concerned as it was with innate ideas and hostile to Aristotelian syllogisms, and the rationalism of Kant, who looked upon concepts and judgments as having related structures (for every concept there was a particular type of judgment) and believed Aristotelian logic to be a pattern of thought. The major distinction in terms of the external dialectic was that Kant was a century and a country away from the Catholic theologians, whose intense conflicts and interests so troubled Descartes, with the result that Kant was sympathetic to Aristotelianism, but took it upon himself in the *Critique of Pure Reason* to construct an organon consistent with eighteenth-century physics.

[6]I have taken much delight in reading Leon Brunschvicg's little book *Descartes*. Although much of my structural schematization of Descartes comes from the ontological grid system I place on his work, my sense of the external dialectics has been greatly influenced by Brunschvicg's perceptive remarks.

Descartes's teacher, Father Fournet (who died January 10, 1638; the *Discours* was published in 1637), during this period corresponded with Descartes until his (Fournet's) death.[7]

Descartes's various contributions have fared badly in the criticisms of contemporary critics who do not share his religious views and who neglect to place him in the outer dialectics of his own period. On the one hand, the question is how could such an acute thinker in mathematics and science be so loose in welding his particular form of theology with seventeenth-century science. Sympathetic critics who tend toward Platonism in philosophy or with strong religious commitments, on the other hand, tend to marvel at the consistency of the method of research, the theory of mind, the general conception of science, and the theology. Critical views of Descartes seem ultimately to be determined strongly by the acceptance or nonacceptance of Platonic-type religious assumptions. In evaluating Descartes's religious rationalism, one must remember that he was trained to defend a conservative religious position and that his task was the development of a new cosmology in which both science and religion could be accommodated. Obviously, early Jesuit training and vigilant Jesuit surveilance were strong constraints in the development of his system of philosophy.[8]

[7]The sociointellectual matrix of Descartes's work can be readily seen in the rather full correspondence published by Vrin and collected and annotated by Adam and Tannery. It will be seen there that a large part of his correspondence was with the clergy.

[8]Descartes had good reasons to fear the power of the Jesuits and at the same time to be identified emotionally with them as a result of his education. The Edict of Nantes of Henry IV, promulgated in April 1598, gave to his Protestant subjects a measure of religious liberty (among other freedoms they could conduct services five leagues from Paris as distinguished from being restrained to ten or more leagues from the city). The point is that the Edict was strongly opposed by the Roman Catholic clergy in general and the Jesuits in particular. In 1685, it was revoked and then followed by the great persecution and migrations of the Huguenots.

As a result of an essentially metaphysical dispute, as distinguished from a purely scientific issue, on the existence of a plurality of worlds, in 1600 Giordano Bruno was condemned to death as a heretic. In 1616, the Congregation of the Holy Office delivered a report that the proposition "the sun is the centre of the world and altogether devoid of local motion" was "foolish and absurd philosophically and formally heretical, in as much as it expressly contradicts the doctrines of Holy Scripture in many places" (quoted in A. C. Crombie, *Medieval and Early Modern Science* (Vol. 2), p. 211). This decree was the major basis of Galileo's condemnation. On hearing of Galileo's arrest, Descartes wrote to Mersenne that "Now I would like to point out to you that all the things that I explained in my Treatise (*Le Monde*), among which was this opinion about the movement of the Earth, depend so much upon the other that it is enough to know that one of them is false, to know that all the reasons which I used are invalid; and although I thought that they were based on

The basic problem of religious thinkers of the seventeenth century was that the growth of mathematics and science was eroding the traditional Aristotelian conceptions of science which, in the Thomistic tradition, had been closely integrated with religious cosmology. The decline of the Aristotelian system brought with it a strong challenge to the theological conceptions closely woven into it. The basic thrust of Descartes's work, although securing the existence of God and the immortality of the soul, was to provide an alternate conception of physics (mechanism over the whole domain), mathematics (geometry by means of algebra and reference systems), and logic (abandonment of syllogistic reasoning for the four-phase scientific method stressing [1] systematic doubt, [2] analysis into elements, [3] synthesis out of elements, and [4] construction of lists to check the adequacy of accounts of phenomena).

The Inner Dialectic

The inner dialectic is between Platonic, Aristotelian and Democritean-Epicurean theories of knowledge, mind, method, and, ultimately, mathematics and physics. I shall stress this inner dialectic first in terms of Platonism and Aristotelianism and then in terms of a conception of the development of Descartes' theory of mind. Table I gives the major ontological positions of the inner dialectics.

The Ontological Alternatives

How one sets up a category system (grid system) for the analysis of the thought of any particular period is, of course, a matter of level generality of the outcomes one expects. Since the time of Descartes, largely owing to his influence, philosophy has gone into what has been called the "epistemological turn." This makes the problem of knowledge central. More specifically, the problem generated by the rise of science has been how is knowledge of the world possible when the basic data are the sense data of the observing scientist. There are many variations proposed as solutions to this problem, and these constitute the problems of epistemology. The view taken here, however, is that what one proposes as an

---

very certain and evident demonstrations, I would not wish for anything in the world to maintain them against the authority of the Church" (*ibid.*, p. 217).

Table I. Five Classical Ontologies in Philosophies of Mind

	What exists? With what are we directly acquainted?
I. Physical events and processes	The world is conceived of as composed of only physical objects and processes. One can distinguish naïve formulations of the principle in which physical objects and processes are seen only in terms of simple (Newtonian) mechanics. And Descartes, Chomsky, and the Gestalters never tire of stressing the limits of mechanical explanation. A sophisticated contemporary physicalism may include causal mechanisms of natural selection for biology, nuclear principles of the shell model of the atom in physics and chemistry, "smart" molecules in biochemistry, etc.
II. Sensory phenomena	That we have direct acquaintance only with sensory phenomena and all else is a construction is a claim of the phenomenologists.
III. Relations	That relations exist and that some relations, particularly in human perception and human performance, influence the properties of the components is a Gestalt position.
IV. Mental acts	Experience is of particular events and may or may not be passive; knowledge is an intellectual construction (a mental act) and is of classes. Mental acts (1) form concepts from an amorphous set of sensations, (2) make judgments (AEIO propositions), and (3) reason with judgments (syllogisms). With the distinctions between concepts, judgments, and reasoning, a "concept rationalism" and a "judgment rationalism" may be distinguished. "Concept rationalism" is associated with Cartesianism, whereas "judgment rationalism" is a later product associated with Kantianism.
V. Forms, ideas, God	Primary existence is a characteristic of forms (squareness) of which we are cognitively aware. These ideas are innate in us. Physical objects participate in these forms but are not a complete realization of them any more than that a statue by Praxiteles is a complete realization of his ideal of beauty. When objective properties are referred to, the term *form* is used. When forms have existence cognitively, the term *ideas* is used. The notion of God as an existent falls into these ontological categories, particularly since the notion of God represents a perfection of all his properties.

epistemological formulation has basic ontological assumptions. These ontological assumptions are logically prior to and determine epistemological positions. The ontological positions presented in Table I were all present in classical Greek thought.[9]

In terms of the ontologies presented, Descartes was engaged in three dialectics. First, he rejected a Democritean materialism espoused by Pierre Gassendi [1592–1655] in physics and Thomas Hobbes [1588–1679] in philosophy. Second, he attacked a teleological biology of the prevailing Aristotelian type by sharply distinguishing between mental and physical states and holding that mechanism held over the domain of physical states. Third, he proposed a highly intellectualized scheme which attempted to be consistent over the problems of religion, mathematics, philosophy, and the sciences. As Brunschvicg notes, this was an intellectual venture which was continued with great clarity by Leibniz.[10] The essential inner dialectic was how much explanatory weight and what

[9]The minor qualification to this statement is the existence of relations, and the implications of this ontological assumption were not clearly perceived until the end of the nineteenth century. As the result of both work in the foundations of mathematics and phenomenology, Bertrand Russell and William James stressed the independent existence of relations. The psychological analogue to this development is to be found in Gestalt psychology; the physical analogue is in the general field equations of electrical phenomena and atomic physics.

It should be clear that ontologies set limits on epistemologies. If there are no mental acts, for instance, then relations between experiences must occur by some strictly deterministic process like a principle of reinforcement or a law of association. If forms do not exist, and are not innate, then there must be some process in mental acts or some sequences of experiences from which abstract terms like the forms can be generated. An important part of the dialectics about cognitive processes is to show that (1) a nonmental act position can account for all the data of thought phenomena or to show that (2) in principle the explanation of thought (or speech) phenomena cannot be reduced to or explained by noncognitive models of mental processes.

It is to be noted that these ontologies in Table I are even today the substructure of the major psychological systematic theories. The first position, that of scientific materialism of either the physiological or Skinnerian type, has as a task the dialectical refutation of the claims of the other ontologies (that phenomena, even if they exist, are not causally associated with behavior, that mental phenomena such as cognitive acts are explained as constructions from processes which do not exhibit any other than physical properties, and that innate ideas are explainable by learning and memory). The second position is that of the phenomenologists and the existentialists. The third position, as mentioned above, is a Gestalt position. The fourth position is central to the Freudian notion of a mind which acts. The taxonomy of the mental acts is given by the "mechanisms." The fifth position, that of innate forms, is in Chomsky's interpretation "innate principles" of grammatical processing.

[10]In 1660, Leibniz, according to Brunschvicg, devoted himself to the task of developing an intellectual system which would be simultaneously an alternative to mechanistic materialism in physics, to teleology in biology, and to empiricism in philosophy. In this orientation his work is a variation within the Cartesian tradition.

functions can be apportioned to external sensations, innate ideas, and reasoning powers. But, as I have previously maintained, how one solves this problem depends on prior ontological assumptions.

The Stress on Mechanism.[11] The seventeenth-century roots of the

---

[11]The general topic of mechanism has a long history. It really should be placed in the seventeenth century and should have as its dialectical opposite a classical science strongly influenced by teleology of the Aristotelian system. There was, of course, a classical influence of Platonism on science, but it was largely in mathematics and geometry and resulted in the subordination of experience (and experiment) to a philosophical investigation of the nature of forms. As an alternative to Aristotelianism, the capacity of mechanistic explanation seemed to intoxicate thinkers of the late seventeenth century. Because of the successes of the Newtonian physics, the development of the mathematics of Fermat, Descartes, Leibniz, and Newton which supported the physical theories and made their confirmation possible, the world seemed to be one large machine. The decline of mechanism has been a topic of many recent books on the "new physics." Both molecular and relativity physics have confined the Newtonian "world machine" into a restricted range of phenomena. The supporting philosophical concepts of the Newtonian system, substance and cause, have been dispensed with, and probability functions and matrix manipulations have been substituted for the old differential equations and scalar mathematics. Determinism, however, has not been abandoned, only given probability formulations. Limits of knowledge have been drawn more narrowly for we have learned to live without a theological quest for certainty in our scientific activities (these are delta-epsilon arguments in calculus).

At any event, there seems to be a Princeton general critique of mechanism and Descartes. The outstanding general, and excellent, analysis of mechanism was W. Kohler's *The Task of Gestalt Psychology* (Princeton University Press, 1969), a series of lectures given in 1966. Julian Jaynes in "Animate Motion in the 17th Century," published in *Historical Conceptions of Psychology* (Henle, Jaynes, & Sullivan, 1973) presents an interesting psychological construction of the source in Descartes's life of the notion of mechanism and the reactions of contemporary biologists to the Cartesian proposals. I abstract his comments as follows:

> [Descartes] a maternally deprived 18 year old suffered . . . several breakdowns . . . hid himself away in Saint Germain for two years . . . [whose] . . . only recreation available were visits to the royal gardens . . . in which there were complicated statues that moved, danced, or even spoke.
> These images . . . perhaps stayed at the very depths of Descartes' thinking. He seems to view the entire physical world as though it were modeled in the Francinis' [the constructors of the statues] work. It was nothing but a vast machine. Just as in the Queen's gardens, there was no spontaneity at any point. He loathed animism. He loved statues. (pp. 169–170)

Jaynes further points out:

> Archaic for its own day, the errors of Descartes' physiology were pointed out one by one as they appeared. The year following the publication of *Traité de l'Homme*, N. Steno (1638–1686) the young Danish theologician and physiologist, found himself obliged to point out . . . the vast difference between Descartes' imaginary machine, and the real machine of the human body'; he showed that the pineal gland existed in animals as well as in man (as had been known before), and in no case had the rich nerve supply which the Cartesian theory demanded. (p. 173)

Although *Traité de l'Homme* was probably written in the early 1630s, it was the second part (Chapter 28) of the withheld *Le Monde*. It was published separately in Leyden mechanism and vitalism controversy are clearly in Descartes's dualism between the mental and the physical, or, as he put it, between substances which exist temporarily but are unextended and characterized by consciousness and those substances which are extended. In the Aristotelian scheme of things, the world was divided into objects which are besouled (animate) and which lack soul (inanimate). The objective manifestation of this distinction was the capacity of the object to be self-moving or only moved by the application of an external force. Thus, within the Artistotelian scheme, all plant and animal kingdoms were viewed as having psyches. There was a vegetive psyche which had the properties of nutrition and reproduction. In the animal psyche, there were, in addition to the vegetive functions, those of sensation, movement, passive memory, and imagination. Only man had all these functions and, in addition, the function of reasoning.

The thrust against Aristotelian theory of mind was to extend the concept of mechanism throughout the physical and biological domain, man as thinker excepted. The Cartesian extension of mechanism broadly across both what we would call today the physical and biological sciences was a bold stroke that fired the imagination of scientists of the succeeding centuries. Its peculiarly attractive feature was the simplicity of the cosmology it proposed as distinguished from the over-ripe *post hoc* patching of Aristotelian science by the scholastic tradition. The Cartesian view had the added advantage that it was consistent with a Platonic hierarchy of reality. In the Cartesian hierarchy, all physical processes (as distinguished from mental rather than as distinguished from biological) are reducible to mechanics; and mechanics is easily reducible to an exemplification of mathematics; and mathematics itself can be reduced to a set of simple, indubitable, innate ideas; and this conception of innate ideas led to a theory of mind as passive which led to the conception of God as the creative source of innate ideas and man as the instrument of his will. Thus, mechanism led to the conception of a world machine designed by God in the manner of Timaeus' Demiurge (Plato, *Timaeus,* pp. 54–56) who creates the universe out of proportions of fire, air, water, and earth and these primary bodies out of triangles arranged to make various solid forms, for example, a cube, a tetrahedron, or a pyramid.

It was important in Cartesianism to exempt mind from this general

---

in 1662 as *Renatus Des Cartes De Homine* by a Florent Schuyl. Clerselier published on April 12, 1664 *L'Homme de René Descartes.*

Hans Aarsleff, Chomsky's vociferous critic, is also from Princeton.

mechanistic account although the mind thus exempted was only a passive
agent of God's will. The ground for the exclusion of the cognitive processes from the mechanistic conception of the world was developed by an
argument which involved a theoretical couple: machines and mind. Mind
was looked upon as a universal instrument which can respond in many
different ways to diverse situations, but the notion of the machine was
that it only responded in a narrow range of responses and only when the
appropriate organ was stimulated. Speech is another differentia between
humans and machines.

In Section V of the *Discours*, Descartes discusses the difference
between animals and men.[12] The first distinction is that, as Chomsky

[12]Section V in the *Discours* reads as follows:

> Et je m'étais ici particulièrement arrêté à faire voir que, s'il y avait de telles machines,
> qui eussent les organes et la figure d'un singe, ou de quelque autre animal sans raison,
> nous n'aurions aucun moyen pour reconnaître qu'elles ne seraient pas en tout de même
> nature que ces animaux; au lieu que, s'il y en avait qui eussent la ressemblance de nos
> corps et imitassent autant nos actions que moralement il serait possible, nous aurions
> toujours deux moyens très certains pour reconnaître qu'elles ne seraient point pour cela
> de vrais hommes. Dont le premier est que jamais elles ne pourraient user de paroles, ni
> d'autres signes en les composant, comme nous faisons pour déclarer aux autres nos
> pensées. Car on peut bien concevoir qu'une machine soit tellement faite qu'elle profère
> des paroles, et même qu'elle en profère quelquesunes à propos des actions corporelles qui
> causeront quelque changement en ses organes : comme, si on la touche en quelque
> endroit, qu'elle demande ce qu'on lui veut dire; si en un autre, qu'elle crie qu'on lui fait
> mal, et choses semblables; mais non pas qu'elle les arrange diversement, pour répondre
> au sens de tout ce qui se dira en sa présence, ainsi que les hommes les plus hébétés
> peuvent faire. Et le second est que, bien qu'elles fissent plusieurs choses aussi bien, ou
> peut-être mieux qu'aucun de nous, elles manqueraient infailliblement en quelques autres,
> par lesquelles on découvrirait qu'elles n'agiraient pas par connaissance, mais seulement
> par la disposition de leurs organes. Car, au lieu que la raison est un instrument universel,
> qui peut servir en toutes sortes de recontres, ces organes ont besoin de quelque par-
> ticulière disposition pour chaque action particulière; d'où vient qu'il est moralement
> impossible qu'il y en ait assez de divers en une machine pour la faire agir en toutes les
> occurrences de la vie, de même façon que notre raison nous fait agir. (Descartes, 1967, pp.
> 628–629)

> And I pause here particularly in order to observe that if there were such machines
> which had the organs and the face of a monkey, or some other animal lacking reason, we
> would not have any means of discriminating if they would not be in all ways of the same
> nature as these animals; instead, if there were some (machines) that resembled our bodies
> and moreover imitated our actions, which conceivably might be possible, we would always
> have two excellent means in order to recognize that they were not true humans. The first
> of which is that they would never be able to use words or signs grammatically as we do in
> order to express our thoughts. For one can well conceive that a machine could be made so
> that it uttered words and even that it uttered some appropriate for those bodily actions
> which caused some change in its organs; for instance, if we touched it in some place, that
> it ask us what we mean; in another, that cries out that we are hurting it, and similar things;
> but not that it arrange them (the utterances) differently in order to respond sensibly to all
> which will be said in its presence, as even the most weak-minded of men can do. And the
> second is that, although they do several things very well, or perhaps better than some of
> us, they would lack infallibly in some other things, from which one would discover that
> they do not act by knowledge but solely by the disposition of their organs. In contrast to
> reason, which is an universal instrument which is able to serve in a variety of situations,
> these organs need some particular disposition for each particular action; therefore, it
> follows that there are not enough variations in a machine in order to make it act in all
> circumstances of life in the same way that our reason causes us to act. [My translation]

(1966, pp. 3–4) notes, animals do not use language grammatically. The second distinction relates to the statues of the Francinis and animals both, namely, that they respond only under the appropriate stimulation of their particular organs and their actions are directly related, one might in later terminology say "instinctively" or "by mediation of reflexes," to the organs originally stimulated. By contrast, humans have the capacity to use reason, the universal instrument, which in many different situations results in appropriate action. Important here is the close relation of speech and reason, as Chomsky continually stresses. The problem is that when the actual discussion gets around to the nature of mind and cognitive processes and the relations of speech, particularly grammatical speech, to these, then the properties given to both reason and mind are hardly sufficient to account for the creative use of language.

The Stress on Innate Ideas. The central feature of Platonic realism is that there exist forms which are the ultimate constituents of the world, which are, by essence, simple (elementary) as distinguished from being composites. By virtue of the property of being simple, they are unchanging and in the case of the psyche, which is a form, immortal. Change, which is a constant characteristic of physical objects, is looked upon as the composition or decomposition of composites from simples. The simplicity requirement of the forms also put some constraints on the characteristics of definitions and knowledge of the forms. Forms, since they are simple, had only one essence and being known at all were known in their entirety.[13] The existence of forms apart from objects which are embodiments of them is the characteristic feature of Platonic realism. Physical objects "participated" in the forms and were a constantly changing and imperfect realization of them.

The separate existence of the forms and that physical objects are only imperfect realizations of them led to the problem of how the forms are knowable. Sense perception is deceptive on three counts: (1) the objects which are sensed are imperfect realizations of the forms, (2) these objects are, moreover, constantly changing, and (3) bodily states interfere with sensations such that, for example, wine tastes sour to the sick man. Yet, that the forms exist there is no doubt, and that they are knowable is also not denied. The existence of geometric forms and of the technical capabil-

---

[13]The phrase "in being known at all is known in its entirety" is one of those frequently used by N. K. Smith to describe Descartes's (also Plato's) conception of the knowledge of the simple, or innate ideas. This schematization is the source of the celebrated Cartesian stress on intuition. When knowledge and perception are structured in terms of the elementary innate ideas, they are beyond reasonable doubt.

ity of reducing complex objects into their simple components (the area of any polygon can be found to be the sum of the areas of triangles of which it can be shown to be composed) is the informing image, the basic pattern of analysis and construction of objects in the world.

To account for the knowledge of the forms, Plato, as was his creative style, created a mythic model, a likely story, corresponding to the elementary ideas. These ideas are in the psyche as a result of prior experience of the psyche in another existence, for the psyche is immortal and only temporarily lodged in the body of an individual. In this other existence, where all forms exist, the psyche had contact (presumably perceptual) with the forms and thus they entered the psyche. In becoming an individual at birth, which is the process of attachment of the psyche to a physical body, the psyche has the ideas innate in it.

Innate ideas come into use in ways which are standard conceptions even today. A sensation is presented to mind, and it is then compared with a mental duplicate, an innate idea. If the sensation is complex, say, a cat is presented, the sensation may be compared with a previously acquired empirical concept of "catness" which is composed of the elementary ideas. If the sensation is not pure and there are no empirical concepts with which to compare it, then the sensation is analyzed down into its elementary components. These elementary components are the innate ideas. Cognitive functions are essentially (1) comparisons of simple sensations with these innate ideas, (2) an analysis of complex sensations into simple ones and then comparison with innate ideas, and (3) then the construction by small, logical, intuitively certain steps of composite concepts, which may be compared with sensations. These mental processes are an internalization of the famous four steps of the *Discours*. Such schemata are used to render cognitively intelligible the stream of sensations presented to the individual.

Perhaps the doctrine of innate ideas and how they function in the Platonic-Cartesian system can be better discriminated by presenting briefly the Aristotelian branch of the dialectic on the nature of mind and the constituents of the world. Aristotle's realism is a naive realism of physical objects as distinguished from the Platonic realism of concepts and forms. For Aristotle, primary existence was given to physical objects. These objects may be conceived to be composed of form and matter immanent in them, but neither the form nor the matter can exist independently of the physical objects. The form is known cognitively, as in the Platonic scheme, but instead of being an innate idea, it is constructed by an act of mind as a generalization from the experience of a number of similar individual objects (particulars). Knowledge for the Aristotelians is of the universal concepts and their relations (class names and their relations) which have been generated from particular instances.

In the Platonic scheme, there is a basic stock of forms, as there is only a small set of basic geometric forms, and the world is constructed as combinations of these elementary components. This method and model of the world have strong appeal to mathematicians. The Aristotelian conception appeals more to those who look upon mind and reason as constructing models of the world from experience. Where theological issues are involved, Aristotelianism has the weakness that reasoning of men compels belief on the basis of experience when compared with the Platonic conception that experience itself is intelligible only on the basis of God granted innate ideas and by means of His grace. The God of the Platonists is the source of our actions and beliefs, that of the Aristotelians is only coherent with our other cognitions. In the Platonic-Cartesian system of thought, only God is creative in generating innate ideas. Humans are only ingenious in their combinations of or analyses of perceptions into innate ideas.

The Development of Descartes's Theory of Mind

To talk about Plato's or Freud's or Descartes's theory of mind leads to disaster unless it is recognized that over their individual careers there was a progressive development of their thought. It is true that there is a Platonistic, a Cartesian, and a Freudian theory of mind that has some historical warrant, in the sense that there has been a general interpretation of their central ideas. But unless care is taken to appreciate the development of their thought, one finds paradoxes in their work and the frequent comment that Plato or Freud or Descartes is not really a Platonist, or a Freudian, or Cartesian, respectively. I shall schematize stages in the development of Descartes's theory of mind and characterize the third period as the historical Cartesianism. I shall then present a hitherto untranslated letter from his correspondence which indicates the features of this theory which I mention. I shall then indicate that Descartes backed away from this position, and in so doing, he moved from a classical Platonism toward an Aristotelian formulation of mind.

First Period (1610–1619). This first period is characterized by the Aristotelianism Descartes learned while at the college at La Flèche. It is the background against which he revolted, although from the contemporary perspective the revolt, as far as theory of the human mind was concerned, was only partial. That is to say that the revolt against classical mathematics and physics was more sweeping than the modifications of the theory of the human mind. For instance, men were by nature or essence all endowed with the capacity to reason. The crisis he went through and its aftermath in which he thought that he was chosen or privileged to have access to the structure of the world is symbolized in the two dramatic dreams he had in 1619.[14] These made a significant transformation of his intellectual orientation so that these events signalled the end of a phase and the beginning of another stage of his development.

Second Period (1619–1628). This stage I conceive of as the development of an alternative to the Aristotelian procedures of science by an application to scientific problems of mathematical methodology. The break from the Aristotelian-scholastic tradition is achieved with the completion of (but not published) *Regulae ad Directionem Ingenii* [Rules for the Direction of the Mind]. In agreement with most scholars, I believe that this was worked out during the period 1627 and the first half of 1628. The point of attack, interestingly enough, was the development of an alternative method to the *Organon* of Aristotle. The *Regulae* is the predecessor to the more famous *Discours de la Méthode* in which the break with Aristotelian methodology is finally consummated. Innate ideas are not mentioned in the *Regulae* nor is the assumption that physical entities reflected in sensations are rendered intelligible by means of a mental duplicate. I follow N. K. Smith's interpretation of this period by holding, as does he, that there is a reliance on (1) the Self as aware of itself as thinking, doubting, affirming, and desiring. For Descartes, nothing can be more immediately present to the Self than itself. In addition, (2) the Self, which in its earthbound life is an embodied self, is no less immediately aware of the physical patterns which external objects, by way of their actions on the sense-organs, imprints on the brain.[15]

---

[14]Descartes's dreams are presented in Smith (1963, pp. 33–39). This is a translation from Baillet's *Vie de Descartes* (1691), Book II, Chapter i, pp. 81–86.

[15]Combined with the dreams, a critical incident while Descartes was still a youth strongly influenced his career. In November 1628, soon after arriving in Paris, he went to a meeting at the house of the Papal Nuncio to hear a talk by a Sieur de Chandoux who was to expound his views of philosophy. These turned out to be an attack against Scholastic philosophy, which powerfully influenced the audience, Descartes expected. Descartes was prevailed upon to give his reaction to the presentation and, with appropriate compliments

Third Period (1629–1646). The difficulties of the formulation of the second stage are repaired in the third stage. The problem is what warrant do we have for the interpretation that the sensations and thoughts we have constitute knowledge and refer to objects in the outside world? The problem is how does one escape from a subjectivity which ultimately leads to solipsism and skepticism? The answer seems to be to adopt the notion of innate ideas, God given, with which we compare sensations and from which we construct our conceptions of the external world. And the God which gives us these innate ideas is a good God who could not, by his nature, deceive us.

This period in Descartes's development is what came to be known as Cartesianism, at least as far as the theory of mind is concerned. It is of some interest that the seeds of this period can be seen in the second half of the year 1629 in Descartes's correspondence with Mersenne on the problems of language. To clarify what is involved epistemologically, the issue is what legitimates knowledge about the external world? To the Platonist, reality, since it is compounded of elementary forms, is knowable directly through the innate idea counterparts of these forms and compounds of these ideas. To the rationalist, there is direct insight into the structure of the world, and the coherence of the structure along with the indubitability of the initial assumptions and the strict logical development legitimates the knowledge of the world. To the empiricist, by contrast, constant recourse to experience as the source of ideas and the confirming instances in experience legitimate claims to knowledge. As an example of how the system worked in *Meditations III*, the following is remarked by Descartes:

---

to Chandoux, proceeded to attack his position mainly on the grounds that it substituded one merely probable position for another. What was needed was better grounds than the probable. He demonstrated the difficulties of the merely probable reasoning by showing that a generally agreed upon true proposition by this reasoning could be looked on as false and a false one given grounds for belief. He, himself, claimed that he could develop, by an application of the methods of mathematics, a set of philosophical doctrines which were clear and certain. The audience was quick to agree with him. Cardinal de Bérulle, who was present and much impressed, later met with Descartes and told him, in effect, that, since God had given him such a fine mind, he ought to use it to good ends, namely, in the development of the philosophy that he had indicated. This injunction from the Cardinal coincided with his own tendencies, and Descartes decided to withdraw from society, to protect his liberty, and to go to some place where the weather was cool (Paris summers being too hot) and where he would be unknown. He then left for Holland for the life of a recluse devoted to study.

> I find present to me two completely diverse ideas of the Sun; the one, in
> which the Sun appears to me as extremely small, is, it would seem, derived
> from the senses, and to be counted as belonging to the class of adventitious
> ideas, the other, in which the Sun is taken to be many times larger than the
> whole Earth, has been arrived at by way of astronomical reasonings, *that is to
> say, elicited from certain notions innate in me, or formed by me in some other
> manner*. Certainly, these two ideas of the Sun cannot both resemble the same
> Sun; and reason constrains me to believe that the one which seems to have
> emanated from it in a direct manner is the more unlike. (Smith, 1963, p. 236;
> italics added)

Fourth Period (1647–1650). Although the grounds for postulating a
fourth stage rest on a rather flimsy evidence, if we can accept that there
was strong evidence for a third stage, then there is certainly a retreat from
this position to a more generalized rationalistic position. What is involved
is the definite deemphasis on innate ideas and a reliance on the powers of
reasoning itself to generate these ideas. This particular docrine is not a
minor shift, for, since it involves a shift from doctrines of innate ideas
which give limited creative powers to the individual to one on which
reason itself generates its major ideas, it is a major concession to the
Aristotelians and a retreat from Platonism. The following quotation of
Descartes is the evidence for the fourth stage:

> I have never either said or judged that the mind has need of innate ideas
> which are anything different from its faculty of thinking . . . in the same manner
> in which we say that generosity is innate in some families and in other families
> certain diseases, such as gout or gavel. In so speaking I am not saying that the
> infants or those families suffer from these diseases in the womb of the mother,
> but that they are born with a certain disposition or faculty of contracting them.
> (Adam E. Tonnery, Vol. 8, pp. 357–358)

Evidence for the Third Period Platonistic Theory of Linguistics

As mentioned above, classical Cartesianism has been identified with
what we have schematized as the third stage of Descartes's development
of a theory of mind. The letter that follows occurred in the beginning of
this stage, and, strangely, has not figured in the discussions of Cartesian
linguistics. I quote the letter extensively to show how it is an exemplification of the application of the Platonic presuppositions to a theory of language in general and grammar in particular. It was written by Descartes
while he was in Amsterdam and dated 20 Novembre, 1629. Apparently the
letter was in response to a previous one from Père Mersenne in which he

had presented to Descartes six propositions about a language project proposed by a M. Hardy.[16]

We can infer from the content of Descartes's reply that Hardy had proposed a multilanguage dictionary in which one common term would then represent *l'amour, aymer, amare, philein*. Descartes responded that interesting as this project was, what prevented people from understanding a language is the grammar. There is no doubt, however, that a simplified and regular grammar could be constructed which would make language learning easy. He then adds that:

> However, I believe one could add to this invention [conception] to com-
> pose the basic words of that language as well as their symbols so that the
> language could be taught in a very little time and this would be by means of the
> notion of order, that is to say, to establish an order[17] between all the thoughts
> which can enter the human mind in the same way that there is a natural order
> of numbers. And just as one can learn in one day all the numbers to infinity and
> to write with them in an unknown language which yet are an infinity of dif-
> ferent words one can do the same for all the other necessary words to express
> all other things that fall within the purview of the human mind. If this order
> could be found I have no doubt whatever that this language would be univer-
> sally understood for there would be a great number of people who would

---

[16]The M. Hardy referred to in this letter has not been identified to my knowledge nor has the original letter from Père Mersenne been found. However, my best guess is that the Hardy referred to in the letter is the mathematician Claude Hardy [1605–1678] who was reputed to have known thirty-six languages. There is a letter from Descartes in Vol. II of *Correspondence* dated June 1638 to this Hardy giving him some support in a controversy he had with Fermat on some geometric properties of a parabola.

[17]In the Platonic intellectual tradition as well as in the general mathematical tradition a sense of intellectual order is of paramount importance. The problem is to determine that which is fundamental from that which is derived. Since the world can be conceptualized as being composite, the problem is to specify the elementary components and how the world is to be analyzed into and further how it is to be constructed out of them. The basic problem is how to start such an analysis. This is the problem of order of ideas. The basic insight is the Platonic notion from *Timeaus* that the objects of the world are really composed of geometric forms. The problem is to do a philosophical analysis similar in outcome to a Fourier analysis of a complex curve.

To show the sense of order generally in Descartes's argument consider the following quotation from Alquié:

> Chacun connâit l'importance de la notion d'ordre chez Descartes. Et nul ne saurait
> nier que Descartes ait toujours présenté sa metáphysique selon un certain ordre qui, au
> moins dans ses grades lignes, est la même dans le *Discours* les *Méditations*, les *Principes:*
> je doute, je pense, je suis, Dieu est, Dieu garantit mes idées et, par conséquent, le science
> du monde est fondée. (Alquié, p. 10)

> Everybody knows the importance for Descartes of the idea of order. And no one
> would deny that Descartes always presented his metaphysics in a certain order which, at
> least in its general aspects, is the same in the *Discours*, the *Meditations*, the *Principes:* I
> doubt, I think, I am, God exists, God guarantees my ideas and, as a consequence, the
> knowledge of the world is grounded. [My translation]

willingly employ five or six days time in order to be able to be understood by
all men. But I do not believe that your author has thought about that simply
because nothing in all his propositions attests to it and the invention of this
language would depend upon the true philosophy for *it is impossible to decide
in any other way all the thoughts of man and to put them in a certain order,* not
solely to distinguish them in such a way that they be clear and simple, which is
in my opinion the greatest secret that one must unlock in order to acquire true
knowledge.

*If somebody had well explained which simple ideas in the imagination of
man are distinct of which all that he thinks is composed and that this be
recognized by everybody I would venture to hope that a universal language
very easy to learn, to pronounce, and to write would result.* And what is most
important is a language which would aid judgment, representing to judgment
all things so distinctly that it would be almost impossible for it to be deceived.
In contradistinction to this situation the words we use have practically only
confused meanings to which the human mind has become accustomed by
tradition so that practically man understands nothing perfectly. Now I believe
that such a language is possible and that one can find the science on which it
depends through which means peasants could better judge the truth of things
than philosophers can at present. But I do not hope ever to see that language in
use. That would presuppose immense changes in the order of things and it
would mean that the whole world were a terrestrial paradise, which is only
good thinking about in [the domain of] novels. (Italics added)[18]

---

[18]I have used Alquié's translation of the seventeenth-century French into modern French
in these notes.

> Au reste, je trouve qu'on pourrait ajouter à ceci une invention, tant pour composer
> les mots primitifs de cette langue que pour leurs caractères; en sorte qu'elle pourrait être
> enseignée en fort peu de temps, et ce par le moyen de l'ordre, c'est-à-dire, établissant un
> ordre entre toutes les pensées qui peuvent entrer en l'esprit humain, de même qu'il y en a
> un naturellement établi entre les nombres; et comme on peut apprendre en un jour à
> nommer tous les nombres jusques à l'infini, et à les écrire en une langue inconnue, qui
> sont toutefois une infinité de mots différents, qu'on pût faire le même de tous les autres
> mots nécessaires pour exprimer toutes les autres choses qui tombent en l'esprit des
> hommes. Si cela était trouvé, je ne doute point que cette langue n'eût bientôt cours parmi
> le monde; car il y a force gens qui emploieraient volontiers cinq ou six jours de temps pour
> se pouvoir faire entendre par tous les hommes.
>
> Mais je ne crois pas que votre auteur ait pensé à cela, tant parce qu'il n'y a rien en
> toutes ses propositions qui le témoigne, que parce que l'invention de cette langue dépend
> de la vraie Philosophie, car il est impossible autrement de dénombrer toutes les pensées
> des hommes, et de les mettre par ordre, ni seulement de les distinguer en sorte qu'elles
> soient claires et simples, qui est à mon avis le plus grand secret qu'on puisse avoir pour
> acquérir la bonne Science. Et si quelqu'un avait bien expliqué quelles sont les idées
> simples qui sont en l'imagination des hommes, desquelles se compose tout ce qu'ils
> pensent, et que cela fût reçu par tout le monde, j'oserais espérer ensuite une langue
> universelle, fort aisée à apprendre, à prononcer et à écrire, et ce qui est le principal, qui
> aiderait au jugement, lui représentant si distinctement toutes choses, qu'il lui serait pres-
> que impossible de se tromper; au lieu que, tout au rebours, les mots que nous avons n'ont
> quasi que des significations confuses, auxquelles l'esprit des hommes s'étant accoutumé
> de longue main, cela est cause qu'il n'entend presque rien parfaitement.
>
> Or je tiens que cette langue est possible, et qu'on peut trouver la Science de qui elle
> dépend, par le moyen de laquelle les paysans pourraient mieux juger de la vérité des
> choses, que ne font maintenant les philosophes. Mais n'espérez pas de la voir jamais en
> usage ; cela présuppose de grands changements en l'ordre des choses, et il faudrait que
> tout le Monde ne fût qu'un paradis terrestre, ce qui n'est bon à proposer que dans le pays
> des romans. (Descartes, 1967, Vol. 1, pp. 230–232)

The italicized sections in the letter to Mersenne indicated the peculiarly Platonic assumptions. The specification of the simple ideas and placing them in an order is the essential problem. Descartes thought that the key to this problem was precisely in the theory and method which he had just worked out. Only the details needed to be specified. It goes without stressing it that we have been waiting for the details of such a proposal since the time of Plato and that Descartes himself never got beyond thinking of the theoretical possibility.

Retreat from the Doctrine of Innate Ideas

How we know the nature of the world is both a function of the structure of the world and the nature of mind, and the conceptualization of both of these, in turn, are a function of the ontological positions one takes as metaphysical presuppositions of science. I have indicated the major alternatives which confronted the thinkers in the various intellectual traditions up to about the turn of this century. The doctrine of innate ideas has a strong emphasis on perception, but yet a distrust of it, and a conception of cognitive processes as consisting of small, step-like inferences, and comparisons of percepts with innate ideas. That the mind generates through mental acts its major concepts because of powers unique to it is an ontological posit of the Aristotelians. That the concepts thus generated have their source in experience and are not innate is the main thrust of the British empirical tradition. This tradition, after Locke, substituted the principle of association for cognitive processes as mechanism by which composite concepts were generated. The crisis that this doctrine led to in the philosophy of Hume resulted in the reconstruction by Kant of a theory of mind in the rationalistic tradition which had innate cognitive powers for giving structure to what was presented to the understanding. The tack taken followed the doctrine of innate powers combined with specific notions of innate ideas. And these innate powers are what was needed to give grammar its flexibility of application. The evolutionary stress on the adaptive modifications and selective survival in the nineteenth century led to the notion that the innate powers reflect not only a philosophical construction but a physiological process. When this phase of development occurred, the issue was clearly no longer one of dispute between methods of philosophically constructing world views but was one of scientific investigation.

Conclusions

I do not wish to inflate a small point to a strategic issue and declare that anyone who does not see its importance is an idiot. The distinction between innate ideas and innate powers is one that cuts deeply, however, for it goes along with different theories of mind, different ontologies, and thus different conceptions of man and science. The talk about innate ideas was always vague, but there was a ready reference to such elements as points, lines, angles, circles, and triangles as was used in geometry. The world forms were thought to be decomposable to simple geometrical forms, ultimately triangles, whose matter was simple stuff on the order of fire, air, water, and earth. This simple stuff became described by Descartes as only having the property of extension. When the theory of mind moved from innate ideas to innate powers, the doctrines which such a theory presumed to explain became harder to test and not so immediately conceivable in terms of an analogy to geometry. These innate ideas, however, found their analogue in Kant's table of categories and the innate powers in his functions of thought in judgment: judgments of quantity, quality, relation, and modality. This is the main line of development of the rationalistic tradition. The transition of the doctrine of innate ideas to one of innate powers can be seen in Descartes and was fully developed by Kant. Running parallel to this development and gaining support from it was the doctrine of grammar "générale." The development of the notion of innate powers was needed to explain the creative use of language.

Polemics arise from many sources, not all of which are rational grounds for disagreement. And the controversy over Chomsky's *Cartesian Linguistics* has generated many complex polemical comments. I add my judgments to this by now, I hope, diminishing literature.

If we have shown anything about both Descartes and about the interpretation of Descartes vis-à-vis British empiricism, it is that the issue of learning language is not one of innate *ideas*. But it is clear, however, that innate *powers* are involved. Even in the British tradition, ideas were generated from experience by powers (conceived by Aristotle) of generating universal concepts from collections of particular instances. It is also clear that there is no difficulty with the concept of a language generating structure, for to have a power of some sort, without it being a property of some structure, strains cognitive capacities. The problem is what particular cognitive properties are given the "powers" which are innate.

Chomsky has discussed this issue in *Reflections on Language* (1975, pp. 137–136). The issue he formulates as either E-powers or R-powers. "E" stands for empiricism; "R" for rationalism. To account for learning of common sense we might postulate R-powers, "a schematism innate to the mind, that is refined and further articulated by experience." Alternatively one might propose E-powers, "the mind is equipped only with the ability to record impressions and retain faded impressions, to construct association among presented impressions, to match impressions (perhaps innately along certain innately given dimensions), to generalize along dimensions that are innate or constructed, to modify the probability of response in terms of contingencies of reinforcement defined in terms of the stimulus space, and so on."

The apparent restriction in the R-E dichotomy is that the schematism is innate in individuals and is not constructible on the bases of experience. Thus, individuals do not, the assertion is, construct the R-schematism from E-powers. It is sometimes said (Kant) that the R-schematism is a presupposition for the operation of E-powers. But, as Piaget proposes, some schematisms can be constructed and function automatically, as if innately. Perhaps Chomsky's version of linguistics is such a schematism.

We are now in a phase in psychology of rapidly expanding our notions of cognitive processes. It is an empirical fact that children have the cognitive powers to extract grammatical rules of different languages with roughly equal facility. Whether the E-powers or the R-powers alone are sufficient is a scientific problem. Chomsky admits the possibility of some combination of both powers is possible. My own preferences are to go for the combination of powers so that we would have, as Aristotle clearly worked out, both memory and inductively determined concepts and hypotheses and deductive systems in which the instances of an implication can also be identified. And the interaction of both these procedures results in schemes which can be tested against experiences of the world.

There are many easy-to-determine differentia between knowing the domains of common sense, language, physics of everyday life, and abstract physics. What is directly seen or heard, within the limits of the "innate" capacities of the organism, may result in some sort of structure and rule properties. Where these capacities' limits are exceeded, recorded speech and other physical events bring past or temporally separate events to mind at one time and thus may be processed by the innate structures. If the "innateness" hypothesis resolves itself into simply determining the properties of the mechanism of language processing, then I judge that the whole "innateness" controversy was a hard way to come to these conclusions.

I judge that, if there had been historically a movement called "Cartesian linguistics," it would have been strongly in the rationalistic movement and thus would have the general characteristics Chomsky attributes to it.

Appendix

CHRONOLOGY OF EVENTS IN DESCARTES'S LIFE*

1596	René Descartes born at La Haye, in Touraine (March 31).
1606	Enters the Jesuit college of La Flèche.
1611	Hears of Galileo's having discovered the satellites of Jupiter.
1614	Leaves La Flèche.
1616	Takes his degree in law at Poitiers.
1618	Goes to Holland to serve in the army under Prince Maurice of Nassau.
	Makes the acquaintance of Beeckman at Breda.
1619	Leaves Holland. Attends the Emperor Ferdinand's coronation.
	Joins the Duke of Bavaria's forces.
	There flashes upon him the idea of extending the method of analytical geometry to other studies (November 10).
1622	Returns to France
1623–25	Travels in Italy.
1625–28	After returning to France, stays sometimes in the country and sometimes in Paris.
1628	Composes the *Rules for the Guidance of the Mind*.
	Leaves for Franeker, Holland, in the autumn.
1630	Moves to Amsterdam. Matriculates at Leyden University.
1632	Moves to Deventer.
1633	Returns to Amsterdam. Learns of Galileo's condemnation by the Inquisition.
1634	Suppresses his treatise on *The World*.
1635	His natural daughter is christened.
	Moves to Utrecht.
1636	Moves to Leyden.
1637	The *Discourse on Method* is published (in June).
	Moves to Santport.
1640	Returns to Leyden.
	Bereaved of his father and his daughter.
1641	Moves to Endegeest.
	The *Meditations* are published (in August).
1641–43	Quarrels with Voëtius, Rector of Utrecht University.

*From Anscombe & Geach, 1954.

1642   Utrecht University officially decides in favour of the old philosophy.
1643   Frequently visits Princess Elizabeth of Bohemia.
        Moves to Egmond-op-den-Hoef.
        Judgment is pronounced against him by the Utrecht magistrates.
1644   Visits France (May to November).
        The *Principles of Philosophy* are published (in July).
        On his return to Holland, takes up permanent residence at Egmond-Binnen near
        Alkmaar, till he leaves Holland in 1649.
1645   After receiving a letter from Descartes, the Utrecht magistrates forbid printed
        discussion of the new philosophy.
1647   Has trouble with Leyden University.
        Visits France in the summer, and talks with Pascal.
        Is awarded (but does not receive) a pension from the King of France.
1648   Again visits France, but leaves hurriedly upon the outbreak of the Fronde rebel-
        lion.
1649   Leaves Holland for Sweden at the invitation of Queen Christina.
        Publishes the *Treatise on the Passions* (November).
1650   Dies at Stockholm on February 11.

References

Aarsleff, H. The history of linguistics and Professor Chomsky. *Language,* 1970, 46(3),
    570–585.
Anscombe, G.E.M. & Geach, P.T. *Descartes.* London: Nelson, 1954.
Atherton, M. & Schwartz, R. Linguistics innateness and its evidence. In S. P. Stich (Ed.),
    Innate Ideas. Berkeley: University of California Press, 1975.
Balz, A.G.A. *Cartesian studies.* New York: Columbia University Press, 1951.
Beck, L. J. *The method of Descartes.* Oxford: Clarendon Press, 1952.
Bergmann, G. *Philosophy of science.* Madison: University of Wisconsin Press, 1956.
Brunschvicg, L. *René Descartes.* Paris: Les Editions Rieder, 1937.
Chomsky, N. *Cartesian linguistics.* New York: Harper & Row, 1966.
Chomsky, N. *Language and mind.* New York: Harcourt Brace & World, 1968.
Chomsky, N. *Reflections on language.* New York: Pantheon Books, 1975.
Chomsky, N. Recent contributions to the theory of innate ideas. in *Synthèse* (Vol. 17),
    Dordrecht, The Netherlands: D. Reidel, 1967. Reprinted in S. P. Stich (Ed.), *Innate
    Ideas.* Berkeley: University of California Press, 1975.
Cordemoy, G., de *A philosophical discourse concerning speech.* (Englished out of French;
    translator unknown.) Printed for the Royal Society, 1668. New York: AMS Press, 1974.
Descartes, R. *Oeuvres philosophiques.* (F. Alquié, Ed.) Paris: Editions Garnier, 1967.
Descartes, R. Notae in programma. In C. Adam & P. Tannery (Eds.), *Oeuvres de Des-
    cartes* (Vol. 8). Paris: Leopold Cerf, 1897–1913, pp. 357–358.
Descartes, R. *Descartes's philosophical writings.* (N. K. Smith, Ed. and trans.) London:
    Macmillan, 1952.
Ewert, A. *The French language.* London: Faber & Faber, 1933.
Henle, M., Jaynes, J., & Sullivan, J. J. *Historical conceptions of psychology.* New York:
    Springer, 1973.
Katz, J. J. *The philosophy of language.* New York: Harper & Row, 1966.
Lanson, G., & Truffau, P. *Manuel illustré de la littérature française.* Paris: Hachette, 1953.

Lyons, J. *Noam Chomsky*. New York: Viking Press, 1970.

Moskowitz, B. A. The acquisition of language. *Scientific American,* 1978, *239*, 92–108.

Plato, Timaeus. In E. Hamilton & H. Cairns (Eds.), *Collected dialogues of Plato*. New York: Bollingen Foundation, 1961.

Quine, W. V. Linguistics and philosophy. In S. Hook (Ed.), *Language and philosophy*. New York: New York University Press, 1969. Reprinted in S. P. Stich (Ed.), *Innate ideas*. Berkeley: University of California Press, 1975.

Smith, N. K. *New studies in the philosophy of Descartes*. London: Russell & Russel, 1963.

Sullivan, J. J. On cartesian linguistics. In *The roots of American psychology* (Vol. 291). New York: Annals of the New York Academy of Sciences, 1977, pp. 287–305.

Verhaar, J. W. M., S. J. Philosophy and linguistic theory. *Language Sciences,* 1971, *14*, 1–11.

10

John W. Black

EDWARD WHEELER SCRIPTURE, PHONETICIAN

The writer is tempted to say that he is naming a new rhetorical device, "successive augumentation," and is illustrating it in this chapter. Scripture ended his autobiography (1936) with the cryptic sentences:

> I notice a paucity of personal details in my account. I have forgotten most of them and I am not interested in the rest; I do not think the reader would be interested either. In order to be dated and placed I have to state that I was born in 1864 in a village in New Hampshire, U.S.A. (p. 261)

The first elaboration follows. E[dward] W[heeler] Scripture, born in Mason, New Hampshire, May 21, 1864, died in Bristol, England, July 31, 1945. Many details of his life, particularly dates, moves, and motivations for the moves are not known, only conjectured. He was graduated from City College in New York, studied at Berlin and Zurich, and after commencing his study in 1888 was granted the Ph.D. at Leipzig. Following a chaotic academic career he earned the M.D. at Munich. The chaotic career was at Yale where he and his Chairman, psychologist George T. Ladd, were dismissed following a decade of intradepartmental and philosophical struggles, essentially armchair psychology versus the laboratory. While at Yale, Scripture published annual volumes of *Studies from the Yale Laboratory* commencing 1892–1893; *Thinking, Feeling, Doing* (1895), which he considered a popular approach to psychology (the second edition, 1907, was written at Columbia and carried the identifica-

---

John W. Black • Professor Emeritus, Department of Speech and Hearing Sciences, The Ohio State University, Columbus, Ohio 43210.

tion M.D.); *The New Psychology* (1898); and *Elements of Experimental Phonetics* (1902), a landmark in phonetics. The *Studies* included reports of recent experiments by Scripture and his students and enlightening sections, "New Apparatus and Methods," by Scripture. Further, the volume for 1900 included a preliminary version of the *Elements*.

The topics of the *Elements* are (a) "Curves of Speech," (b) "Perception of Speech," (c) "Production of Speech," and (d) a vague term, "Factors of Speech." (a) The "curves" treats measurement, but more particularly the obtaining of the records (curves) as a preliminary to measurement. Scripture appreciated the rate of change from one event to another in talking and the need for delicate equipment that could follow the attending movements. Optical systems were to be preferred over mechanical ones. The artisan-character of Scripture unfolds throughout this portion of the *Elements*. (b) "Perception of speech" leaves much to the reader and the future. Scripture acknowledges the ear as the first agent in hearing and is respectful of Helmholtz's explanation of hearing. Then he posits association as an important aspect of perception, first associations of sound and second ones of meaning. (c) The "production of speech" returns to Topic 1 and reliance on the Marey tambour. Both the articulation of sounds (palatography) and the study of respiration require precise mechanical equipment. The treatment seems to anticipate Stetson's work (1957) with mechanical and early electronic equipment. (d) "Factors of speech" is a topic that permits a range of skepticism and discussions of relevant theoretical matters. The popular classifications of speech sounds are thrown open to question. Voice—its loudness, duration, and melody—is treated at length. The inharmonic notion of vowel production and the concept of the centroid (borrowed from mechanics) are presented.

Scripture's *Researches in Experimental Phonetics: The Study of Speech Curves* (1906) was his epochal work after the *Elements*. This was an elaboration of earlier "positions," "hypotheses," and methods. The procedure for determining the "mouth resonance" (inharmonic) is clearly spelled out, sufficiently so for an undergraduate student to follow if he has a speech curve before him.

Scripture's interest in speech pathology was evident in the *Elements*. Carl Seashore was Scripture's only student who "carried on." He, in turn, was a guiding influence for Travis and a host of speech pathologists who "grew up" academically in the Midwest of the United States. The possibility is tantalizing that Wundt (Leipzig) held this a topic of interest, too. However, aided by research grants from the Carnegie Institution, Scripture had a second opportunity to study in Europe and to note carefully the relation between medicine and speech. He studied medicine, concentrating on speech pathology, and was granted the M.D. degree (Munich) by 1907. He practiced in New York, Austria, and England until interrupted by war and age. His works included *Stuttering and Lisping* (1912) with the second edition titled *Stuttering, Lisping, and Correction of the Speech of the Deaf* (1923), and *Study of English Speech by New Methods of Phonetic Investigation* (1923).

Scripture is known as an "inharmonic vowel theorist." This identification ignores the mathematician, the artisan, the creator of a speech laboratory, the student of speech perception, the patient "surveyor" of microscopic areas, and the medically trained practicing speech pathologist.

The remainder of this chapter is a further augmentation of the foregoing. Scripture's first interest was speech, the behaviors of speaking and listening. Both the words *psychology* and *experimental phonetics* were new. He could do the same work under either banner. He chose *experimental phonetics* and for his laboratories simply *phonetics*; hence the emphasis in this elaboration will be on the phonetician and the book that placed him at the pinnacle of experimental phonetics: *The Elements*. Three questions are asked: What is experimental phonetics? What characterized Scripture as a dominant force in the rise of experimental phonetics? What shaped the topics of his *Elements*? These are convenient questions. Underlying the treatments of them are observations the thrust of which implies dimensions of a giant (Scripture) and the inseparability of his topic (language) and human behavior.

Intentionally or not, Scripture influenced the scope of *experimental phonetics*. This domain of academicians who hold singular interests in the production, transmission, and reception of speech he treated broadly and in a pioneering manner. Perhaps he mirrored relationships and activities that were taken for granted in Wundt's laboratory at Leipzig. In any event, he has helped scholars on at least two continents organize a variety of research interests and teaching activities under experimental phonetics. Relatively few writers in this field have ventured to cope with such a vast array of interrelated topics as did the multifaceted Scripture.

Curtis, in his essay, "The Rise of Experimental Phonetics" (1954), treated his subject with awe, emphasizing that experimental phonetics is

generic and subtends the interest of many contributors who do not view
themselves as phoneticians:

> The field is hard to define and circumscribe ... in part because the terms have
> different meanings for different people, and, in part because many of the
> important contributors to the field have been, and still are, persons who have
> not regarded themselves primarily as experimental phoneticians. Some of the
> most important contributions have come from physicists, psychologists, and
> physiologists, and communications engineers, as well as from researchers in
> speech and linguistics. (p. 349)

Other writers who have ventured to use the title experimental phonetics
without a restricting modifier include Gray (1936), Panconcelli-Calzia
(1924), and Rousselot (1894). It was also the title chosen by Miron under
which to publish selected papers of Fairbanks (1966). Two issues of the
short-lived *Archives of Speech* carried papers under the heading "Studies
in Experimental Phonetics" (Tiffin, 1934, 1937) and a third might well
have done so (Cowan, 1936). Some of these broad-spectrum publications
have a direct and probably real significance in the present context. Doubtless Scripture's closest bond with psychology subsequent to his career at
Yale was through Carl E. Seashore who, in his dual position of psychologist and long-time dean of a graduate school, did much to foster experimental studies in speech. As a teacher and through other intermediate
ones he influenced the directions and methodologies of many authors
named here and others who studied at Iowa and related laboratories after
1897.

It would be futile to attempt to enumerate all the titles of scholarly
works that relate to segments of experimental phonetics. Ladefoged was
precise in his title *Three Areas of Experimental Phonetics* (1967). The
writer has made many imaginative quests and ventured speculations
about the origin of the name *experimental phonetics*. Persons who
worked with Stephen Jones, University of London, are quite likely to use
it in their shop talk. The few students who studied with Jones and
Seashore simultaneously during a brief spell in Iowa City may have been
unaware that the term was not universal jargon. Only now, too late, the
question arises: Whence came experimental phonetics with the scope
accorded it be Scripture? It is common currency in Belgrade (Djorje Kos-
tič); he studied with Jones. Was Scripture the progenitor? Rousselot?[1] Or

---

[1]Millet (1925) quotes Scripture, "[Rousselot] père de la phonétique expérimentale" (p. 31).
Tagliaviani (1966) makes a similar attribution; however, this one seems to relate to a small
study of a dialect of pronunciation.

did it all start with Wundt? Sweet used the term in 1899 (Fry, 1969). The
writer turned to Svend Smith. He produced half a dozen interesting titles
from his university library (Hamburg). All fell within a limited span, 1890
plus or minus three. No claim is being made that Scripture invented the
term, only that he helped to shape the subject matter. The Ladefoged
contribution is of special interest. His first two "areas", respiration and
vowel quality, are normal ones for a treatment of experimental approaches to speech. The third one, "Units in the Perception and Production of Speech," suggests a psychology laboratory, possibly Wundt's.
One of the hallmarks of the term after Scripture, whatever else its scope,
is a psychological bent.

One offshoot of Scripture's experimental phonetics was Seashore's
application of the methods to music and the development of an approach
to the psychology of music. Berry (1965) includes the tonoscope and the
Iowa pitch–range audiometer, among the tests and psychological apparatus that he [Scripture] devised, alone or in collaboration. Importantly, Seashore's pioneering work and the attending series of studies
summarized in the *Psychology of Music* (1938) coincided with the development of doctoral study in the field. The effect was felt throughout
the United States. Whether one was studying the vibrato in singing (Metfessel, 1932) or speaking (Gray, 1926), the genesis lay with Scripture. This
is only illustrative of the many lines that emerged from experimental
phonetics and added subject matters for inquiries and teaching.

Another offshoot was speech correction or speech pathology. This
was a recurrent topic in Scripture's book and one that was nurtured by
Seashore and developed largely through his efforts. Material was drawn
for the *Elements*, as convenient, from the behaviors of stuttering and
aphasia. For Scripture these provided appropriate topics for both the
psychology laboratory and experimental phonetics. This relationship continues in many continental centers with both subject matters being associated with the curricula of medicine. In the 1920s, the study of abnormal speech became a specialization in the United States and concurrently—
and almost independently—became one for Scripture, who was to spend a
considerable portion of his adult life as a medically trained logopedist and
phoniatrist in Europe.

These "offshoots" may be seen also as seminal from the viewpoint of
Scripture. The preface of *The New Psychology* (1905) dated 1897, ends
with an ackknowledgment of the contributions of "Dr. C. E. Seashore,
my friend and assistant." This is restated in a relevant substantive context

in an autobiographical essay (1936) tempered by the insights and distillations gained subsequently during three productive decades:

> This line of work aroused much interest at the time; my pupil, assistant, and friend, Seashore, with his group in Iowa has continued it in his brillant investigations of speech and vocal music. *I have never been able to understand why experimental psychology never attempts to use the methods of experimental phonetics for investigating the most complete form of expression that the mind possesses.* (p. 242, italics added)

Clearly, for Scripture, the experimental study of the production of language was equivalent to the study of man himself.

Apart from recent broad treatments of oral-language behavior designated experimental phonetics and Ladefoged's book, several segmental ones seem to reflect parts of Scripture. Three of these are termed merely phonetics. Kaiser's (1957) represents the interests of a physiologist who admittedly turned phonetician. Malmberg's terse systematic treatment (1954, French; 1963, English) is similarly scientific with an overlay of humanistic study. Rosetti (1967) writing for a Roumanian audience, retains the scientific orientation and adds more humanism than Malmberg. Lehiste (1967) restricts her focus to acoustic phonetics, as does Ladefoged (1962) and Pulgram (1964). Trendelenburg (1950), Fant (1960), and Flanagan (1965) from one to the next present increasing depth in treatments of the acoustics of speech, with Flanagan including considerable perceptual data. Russell (1928), Jensen (1961), and Castle (1964) illustrate approaches to singular elements of experimental phonetics the vowels, the tonemes of "nonphonemic language" (Norwegian), and the perception of filtered vowels, respectively. Illustrative of other extremes are the encyclopedic works of Tagliaviani (1966) and Malmberg (1968). The former gives a "history of continental phonetics in biography" and the latter adds unity in point of view to Kaiser's long-awaited anthology of phonetics (1957). Moses (1964) presents an organized compendium of names and topics associated with phonetics, in many regards an elaboration of Curtis's terse essay.

Obviously, there is hardly a single field of experimental phonetics. Realizing this, one looks again at the title coined by Scripture and appreciates anew the plural form *Elements*. A prevailing model at Leipzig was provided by the burgeoning science of chemistry. This was to lead Titchenor to the elements of psychology and a dominant school of psychology in America and to provide a pattern of organization for several other "schools" for three or more decades (Wickens, 1968). Thus, through substituting equals for equals, one might read in Scripture "a systematic treatise'' or experimental approaches to human behavior. Only a brave man would have treated as many elements as he did. This bravery was tempered with caution, the caution that attends respect for facts. For example, he was reluctant to attibute primacy to a single name: "The original machine for reproducing speech *seems* to have been the phonograph of Edison" (1877, p. 32). "The resolution of an empirically obtained speech curve into a series of harmonics by the Fourier analysis *seems* to have been first performed by Schneebeld" (1878–1879) (p. 75, italics added).

The thrust of this chapter has been to delimit the wide scope of experimental phonetics as viewed by Scripture. The overtones relate to both Scripture the man and his treatment of specific topics. In turn, later discussions of these will also relate to the range of Scripture's topic.

Who was Scripture? In writing of himself he describes a psychologist and a psychophysicist (1936):

> Entering Wundt's psychological laboratory in Leipzig in 1888, I learned to listen to little ivory balls striking a board and to say whether I perceived a difference between two sounds or not. . . . *The logical conclusion is: only statements based on measurements are reliable.* The corollary is: "statements without measurements are not worth listening to." (pp. 231–232)

It is not surprising, then, to find mathematical equations used generously in this autobiography:

> While at Yale I wrote a popular book, *Thinking, Feeling, Doing*, in which I showed that knowledge of mental life could be obtained only by making experiments and that the productions of the arm-chair psychology had no more value than medieval speculations concerning how many angels could dance on the point of a needle. . . . A second book, *The New Psychology*, was an exposition of the psychology of consciousness from a strictly experimental point of view. A third book, *Elements of Experimental Phonetics*, was a systematic treatise on this science in which I aimed to include everything that has been done in the experimental investigation of speech. My work at Yale on speech was essentially psychological; my book on experimental phonetics might have just as well been designated as one on the experimental psychology of speech. (pp. 241–242)

Scripture was a humanist as well as a scientist. His allusions to Shaw, Milton, Goethe, Hardy, Burton, Socrates, Bridges, Browning, and Herrick, among others, reflect a penetrating and sympathetic understanding of the artist-philosopher. In his *Analysis of Speech Curves*, he published detailed measures of speech. These were not based on "the speech of the town crier" or utterances of the vernacular but on representative samples of the speech of acclaimed artists in use of the voice, for example, Joseph Jefferson. The writer recalls a conversation with Agostino Gemelli, experimental phonetician of Milan, "I chose to work with vowels because the best voices in the world come here to sing at La Scala. They record vowels for me."

Scripture was a perfectionist and demanded to know the cause of human behavior to the extent that it is possible that this can be probed. As he says, he became so interested in learning about human beings anatomically, physiologically, and pathologically that he took up the systematic study of medicine. This was late in his professional life and led to his specialization in matters of speech correction. This enthusiasm for speech as the most informative behavior to trace to its sources might have been anticipated from the *Elements*. The references there to his son's developing speech seem to be ones of a perfectionist-observer working as an amateur. Possibly he will drive himself to do what is necessary to heighten his exactness.[2]

By 1929, he had established himself as a Professor of Experimental Phonetics at the University of Vienna. He continued to hold his position until 1933 when he took up residence in London. Articles by him appeared in *Nature* and other British journals as contributions from the Phonetics Laboratory, University of London (Berry, 1965).

This was not his first residence in England: "In 1912 I transferred my work to London and founded a Laboratory of Speech Neurology" (1936). Indeed, Professor Abercrombie is only one person of many having difficulty in keeping track of the peripatetic Scripture. His son, the late Edward W. Scripture, Jr., doubted (1963) the records of Vanderbilt Clinic, New York City which showed the father to be in New York in 1917 to 1918. The son served in the AEF in France during World War I and relished the British cigarettes his father sent him from London. He also heard that his father "subsequently spent some time in Vienna and in Russia." The son served in the armed forces during World War II as well and visited his father in England "two or three times" (1969).

Doubtless Scripture's professional career was greatly influenced by the conflict at Yale that terminated the services of both him and Ladd. Some insight into this comes from Seashore's autobiography (1930). The

---

[2]Scripture's whereabouts from year to year are hardly of first-order concern in a treatment of his contribution to phonetics. Abercrombie notes:

> He [Scripture] attended the Second International Congress of Phonetic Sciences in London in 1935, which is where I first saw him, I think. In the program of papers (he spoke on "The Nature of Speech") he was described as being from Vienna, though a list of participants gives him a rather strange address: The Phonetic Laboratory, 62 Leytonstone Road, London (1969).

classical struggle between Ladd and Scripture at Yale was one that recurs in academic sectors. The traditional known professor, Ladd, is challenged by the junior upstart, Scripture:

> In May, 1895, I turned in my thesis to Ladd, not to Scripture, although the work was all done under him and had his approveal. Again the President should have recognized in Scripture the new approach to mental science, of which Scripture was champion. Instead he threw the baby out with the bath. Scripture came to Yale with good training and a splendid grasp of the approaches to the "new psychology." He was temperamental and enthusiastic. With the students he was both patient and critical. . . . I am the only one of his pupils in that earliest period who survived the ordeal and remained clearly in the field of experimental psychology. (p. 251)

What did Scripture write as experimental phonetics? The *Elements* (1902) is uneven from one to another through four topics. The first one, "Curves of Speech," is superb. Scripture blends the skills of a watchmaker with the erudition and exactness of a historian who is able to relate and interpret people and events; he states clearly—and often restates in mathematical terms—the accelerating series of psychological and physical explanations of the sound waves that accompany speech. His documentation is complete. Of special significance, the graphic explanations of successive devices for studying the speech waves should lead the novice to understanding them—and overcome a possible awe and fear of devices and sound waves—without treating the expert deferentially. The authenticity that comes from making appropriate adjustments of every device that is described and of evaluating every output is evident.

In the treatment of "Curves of Speech" Scripture reveals much that is part of the Scripture legend. First, he looked for evidence at different levels or more specifically at the appropriate level:

> Many of the main features of the speech curves can be obtained by inspection without measurment; very much more can be obtained by simple measurements. (p. 63)

The chapters point to ever-increasing exactness in measurement with the successive instrumental developments. Second, although he was respectful of the Fourier analysis, he leaned toward an inharmonic explanation of the physical dimension of quality or timbre of a vowel:

> The Fourier analysis is often the only way of locating the tone or tones in a complex, even though they do not stand in harmonic relations. (p. 75)

Third, his reputed skill as an artisan is substantiated over and over. How it is that this respect for exactness and patience in handling miniature hardware was to be perpetuated to his students and their students cannot be read, but it can be imagined to be the effect of the "weight of the idea" as generated and expressed by an innovative philosopher-craftsman (the words "weight of the idea" come into the following paragraph).

The treatment of the second topic, "Perception of Speech," is somewhat speculative and reaches the levels of credibility of the earlier discussion only when the author can rely on his experience in the laboratory. This occurs with explanations of the properties of tone (pitch, duration, and intensity) and with tangential allusions to verifiable psychophysical measures. The references to behaviors of stuttering and to ones that attend aphasia are of interest largely to the extent that they anticipate Scripture's subsequent identification with medical study and a career in speech correction. The speculations of this section incorporated the "weight of the idea" used above. This phrase illustrates the frequent recourses to mechanics that Scripture used in explaining perception. Such analogies are not limited to one historical period. They were common, however, with him. The "time required" to achieve perception was another, and more tangible, measure. More profitable lines of explanation led to reliance on various associations. Although this topic continues to be fruitful, it would be merely opportunistic to credit Scripture with instances that remain in vogue and ignore the remainder.[3]

Scripture's basic attribution of the perception of speech was to the ear. Without considering any explanation of speech perception as final, he was tolerant of the theory advocated by Helmholtz:

---

[3]The writer tested two topics of Scripture's treatment of association, namely that words perceived in response to aural stimuli are (a) similar in sound to the stimuli, and (b) similar in meaning to the stimuli. Panels of judges appraised the errors made by listeners in responding to each of 100 words. The judgments were made on a 1 to 9 equal-appearing-intervals scale with 1 indicating "close" relationship and 9, "no discernible" relationship. The mean score assigned by a panel of 15 judges, all students of phonetics who worked independently, to the error-responses in the instance of "sounding alike" was 4.8; and by another panel, all students of psychology who worked independently, in regard to meaning was 7.5. There were 3,180 error-responses representing 1,561 different errors. The assigned ratings were weighted by frequency of occurrence for computing the means. Obviously association in regard to the sound of the word is real. Incorrect responses resemble the correct one in sound. A third test of the power of association is underway. Pairs of syllables are being viewed for 1.5 s/pair. After viewing six pairs, subjects are shown one member of each pair and asked to reproduce the other member. The effects of recency and primacy are evident. Also some of the pairs of nonsense syllables form English words. There is obviously a strong influence of association. The work is also being conducted in English. The strength of association will be compared to the power of both recency and primacy.

The manner of analysis by the nerve endings in the internal ear is largely
unknown; tones like those from some musical instruments are supposed to be
analyzed into a harmonic series on a principle of resonance. The complicated
vibrations in speech sounds, especially in the consonants, presents difficulties
to such a harmonic analysis; *these difficulties may not be fatal and the theory
is still a plausible one*. (1902, p. 82, italics added)

The third topic, "Production of Speech," is discussed largely in the
context of the Marey tambour (1878) and palatography. The former relates to movements and registering them, especially ones that accompany
respiration and articulation; the latter, palatography, provides a tool to
differentiate among languages and dialects of pronunciation. In treatments that relate to his own practices in his laboratory, Scripture seems to
anticipate *Stetson* (1951), but no connection has been found. The possibility of mutual indebtedness to Rousselot remains. The craftsmanship in the
use of the tambour that is evident from the vivid descriptions is impressive. Readers in an electronic era may well view Scripture's treatments of
the procedures of a mechanical age as a prelude to practices that attend
electromyography, X-ray laminography, and high-speed motion pictures,
and many sense that the eras have more in common than is often implied
by *current practice* versus *former practice*. In the instance of palatography, exhaustively treated by Scripture—in spite of the efforts of many
researchers, past and contemporary, and the apparently valid logic of the
approach—there remains a gulf between the evidence at hand and that
which would be admissible in a courtroom.

The fourth and final topic, "Factors of Speech," is one that permits
Scripture the phonetician to question the vogue in classifying phonemes
and to theorize about the nature of speech sounds. This is a topic that is
central in the Scripture legend. He is viewed as an iconoclast. Many
sounds, including the vowels, he took to be comprised of a cord tone and
a mouth tone, independent in pitch. Of Helmholtz and his contrary view
he wrote, "[Helmholtz] was greatly influenced in his theory by his views
of the action of the ear." Many of Scripture's apparently unorthodox
views relative to categorizing sounds would go unchallenged by contemporary writers of textbooks in the field of phonetics. (1) Since a vowel is
changing continuously, why distinguish vowels from diphthongs on the
basis of change? (2) / m, n, ŋ, r, l / are not vowels, but it is unfortunate to
name them merely consonants. (3) Whispered sounds are not synonymous with surd sounds. These few evidences of an interest in transcription
phonetics must be viewed alongside: "[Speech is] not made up of separate
elements placed side by side like letters," or again, "I do not believe,

however, that a division of the flow of speech into separate blocks (termed syllables) has the slightest justification or the slightest meaning." Lest the reader conclude that Scripture was characteristically negative in his approach to phonetics, special note should be taken of his support of melody and rhythm in speech. He viewed these as functions of pitch, duration, and stress, and his treatments of them mark important pioneering efforts.

Obviously, for this writer the high point of *The Elements* lies in "Curves of Speech." Fortunately, Scripture demonstrated that his reatment of this topic was no passing fancy; he made it the topic of his next book (1906). This book may have more wave-to-wave illustrations than any other phonetics book. They illustrate the quality of work that was possible with a Marey tambour and a kymograph. Perhaps one must go to Gemelli to find the equivalent curves obtained by photographing the output of an oscilloscope. Another feature of *Researches in Experimental Phonetics* is a step-by-step guide to an analysis of a speech curve. The writer made a mechanical analysis of the successive waves of vowels in the mid-1930s. The analysis was made with the help of a Henrici analyzer, a photograph of which appears in Seashore (1938). The curves that were analyzed were preserved. Successive classes of students reanalyzed the curves, following the procedures spelled out by Scripture. The exercise completed, students could read *Researches* insightfully.

What is the impact of Scripture? His influence goes beyond the *Elements*, but the intent of the present chapter restricts the discussion of his influence to that of the areas treated by the *Elements*. Largely on the basis of the *Elements* he has influenced the character and name of an academic specialization, experimental phonetics. He has aided in linking speech and psychology among students and teachers of both. Through emphasizing and dignifying shopwork, he has added to the responsibilities of many teachers' tasks that might in another tradition have been assigned to laboratory technicians and assistants. Although Scripture learned some terminology from other workers, he seems to have originated several terms. Students make melody curves, a heritage from "curves of melody," and refer to "simultaneous and successive fusion," possibly unaware of Scripture's legacy to Seashore and in turn to Metfessel. Some use the word *centroid* as a calculated measure related to a formant. Here the lineage is from Scripture and through Seashore and Tiffin, and the computation is a weighted mean. This, however, is an analogy, an appropriate one, drawn from either of two uses by Scripture: (a) "maximum energy in on-going speech'' and (b) the relative weight or intensity of an idea. In either of these senses one might draw another analogy to say that Scripture himself was something of a centroid. He was a high point, a concentration of energy, and a generator of maximum ideas in the history of a science of speech.

It is dangerous to try to describe the personality of Scripture, a scientist, humanist, and humanitarian. Photographs suggest that he was a neat, perhaps dapper, man who might be at home with a monocle. Two rifts are open history, the one with Ladd at Yale and the legal separation from May Kirk Scripture whom he had married in Germany and who was the mother of his three children. Berry described him as "of a restless wide ranging intellect and of a restless, dynamic, albeit somewhat turbulent personality." Edward Wheeler Scripture, Jr., liked the words so much that he sent them back to Professor Berry in quotation marks and with praise for her writing. Let the case rest with the good fortune of phoneticians to have inherited Scripture's experimental works from the turn of the century.

References

Abercrombie, D. Personal correspondence, December 8, 1969.

Berry, M. F. Historical vignettes of leadership in speech and hearing: I. Speech pathology. *Asha*, 1965, 7.

Castle, W. E. *The effect of narrow-band filtering on the perception of certain English vowels*. The Hague: Mouton, 1964.

Cowan, M. *Archives of speech: Pitch and intensity characteristics of stage speech*. Iowa City: University of Iowa Press, 1936.

Curtis, J. F. The rise of experimental phonetics. In K. Wallace (Ed.), *A history of speech education in America*. New York: Appleton-Century-Crofts, 1954.

Fairbanks, G. In S. Miron (Ed.), *Experimental phonetics: Selected articles*. Urbana: University of Illinois Press, 1966.

Fant, G. *Acoustic theory of speech production*. The Hague: Mouton, 1960.

Flanagan, J. L. *Speech analysis synthesis and perception*. New York: Academic Press, 1965.

Fry, D. B. Personal correspondence, November 19, 1969.

Gray, G. W. An experimental study of the vibrato in speech. *Quarterly Journal of Speech Education*, 1926, *12*, 296–333.

Gray, G. W. (Ed.), *Studies in experimental phonetics*. Baton Rouge: Lousiana State University Press, 1936.

Jensen, M. K. *Tonemicity*. Bergen-Oslo: Norwegian Universities Press, 1961.

Kaiser, L. *Manual of phonetics*. Amsterdam: North Holland, 1957.

Ladefoged, P. *Elements of acoustic phonetics*. Chicago: University of Chicago Press, 1962.

Ladefoged, P. *Three areas of experimental phonetics*. London: Oxford University Press, 1967.

Lehiste, I. *Readings in acoustic phonetics*. Cambridge: M.I.T. Press, 1967.

Malmberg, B. *La phonétique*. Paris: Presses Universitaire de France, 1954.

Malmberg, B. *Manual of phonetics*. Amsterdam: North Holland, 1968.

Metfessel, M. *The vibrato in artistic voices*. Iowa City: University of Iowa Studies in the Psychology of Music, *I*, 1932.

Millet, A. *Précis d'expérimentation phonétique*. Paris: Henri Didier, 1925.

Moses, E. R., Jr. *Phonetics: History and interpretation*. Englewood Cliffs, N.J.: Prentice-Hall, 1964.

Panconcelli-Calzia, G. *Die experimentelle Phonetik und ihre Anwendung auf die Sprachwissenschaft*. Berlin, 1924.

Pulgram, E. *Introduction to the spectography of speech*. The Hague: Mouton, 1964.

Rosetti, A. *Introducere in fonetica*. Bucharest: Editura Stiinfica, 1967.

Rousselot, P. La phonétique expérimentale. *Bulletin de l'Institut Catholique de Paris,* 1894.

Russell, G. O. *The vowel*. Columbus: Ohio State University Press, 1928.

Russell, G. O. *Speech and voice*. New York: Macmillan, 1931.

Schneebeli. Expériences avec le phonoautograph. *Archives des Sciences Physiques et Naturellas de Genève*, 1878 (Nouvelle période) *LXIV*, 79.

Schneebeli. Sur la théorie du timbre et particulièrement des voyelles. *Archives des Sciences Physiques et Neturelles de Genère*, 1879 (III période) *I*, 149.

Scripture, E. W. *Thinking, feeling, doing*. New York: G. D. Putnam's Sons, 1895. (Second edition, 1907.)

Scripture, E. W. *The new psychology*. New York: Charles Scribner's Sons, 1898. (Second edition, 1905.)

Scripture, E. W. *Elements of experimental phonetics*. New York: Charles Scribner's Sons, 1902.

Scripture, E. W. (Ed.), *Studies from Yale psychological laboratory* (Vols 1–10). New Haven: Yale University Press, 1893–1902.

Scripture, E. W. *Researches in experimental phonetics: The study of speech curves*. Washington: The Carnegie Institution of Washington, 1906.

Scripture, E. W. Treatment of stuttering. *Journal of the American Medical Association*, 1911, 1168–1171.

Scripture, E. W. *Stuttering and lisping and correction of the speech of the deaf*. New York: Macmillan, 1912. (Second edition, 1923).

Scripture, E. W. Study of English by new methods of phonetic investigation. London: Oxford University Press, 1923.

Scripture, E. W. Autobiography. In C. Murchison (Ed.), *History of psychology in autobiography* (Vol. 3). Worcester: Clark University Press, 1936.

Scripture, E. W., Jr. Personal correspondence between E. W. Scripture, Jr., and M. F. Berry, 1963 and 1969.

Seashore, C. E. Autobiography. In C. Murchison (Ed.), *History of psychology in autobiography* (Vol. 1). Worcester: Clark University Press, 1930.

Seashore, C. E. (Ed.). *Studies in the psychology of music: Psychology of the vibrato in voice and instrument and objective analysis of musical performance*. Iowa City: University of Iowa Press, 1936–1937.

Seashore, C. E. *Psychology of music*. New York: McGraw-Hill, 1938.

Stetson, R. H. *Motor phonetics* (2nd ed.). Amsterdam: North Holland Publishing, 1951.

Sweet, H. *The practical study of languages*. New York: Henry Holt, 1900.

Tagliavini, C. *Glottologia* (6th ed.). Bologna: Patron, 1966.

Tiffin, J. (Ed.) *Archives of speech: Studies in experimental phonetics*. Iowa City: University of Iowa Press, 1934 and 1937.

Trendelenburg, F. *Akustic*. Berlin-Göttingen-Heidelberg: Springer Verlag, 1950.

Wickens, D. D. Personal conference, May, 1968.

11

James H. Stam

AN HISTORICAL PERSPECTIVE ON 'LINGUISTIC RELATIVITY'*

What is now commonly called the "principle of linguistic relativity" asserts a correlation between language and thinking either with regard to the specifics, the structure, the categories, or some other generalities of each. In its stronger form, it postulates that in some way the language of any given culture is the causal determinant of the patterns of thinking in that culture. In still another variation, "linguistic relativity calls attention to differences in cultural pattern, and to their importance for linguistic experience and.behavior" (Hymes, 1966, p. 114), or language and culture are viewed as reciprocally or co-determined. The principle is now best known from the works of Edward Sapir [1884–1939], professor of anthropology and linguistics in the Universities of Pennsylvania, Chicago, and Yale, and Benjamin Lee Whorf [1897–1941], a fire-prevention engineer in Hartford, Connecticut, by profession and a linguist by passionate avocation. The pertinent works were composed mainly during the 1920s and 1930s, and the hypothesis reached a broader audience through publication of collected essays by both men during the 1950s. It

*This article is a revision and expansion of a paper first delivered at the conference "The Roots of American Psychology: Historical Influences and Implications for the Future," April 28–30, 1976, sponsored by The New York Academy of Sciences. It was published in the *Annals of the New York Academy of Sciences*, 1977, *291*, pp. 306–316. Permission of The New York Academy of Sciences is gratefully acknowledged.

James H. Stam • Department of Philosophy and Religion, Upsala College, East Orange, New Jersey 07019.

was then that the position received more extensive discussion, criticism, and evaluation by anthropologists, linguists, psychologists, and philosophers. Similar hypotheses have been recurrent in the history of the philosophy of language since the eighteenth century. It is the purpose of this chapter to see what some of these previous attempts can tell us about the nature of the alleged correlation: the problems it is meant to illuminate and the errors it is intended to dispel. We will first summarize the hypothesis in the formulations of Sapir and Whorf and roughly sketch the historical links whereby it traveled from eighteenth-century Königsberg to twentieth-century Connecticut.

The best statement of the principle by Sapir is from a paper delivered in 1928 and published in 1929, "The Status of Linguistics as a Science:"

> Language is a guide to "social reality".... It powerfully conditions all our thinking about social problems and processes. Human beings do not live in the objective world alone, nor alone in the world of social activity as ordinarily understood, but are very much at the mercy of the particular language which has become the medium of expression for their society. It is quite an illusion to imagine that one adjusts to reality essentially without the use of language and that language is merely an incidental means of solving specific problems of communication or reflection. The fact of the matter is that the "real world" is to a large extent unconsciously built up on the language habits of the group. No two languages are ever sufficiently similar to be considered as representing the same social reality. The worlds in which different societies live are distinct worlds, not merely the same world with different labels attached. (p. 162)

It is evident that a causal relationship of some kind is here clearly suggested: Language *conditions* our thinking; we are *at its mercy*; and so on. It should be noted, however, that whereas the phrases "social reality" and "real world" are put into quotation marks, the *distinct worlds* to which language is related is not so set off: Sapir's stylistic device here suggests that he is simply calling upon our confused popular understanding of the former, but that he intends something more clarified with the latter. It will also be remarked that the alleged correlation is at this point very general indeed.

Sapir continues:

> The understanding of a simple poem, for instance, involves not merely an understanding of the single words in their average significance, but a full comprehension of the whole life of the community as it is mirrored in the words, or as it is suggested by their overtones. Even comparatively simple acts of perception are very much more at the mercy of the social patterns called words than we might suppose. If one draws some dozen lines, for instance, of different shapes, one perceives them as divisible into such categories as

> "straight," "crooked," "curved," "zigzag" because of the classificatory
> suggestiveness of the linguistic terms themselves. We see and hear and oth-
> erwise experience very largely as we do because the language habits of our
> community predispose certain choices of interpretation. (p. 162)

Applications of the principle are here more specific, but are of very different sorts. In the first example, the meaning of the parts—the words of a
poem—is said to derive from the whole of a language and the whole of the
relevant culture. Only in the last example is a correlation of part to part
proposed, that between word and figure identification.

A few paragraphs later, it is to the general correspondence that Sapir
returns:

> We may suspect that linguistics is destined to have a very special value for
> configurative psychology ("Gestalt psychology"), for, of all forms of culture,
> it seems that language is that one which develops its fundamental patterns with
> relatively the most complete detachment from other types of cultural pattern-
> ing. Linguistics may thus hope to become something of a guide to the under-
> standing of the "psychological geography" of culture in the large. (pp. 164–
> 165)

Sapir wrote this in the context of differentiating functional from symbolic
activities, wherein he approached without ever exactly formulating the
distinction sometimes made between sign and symbol (cf. Cassirer, 1923/
1953; Langer 1942; Percy, 1975). Although the passage is not fully clear, it
is evident that Sapir sees as the distinctive character of human language
its ability to transcend functional and one-to-one relationships, relationships in which a single sign stands for a single thought, object, or perception as a *quid pro quo*.

Whorf was more specific than Sapir in his attempts to apply the
principle to contrasts between American Indian languages and Standard
Average European—as he called everything from Italian to English—but
his formulations are also much more varied. He was apparently groping
for a philosophical terminology adequate to his meaning and, in general,
he does not display any broad or thorough acquaintance with modern
philosophical literature. Language, says Whorf, involves a "connection
of ideas" (1927b/1956, p. 35), a "segmentation of nature" (1941/1956,
p. 240), an "organization, classification, or arrangement of experience"
(1936b/1956, p. 55), "a 'geometry' of form principles characteristic of
each language" (1942/1956, p. 257). Underlying every language is a
"metaphysics" (1950/1956, p. 59), an "idea-map of language" (1928/1956,
p. 25). In Whorf, the principle of linguistic relativity is typically affirmed

in the context of such images and phrases:

> Segmentation of nature is an aspect of grammar. . . . We cut up and organize
> the spread and flow of events as we do, largely because, through our mother
> tongue, we are parties to an agreement to do so, not because nature itself is
> segmented in exactly that way for all to see". (1941/1956, p. 240).

Or again:

> We cut nature up, organize it into concepts, and ascribe significances as we do,
> largely because we are parties to an agreement to organize it in this way—an
> agreement that holds throughout our speech community and is codified in the
> patterns of our language. (1940c/1956, p. 213).

Consequently the grammarian must analyze "covert as well as overt
structure and meaning," because language and thinking both involve
covert as well as overt categories and classes, cryptotypes as well as
phenotypes (1936a–1956, p. 79; cf. 1945a/1956, pp. 88–89, 93; 1937/1956,
p. 105). And thus the purpose of "scientific grammar" must be a "deep
analysis into relations" (1945b/1956, p. 68). The correlation of language
and thought is in several places said to be unconscious: "the forms of a
person's thoughts are controlled by inexorable laws of pattern of which he
is unconscious. These patterns are the unperceived systematizations of
his own language" (1942/1956, p. 252). "The phenomena of a language are
to its own speakers largely of a background character and so are outside
the critical consciousness and control of the speaker" (1940c/1956,
p. 211). "We all, unknowingly, project the linguistic relationships of a particular language upon the universe, and SEE them there" (1942/1956,
p. 262). Throughout there is an emphasis upon pattern. What is needed,
writes Whorf, is a "Gestalt technique" to show how "different languages
differently "segment" the same situation or experience" (1940a/1956,
pp. 160, 162). Basic to language is a "configurative or pattern aspect"
(1942/1956, p. 250), "a systematic synthetic use of pattern" (1941/1956,
p. 237), "a sway of pattern over reference" (1942/1956, p. 261).

What emerges from these varied and often loose formulations is that
Whorf's point concerns the relationship of something general in language
to something general in thought and culture; only incidentally, and in
hesitant application, does it concern the correspondence between any
linguistic particular and any particular perception or conception. Allowing
Philip Wheelwright's characterization of referential—as opposed to
expressive—language as being univocal and sharp-focused (1968, 1962),
one would have to admit that there is in Whorf's own philosophical language "a sway of pattern over reference." Whorf may have lacked either

the rigor or the philosophical nomenclature to make the hypothesis more lucid, but it was such generalities of pattern that he was driving at. This is consistent with the applications Whorf himself did undertake, which involved such phenomena as the awareness of time, the awareness of agency, and the like. And it is consistent with his more direct formulation of the linguistic relativity principle itself:

> the background linguistic system (in other words, the grammar) of each language is not merely a reproducing instrument for voicing ideas but rather is itself the shaper of ideas, the program and guide for the individual's mental activity, for his analysis of impressions, for his synthesis of his mental stock in trade. . . . We dissect nature along lines laid down by our native languages. The categories and types that we isolate from the world of phenomena we do not find there because they stare every observer in the face; on the contrary, the world is presented in a kaleidoscopic flux of impressions which has to be organized by our minds—and this means largely by the linguistic systems in our minds. . . . We are thus introduced to a new principle of relativity, which holds that all observers are not led by the same physical evidence to the same picture of the universe, unless their linguistic backgrounds are similar, or can in some way be calibrated. (1940c/1956, pp. 212–214)

Or elsewhere:

> Users of markedly different grammars are pointed by their grammars toward different types of observations and different evaluations of externally similar acts of observation, and hence are not equivalent as observers but must arrive at somewhat different views of the world. . . . The participants of a given world view are not aware of the idiomatic nature of the channels in which their talking and thinking run" (1940b/1956, pp. 221–222)

We here find the same pattern of vocabulary: the *picture* of the universe, *view* of the world, *channels* of our thinking.

Let us then turn to the historical background of the hypothesis. Ignoring Vico, whose influence outside of Italy remains a somewhat misty question, we can locate the beginnings of the line leading to the Sapir–Whorf formulation in Germany during the 1760s and 1770s, particularly in the writings of Johann Georg Hamann and Johann Gottfried Herder. To his contemporaries, the obscure Hamann represented an outspoken protest against the Enlightenment in both its rationalist and empiricist versions. Although he is a most difficult writer to paraphrase or even to quote properly—he was popularly known as "the Magus of the North"—his objections as they relate to language can be summarized. Hamann ridiculed universal grammarians among the rationalists for their attempt to isolate the abstracting function of language and force its compliance with the rational and logically discursive faculties of the mind. Universal grammar, Hamann felt, tells us more about formal logic than it does about speech, and least of all does it explain the foundations of language. In an enticing epigram Hamann wrote that "poetry is the mother-tongue of the human race" (1762a/1949–1957, p. 197). Primitive poetry—which at this time referred primarily to Homer and the Old Testament—was written in a sensuous, metaphorical, sometimes ecstatic language, more allied to music and dance than to syllogistics, expressive of a different scale of human values and a distinct outlook on the world and on human existence. In such poesy Hamann found a kind of primordial wisdom embedded more deeply in the human psyche than the axioms of mathematicians or the innate ideas of metaphysicians. The empiricists did, to be sure, draw parallels between stages of language and states of mind, and thinkers like Condillac (1746) and Turgot (1750/1808–1811) projected this psychological development as the pattern for the historical progression of the human race. But for them, too, abstract reasoning was the implicit goal of this evolution: as the individual becomes more rational with maturity, so human language ages into a mechanism more efficient, more clarified, more scientific. Hamann and Herder insisted that language is not a mechanism at all and that its metamorphoses constitute differences, not improvements. Their contrast of ancient with modern languages involved an appreciation of "primitive mentality and culture," a protest against modernist ethnocentricity, no less than did Whorf's comparisons of Hopi or Shawnee with Standard Average European.

Hamann and Herder took a phrase which had been used casually in the English and French literature, "the genius of a language" or its *esprit*, and made of it something more systematic. Each language, indeed each stage in the growth of language, has its own peculiar genius, a *Sprachgeist* corresponding to the *Volksgeist* (cf. Hamann, 1762b/1949–1957, pp. 122–123; Cassirer, 1923/1953, Vol. I, pp. 143–155). Since each language has its own genius, each must be understood on its own terms, "from the inside," so to speak, as an integral whole representing a comprehensive world or view. The political implication is clear: Herder's insistence that each national character has its own integrity expressed in its language is a dissent from the then prevailing cosmopolitanism and Francophile cultural imperialism. Underlying this theme is the notion that language must be understood in organistic rather than mechanistic terms and the rejection of any functionalist explanation of language as a tool: language is not applied to a separable reality or expressive of a separate thought process, but is inextricably connected with the delineation of that reality and the shaping of such thought. This motif is continued in German romantic thinkers, in Humboldt, in Steinthal, and evident in the pages of Sapir and Whorf themselves. For example, Whorf: "We are inclined to think of language simply as a technique of expression, and not to realize that language first of all is a classification and arrangement of the stream of sensory experience which results in a certain world-order...." (1936b/ 1956, p. 55).

Similar themes abound in the writings of Wilhelm von Humboldt, though with an important Kantian ingredient. "One must not consider language as though it were a dead product," Humboldt wrote, "but far more as a producing.... Language itself is not a work (*érgon*), but an activity (*enérgeia*)" (1835/1903–1935, p. 44, p. 46). Humboldt repeatedly emphasized the active, formative character of language:

> The mutual dependence of thought and word the one upon the other makes it clear that languages are not in fact means for the presentation of a truth already recognized, but rather for the discovery of a truth previously unknown. Their diversity is not one of sounds and signs, but a diversity of the world-views themselves. (1820/1903–1935, p. 27)

In its "subjective" aspect, language is the mediation between one individual and the other individuals in his community and nation on the one hand, between the individual and the external world on the other. The various languages of different peoples, in "objective" turn, are the mediation between those peoples and universal humanity on the one hand and universal reason on the other. Thus, every language relates both "downward" to individuals and "upward" to universal rationality and humanity. Every language both generalizes and particularizes: It involves the individual speaker in something more general than himself and it particularizes common rationality in a specific world view. Within these parameters every language places its speakers within a charmed circle, which simultaneously presents a view of the world and limits the horizons of that same view (cf. 1820/1903–1935, p. 22).

The line from Humboldt to Sapir and Whorf is reasonably clear. Humboldt's philosophy of language was taken up by dozens of German authors during the nineteenth century, most eminent among them Haymann Steinthal and Friedrich Max Müller. Steinthal edited Humboldt's posthumous works, and although he tergiversated on many issues and came under the sway of Herbartian psychology, the ethno- and psycholinguistic questions, in the literal sense of those terms, always remained in the forefront of his concerns. Although Max Müller has now fallen under a nearly universal ill-repute, in his own day he was, after his emigration to Oxford, unrivaled in the English-speaking world as a popularizer of trends in linguistics and the philosophy of language. In addition, references to Humboldt and his predecessors are scattered throughout general works on language—in English and widely read—by A. H. Sayce, Abel Hovelacque, and Dwight Whitney. In 1885, Daniel G. Brinton translated and explicated one of Humboldt's articles. Accessibility in English was not that important, however, since both Sapir and his teacher, Franz Boas, were German-born. The latter knew Steinthal personally while still a student in Berlin and had an extensive acquaintance with the tradition under discussion (cf. Roger Langham Brown, 1967, pp. 13–16). In his introductory volume to the *Handbook of American Indian Languages*, Boas argued against Brinton and against the "Hypothesis of Original Correlation of [Physical] Type, Language, and Culture" (1911, pp. 11–14; cf. pp. 64–73), but it should be said that both Sapir (1933/1949, pp. 26–27) and Whorf (1936a/1956, pp. 65–73, 77–79) also rejected superficial correlations such as those Boas there rejected. Sapir did his undergraduate and early graduate work in Germanistics at Columbia before turning to anthropological studies under Boas. An early article about Herder's *Prize Essay Concerning the Origin of Language* (1907), based on his master's thesis (1905), also discussed Hamann and Humboldt. Whorf arrived at his formulations more independently: it was relatively late that he came into close contact with Sapir and became somewhat more aware of the historical background for his own hypothesis. Meanwhile, in Germany, there was a continuous parallel tradition relating language to thought and culture and coming into the twentieth century in the works of Walter Porzig, Ernst Cassirer, Jost Trier, and Leo Weisgerber (cf. Gipper, 1972; Jost, 1960; Robert L. Miller, 1968).

Three general points should be made regarding this historical sketch. First of all, it is incomplete, and especially so with regard to a French tradition going back to the seventeenth century and including what is now referred to—for better or worse—as "Cartesian linguistics" (Chomsky, 1966). So long as we leave the hypothesis in the vague terms of a correlation between language and thought, this can be found as well in the writings of an avowed Cartesian like Cordemoy, or in the *Port-Royal Grammar* or *Logic*, or in the sundry *Grammaires raisonnées* (cf. Harnois, 1928, pp. 29–42; Juliard, 1970, pp. 45–58; Kuehner, 1944). Two generalizations, however, show the contrast between these and the works of the "German tradition." First, these French works do not emphasize the ways in which the correlation is specific to individual cultures and their languages. The specifically cultural understanding of the relationship between language and thought was in the main a German contribution. Second, in these French works language is generally taken to be the mirror or reflection of thought, whereas among the Germans language and language-making are themselves formative factors in thought and in the thinking process. However much Sapir and Whorf may have hedged on this causative factor, something of it seems to be an essential ingredient in the linguistic relativity principle.

Furthermore, this rough history presents us with an apparent anomaly. Opponents of the Sapir–Whorf hypothesis have drawn, at least in part, upon the very same tradition and especially on Humboldt. To take a recent example: In *After Babel* (1975, pp. 73–109), George Steiner contrasts the tradition we are here discussing—and for which he shows great sympathy—with the universalism of Chomsky and his antecedents. Yet, Chomsky, quite properly, considers some of the same thinkers among his own philosophical forebears (1964, pp. 17–21; 1966, pp. 19–30, 57–65). His admiration for Humboldt, for example, is as much in evidence as is his distance from the Sapir–Whorf hypothesis. At the least, this paradox should awaken us to the principle of the relativity of our perspectives on the history of linguistics.

Finally, when the linguistic relativity principle is presented in its historical context, the less appropriate to it seem many of the varied psychological experiments and other devices designed since the 1950s to test its validity and probe its applications.[1] Most of the experimental probing of the Sapir–Whorf hypothesis has been done in the context of research designs which have tried to match verbal particulars (names) with perceptual particulars (colors, figures, and the like), physical stimuli with linguistic responses. For instance, Eric Lenneberg casually remarked: "Suppose, for example, that we subject English speakers to a set of physical stimuli and record their linguistic responses" (in Hoijer, 1954, pp. 266–267). This strategy for testing the hypothesis, however, is only as

---

[1]There is a convenient review of the psycholinguistic literature on the problem in Diebold (1965), pp. 258–267. Cf. also the surveys of research and literature in Roger Brown (1958), pp. 229–263; de Vito (1970), pp. 199–206; Slobin (1974), pp. 120–133; and Church (1961), pp. 123–146. For an overview of anthropological interest in the question, cf. Kroeber (1953), Tax, Eisely, Rouse, and Voegelin (1953), and Hoijer (1954). For some philosophical perspectives, cf. Part I of Hook (1969). Saporta (1961) has reprinted a number of the more important papers on linguistic relativity.

valid as the behaviorist or mechanist assumption that language is, in fact, a set of behavioral responses to physical stimuli. Yet, Whorf himself (1927a/1956, p. 41) explicitly rejected these behaviorist assumptions from his earliest writings on. Absent those assumptions, only relatively few and rather marginal utterances are obviously comparable to reactions which humans and laboratory animals roughly share when experiencing electric shocks, hot stoves, warning buzzers, and the like. "Ouch!," "Damn it!," and similar ejaculations are linguistically marginal because of their basic thoughtlessness. But it will hardly suffice to try to prove or disprove the correlation between language and thought by using as evidence language in its least thoughtful manifestations.

Many of the psychological experiments have involved color identification, recognition, and memory and color name "codability" (Brown & Lenneberg, 1954; Burnham & Clark, 1955; Rosch Heider, 1971, 1972, 1973; Lenneberg, 1953, 1961; Lenneberg & Roberts, 1956). Here again, the relation between particular perceptions and particular designations is made the test of a thesis which primarily concerns the relationship between the framework of thought and the generalities or structure of language, or even "cognitive styles" (cf. Hymes, 1961). It is vaguely like an attempt to evaluate Kant's theory of space and time as *a priori* forms of perception by measuring the differential time-lapse awareness of subjects exposed to varying conditions of stress. Most important, all of the experimentalists' concern with the Sapir–Whorf hypothesis has been directed toward overt linguistic behavior. Thus, Brown and Lenneberg (1954, p. 455):

> Psychologists ordinarily infer perceptual discrimination when a subject is consistently able to respond differently to distinctive stimulus situations. The subject may be rat, dog, or man. The response may be running, salivation, or—speech. Words are used meaningfully when they are selectively employed with reference to some kind of environment—whether physical, social, or linguistic.

Yet, Whorf (1937/1956, 1938/1956) distinguished both overt and covert categories, "cryptotypes" as well as "phenotypes," just as Herder had spoken of "inner language" and Humboldt dealt with the "inner form of language" (cf. Basilius, 1952; Beneš, 1958; Porzig, 1923; Schmidt, 1968; Waterman, 1957; Weisgerber, 1926). Experimental tests, perhaps by necessity, measure overt behavior. If, however, the principle of linguistic relativity is not really about overt behavior, then tests of such behavior can constitute neither its confirmation nor its refutation.

A more basic question about the hypothesis would be whether it is verifiable or falsifiable at all, when understood in the breadth that its authors and their predecessors apparently intended. According to recent philosophers of science, potential disconfirmability is a necessary prerequisite for the scientific status of any theory. In other words, for any hypothesis to be genuinely scientific, it must be logically possible that there could be some item of empirical evidence which would refute it, for a theory which can apply equally well to all contradictory evidence is an inherently contradictory theory. Even if the Sapir–Whorf hypothesis were nonfalsifiable, however, that would not as such–unless one adds additional and debatable premises–make it either false or meaningless. It would also not make it either clear or true.

It is crucial to clarify what is and was meant by the terms "thought" and "reality" as they are said to correlate with language. Here again our historical material sheds some light. In 1759, Johann David Michaelis received the prize of the Berlin Academy of Sciences in its essay contest concerning the topid: "What is the reciprocal influence of the opinions of a people upon its language and of language upon its opinions?" Michaelis documented such influences and distinguished the deleterious from the beneficial varieties thereof, suggesting remedies for overcoming the handicaps presented by linguistic limitations. The academy's topic seems directly to pose the question of what we now call the "linguistic relativity principle." Despite its coronation, Michaelis's prize essay received a cool reception from Hamann and from Moses Mendelssohn, and both of their reviews are specifically critical of the way in which the question had been formulated in the first place.

Mendelssohn pointed to both a circularity and an inconsistency built into the question as phrased. There is circularity insofar as it is assumed that linguistic evidence can be used to document the linguistic influence upon opinions—a point reiterated by numerous commentators on Sapir and Whorf. There is inconsistency inasmuch as the theme proposed assumes that language does indeed limit and direct our thinking; but if that is in fact the case, then, says Mendelssohn, we are not in a position to see how language limits and directs it, for we are caught under the spell that we are trying to investigate. "As little as the eyes in their natural state can clearly perceive the instrument of sight, the light rays, perhaps just so little can the soul investigate language, the instrument of its thoughts, back to its origin" (1759, Vol. IV, pp. 365–366). If language limits our thinking, then we are unconscious of that fact; but "the limitations of

language are no longer limitations, as soon as we recognize them as such"
(p. 370). To express our awareness of the boundaries of language, we
resort, in turn, to language—"metalanguage," as we might say today—
and this language may have limits of its own, so that we are faced once
again with the same problem, but we are faced with it at a critically
different remove and from an altered level of linguistic consciousness.
Both Michaelis and the academy itself failed to make the fundamental
distinction between that sort of unphilosophical thinking or opinion which
is but dimly aware of the language it is employing and that more reflective
kind of thinking—to be observed often enough in the works of
philosophers, poets, mystics and others—which consciously expresses its
awareness of the limits of language and which manifestly wrestles with
those very limitations. Even with "philosophy" so loosely defined as it is
here, if a distinction is to be allowed between philosophical and
nonphilosophical—or, for that matter, scientific and nonscientific—
thinking, the relationship between language and thought would have to be
investigated differently in the respective cases.

Hamann's review of Michaelis's prize essay is more outspoken,
though it is replete with the enigmas and tropes so typical of Hamann's
style. Hamann also demanded a clarification of the question:

> In my opinion it would be easier to survey the discussion of the question
> concerning the reciprocal influence of opinions and language, if the topic itself
> were explained before plunging into solutions to it. But since scholars do not
> require such tedious thoroughness in order to make themselves understand-
> able to one another, or perhaps because they can write most affluently and yet
> with the least cost to themselves about the vague propositions, common
> readers may be done a service if this deficiency . . . is pointed out in the present
> pages. (1762b/1949–1957, p. 121)

In particular, "the meaning of the word "opinions' (*Meynungen*) is ambiguous, since the same are sometimes equated with truths and sometimes
taken as the opposite of truths" (p. 121). Hamann refers to Plato's explanation of opinion (*dóxa*) as unexamined thinking and as the median stage
between total ignorance and demonstrable knowledge. Opinion, for Plato,
represents a type of limited thinking—thinking without really thinking
about it—which is cave-bound, sense-bound, city- or culture-bound, and
in these regards also specifically language-bound: i.e., it is tied up with
and down to the limitations of a particular language. But it is Plato's point
that such thinking is the antithesis of philosophy, that it is not genuine
thinking at all.

Hamann himself makes somewhat more complicated distinctions along these Platonic lines (1762b/1949–1957, pp. 122–125; cf. Stam, 1976, pp. 106–109). His main point is clear: The correlation between language and thought is only as good as the clarity of our explanation of the kind of thought and language we are talking about. Hamann allows that there is—as he calls it somewhat confusingly—a "natural mode of thinking" upon which are based the relative wealth or poverty of a language, its peculiar characteristics, its *genius*:

> If our conceptions are given direction by the point of view of the soul and if this in turn . . . is determined by the condition of the body, then something similar can be applied to the body of the entire *Volk*. The lineaments of its language will then correspond to the direction of its mode of thinking; and every *Volk* reveals the same through the nature, form, laws, and customs of its speech as well as through its external form and a whole drama of public activities. (p. 122)

This last sentence is noticeably similar to a loose formulation of the Sapir–Whorf hypothesis. But it should be remarked, first, that thought patterns are here correlated with a wide range of manifestations, not language alone; and, second, that Hamann here suggests a correlation merely, not a cause-and-effect relationship in which language is the determining factor. From this "natural mode of thinking," however, Hamann distinguishes an "artificial or accidental mode of thinking"— temporary vogues of popular mind, prejudices, intellectual fashions. And from these, he still further differentiates scientific, poetical, or philosophical thinking and language.

Whorf has been ridiculed for his contention in "An American Indian Model of the Universe" (1950, posthumous) that there is some parallel between the language of the Hopi and the physics of relativity, and his apparent implication that Einstein and Planck might better have expressed themselves in Hopi than in Standard Average European. Indeed, many critics take as *prima facie* proof of the implausibilty of the Sapir–Whorf hypothesis the fact that the principle of relativity in physics was first discovered and articulated by Europeans, and that no Hopi Indian ever even chanced upon its formulation. Before addressing this, we should see what Whorf actually said about the matter:

> I find it gratuitous to assume that a Hopi who knows only the Hopi language and the cultural ideas of his own society has the same notions, often supposed to be intuitions, of time and space that we have, and that are generally assumed to be universal. In particular, he has no general notion of TIME

as a smooth flowing continuum in which everything in the universe proceeds at an equal rate, out of a future, through a present, into a past; or, in which ... the observer is being carried in the stream of duration continuously away from a past and into a future.

... the Hopi language contains no reference to "time," either explicit or implicit.

At the same time, the Hopi language is capable of accounting for and describing correctly, in a pragmatic or operational sense, all observable phenomena of the universe. Hence, I find it gratuitous to assume that Hopi thinking contains any such notion as the supposed intuitively felt flowing of "time," or that the intuition of a Hopi gives him this as one of its data. Just as it is possible to have any number of geometries other than the Euclidean which give an equally perfect account of space configurations, so it is possible to have descriptions of the universe, all equally valid, that do not contain our familiar contrasts of time and space. The relativity viewpoint of modern physics is one such view, conceived in mathematical terms, and the Hopi Weltanschauung is another and quite different one, nonmathematical and linguistic.

Thus, the Hopi language and culture conceals a METAPHYSICS, such as our so-called naïve view of space and time does, or as the relativity theory does; yet it is a different metaphysics from either. . . .

In this Hopi view, time disappears and space is altered, so that it is no longer the homogeneous and instantaneous timeless space of our supposed intuition or of classical Newtonian mechanics. At the same time, new concepts and abstractions flow into the picture, taking up the task of describing the universe without reference to such time or space—abstractions for which our language lacks adequate terms. . . . The Hopi postulates equally account for all phenomena and their interrelations, and lend themselves even better to the integration of Hopi culture in all its phases. (1950/1956, pp. 57–59)

Whorf then goes on to expand on this Hopi "metaphysics" and contrasts it with Western views of space and time which, he claims, are embedded in the grammatical structure and tense systems of modern Indo-European languages.

There are two things clear about the above passage. First, Whorf does not quite say what his detractors would have him say. Second, whatever it is that Whorf does say, he does not say it clearly. At any rate, Whorf does not state his thesis in anything like a satisfactory philosophical terminology, as is evident from his usage of two terms: "metaphysics" and "relativity." "Metaphysics" is used to refer to an unclarified, if not unconscious, world view, on the one hand, and to a philosophical and scientific system on the other. It may be that Galileo, Kant, and Einstein, Homer, Dante, and Shelley, the average Athenian citizen, the average medieval faithful, and the standard average European businessman all had discernible world views or Weltanschauungen or ideologies in some sense or other, but they most certainly did not all have a coherent metaphysics or philosophy. And regarding the relationship which his thought has to his language, Dante is probably closer to Homer or Shelley than to his simply pious contemporary; and Kant was certainly closer to Galileo or Einstein on that score than he was to the typical Königsberg burgher. Had Whorf simply availed himself of Hamann's differentiation among modes of thinking and their different relationships to language, or of a number of alternative dichotomies from the history of philosophy, his conjecture on this matter might have had greater plausibility. Whorf himself edges toward some such distinction when he says that modern physics is "conceived in mathematical terms, and the Hopi Weltanschauung is... nonmathematical and linguistic" (1950/1956, p. 58). Here he implicitly removes modern physicists from the language–thought axis, but he never follows through on the implications.

Second, relativity (as in Einsteinian physics) and relativism (as in Protagorean philosophy) should not be identified, as they are loosely in the above passage. Aristotelian, Galilean, and atomic physics are definitely not "descriptions of the universe, all equally valid." On some points they are directly contradictory, so that one supplants the other; but on other issues they are not even in competition: a particular theory of nuclear particles, for example, does not contradict a theory in which there is no notion of the nucleus in the first place. Matters stand quite differently when it comes to alternative "world views." A timeless universe certainly does contradict a space–time continuum; and different mythical accounts of genesis or cosmology are not "all equally valid" in any scientific or philosophical sense. What different Weltanschauungen or ideologies or mythologies *might* have is equal coherence or integrity, not equal validity. Again, it is the failure to draw elementary distinctions which makes Whorf so vulnerable to the scoffers' derision. If, however, one takes into account that the Europeans of whom Whorf speaks were indeed engaged in scientific and philosophical thinking, a mode of thinking which already removed them from their "natural mode of language," and that perhaps no Hopi Indians were engaged in scientific thinking at all—at least not in the Hopi language—then Whorf's conjecture may not be so patently absurd at all. All of which would not make his assertion true either, of course, and its possible validity would only be as strong as its ability to account for levels of thought and of language.

In his references to our "supposed intuitions of time and space" throughout "An American Indian Model of the Universe," Whorf was presumably attacking Kant: "Intuitions" was the somewhat misleading translation of Kant's "*Anschauungen*" employed by the early translators of *The Critique of Pure Reason*, J. M. D. Meiklejohn and F. Max Müller. Whorf's criticisms of everyday assumptions about the space–time framework in many other essays also seem to be directed against Kant. Curiously, however, there are many other passages in Whorf, especially those concerning the organization of our experience, which have a vaguely Kantian flavor to them. There is no evidence that Whorf ever read Kant extensively or carefully, and probably most of his acquaintance was second hand. Nonetheless, our historical perspective can again shed some light on the seeming discrepancy.

After the publication of Kant's first *Critique* in 1781, Hamann and Herder both began to work on *Metacritiques*. Because of the interrelated text history of Hamann's brief and Herder's lengthy work, we will here treat the two as one and emphasize their common charges against Kant.[2] Their attack centered around two broad points: first, Kant's adherence to a discredited faculty psychology; second, Kant's failure to understand the role of language. In earlier treatises, Herder had argued against any psychology that isolates the different faculties of the mind from one another, as though they performed separable operations (cf. 1770/1877–1913, 1778/1877–1913). Hamann particularly protested such an isolation of reason and, he felt, the consequent idolatry which enlightenment *philosophes* practiced in homage to the abstraced faculty (cf. Alexander, 1966, pp. 137–149; Leibrecht, 1966, pp. 161–171; Unger, 1925). Instead, Herder maintained, the psychologist must try to explain the total disposition of all the faculties, the specifically human element in the operation of each. Only when we concentrate upon the integration and relatedness of all these faculties do we begin to understand thinking *as a whole* and see what is human about human thinking.

A great bulk of Hamann's and Herder's criticisms concern language.

---

[2]Both Hamann and Herder conceived metacritiques after first reading Kant's *Critique* and discussed their common ideas in correspondence. Herder received and kept a copy of Hamann's unpublished manuscript, *Metakritik über den Purismus der Vernunft*, after the latter's death in 1788. In 1799, Herder published his own *Vernunft und Sprache: Metakritik zur Kritik der reinen Vernunft* in two volumes and in 1800 his *Kalligone*, a metacritical response to Kant's *Critique of Judgement*. F. T. Rink (1800), an avid Kantian, thereupon accused Herder of plagiarism and published Hamann's piece as his evidence. In quick succession other works appeared by Kiesewetter (1799–1800) and Cramer (1800). In fact, however, Herder's role was essentially innocent: his own and Hamann's works simply shared a common reaction to the Kantian tendency. Cf. Suphan (1881/1877–1913), pp. v–xxv, and Robert T. Clark (1955), pp. 396–412.

They both accuse Kant of a misuse of language, of a forced style and vocabulary, which alone permit his conclusions:

> It is not presumptuous to contradict presumptions. To oppose a vain dialectic, which ... would impose its word-schemes on us as the completed, most elevated results of all thinking, and to cleanse such misused language of its rubbish... : this is not presumption, but a duty. Whoever through artifice spoils a nation's language—no matter the acumen with which it is done—he has corrupted and injured the instrument of its reason. (1799, p. 12)

More important, Kant failed to take account of language and the role it plays in the shaping of perceptions, the formation of judgments, and the construction of ideas. This neglect leaves Kant open to a charge which would be devastating to the arguments of the *Critique*, namely that the *a priori* forms of perception and of judgment and the ideas of reason themselves are all linguistically derived categories. If true, the charge would not as such entail that those categories are "relative," nor would it even mean that they could not be *a priori* in some modified sense (especially since Kant himself already used the *a priori* in a somewhat modified sense); but it would mean that neither the categories nor reason itself is autonomous. Operations of reason could not be understood independently of considerations of language.

Despite the metacritical attacks on Kant by Hamann and Herder, there is an important common element in their respective views of reality. That agreement is as fundamental to an understanding of the language–thought correlation as are the differences among them. None of them takes reality to be something which is given independently of human consciousness. All three reject the early modern model of objectivity, or the thoroughgoing separation of subject and object, implied in Galilean physics and Cartesian metaphysics—a model which has now been superseded in twentieth-century physics as well. Rather, "subjective mind" and "objective reality" must be understood in their interrelationship and interactivity. The question of objectivity, for Kant, is not simply a question concerning the object detached from any observer, but a problem about what can constitute an object for an observer in the first place. For Kant—even more clearly than for Hamann and Herder—reality is not a *Gegebenes*, but an *Aufgegebenes*; not simply given, but given as a task; not set down, but offered up; not a *datum*, but a constructive project. The example of Kant makes clear, however, that this certainly does not entail a dismissal of science or of empirical evidence; nor does it imply relativism in the accepted Protagorean sense. On one interpretation Kant was a subjectivist, but he clearly was not a relativist, which would have been incompatible with such fundamental concepts in his philosophy as transcendental analysis, the *a priori* forms of intuition and of judgment, and universal laws—to name but some. To a considerable extent, the label "linguistic relativity" misses the point, since the correlation of language and thought, even with a causative factor, can be based upon a belief in linguistic universals, as is the case in Humboldt.

Cassirer (1923; 1923/1953, Vol. I, pp. 155–163; 1945) has amply documented the decisive influence that Kant had upon Humboldt's philosopy of language. According to Kant, the objects of cognition are first constituted as objects in the act of cognition and in particular through the synthetic judgments of the understanding. Humboldt sought to complete the Kantian philosophy and rectify Kant's own neglect of language by assigning this synthetic function to the formative (*bildende*) powers of language itself, and in turn by relating this to the nature of language as *enérgeia* and to the nature of man as *Streben* (aspiration) and *Geisteskraft* ("spiritual or mental power," roughly translated). The reciprocal interrelationships between thought and word, as Humboldt understands them, cannot be understood on a simple one-dimensional axis of the relative versus the absolute, the subjective versus the objective. Any given language is subjective relative to universal rationality and humanity, but objective relative to the individual speaker, since language always mediates. Thus Cassirer (1923/1953, Vol. I, p. 159): "Each language is a note in the harmony of man's universal nature"; and Humboldt himself (1820/1903–1935, Vol. IV, pp. 27–28):

> The mutual dependence of thought and word the one upon the other makes it clear that languages are not in fact means for the presentation of a truth already recognized, but rather for the discovery of a truth previously unknown. Their diversity is not one of sounds and signs, but a diversity of the world-views themselves. . . . The sum total of the knowable, as the field to be worked over by the human mind, lies in between all languages, independent from them, in the middle; man can approach this purely objective sphere in no way other than via his own manner of knowing and perceiving, thus along a subjective road. . . . This is only possible with and through language. Language, however, as a work of the nation and of bygone times, is something alien for the [individual] man: on the one hand he is restricted by it, but on the other he is enriched, strengthened, and stimulated by that which has been stored in it by all previous generations. Just as language stands over against the knowable as something subjective, so it stands over against man as something objective. For every language is a reminiscence (*Anklang*) of the universal nature of man; and even if the epitome of all of them can never become a perfect imprint of the subjectivity of humanity, nonetheless languages constantly move toward this

goal. But the subjectivity of *all* humanity becomes in turn, *per se*, something objective. The original harmony between man and world, on which the very possibility of all knowledge of the truth rests, is thus also regained gradually and progressively along the road of appearances. For it is always the objective which is that actually to be achieved, and if man approaches that on the subjective path of his individual language, then his next effort, in turn—even if it is only through the exchange of one language-subjectivity for another—is to isolate the subjective and to separate the object as purely as possible from it.

As clearly as the beginning of this passage provides background material for the "linguistic relativity principle," just as clearly does the end of the passage show that Humboldt was not enunciating any simple relativity principle at all. Just as clearly too, Humboldt—unlike Sapir and particularly Whorf—stands in a continuous though varied tradition with the universal grammarians of the seventeenth century, with Kant and Hegel and the German Idealists, and with twentieth-century thinkers such as Chomsky who have reopened the question of innateness and the *a priori* with regard to language. The correlation between language and thought as proposed by Humboldt, Herder, and Hamann must be understood in the context of a redefinition of the *a priori* and of an explanation of objective reality which attempts to go beyond the subject–object division in Galileo and Descartes, and which already presupposes those Kantian moves. It is the failure to so understand it—both by Sapir and Whorf themselves and by most of their critics—which accounts both for the historical anomaly to which we have alluded earlier and for the inappropriateness of the experimental tests of the Sapir–Whorf hypothesis to the hypothesis itself.

The title of Whorf's compiled essays, *Language, Thought, and Reality*, serves as a shorthand version of the "linguistic relativity principle" as a whole. When we place that principle in historical perspective, we find that earlier thinkers tried more carefully to distinguish just what should be meant by "thought" and by "reality" in such an equation. Both Sapir and Whorf, as well as some of their critics and supporters, tried to specify which linguistic elements they thought pertinent to the correlation: lexation or grammar, phonetic or semantic components, even surface or deep structure; but they are more careless when they speak of thought and of reality, and when they indulge a vacuous vocabulary in which world view and presupposition become synonymous with metaphysics and philosophy. Either the demonstration or the refutation of the hypothesis requires greater clarity about its terms. Otherwise, we will as easily be entrapped by the magic spell of our respective methods, as this tradition claims that we can become enwebbed in the magic circle of our language.

Reference

Alexander, W. M. Johann Georg Hamann: Metacritic of Kant. *Journal of the History of Ideas*, 1966, *27*, 137–149.

Basilius, H. Neo-Humboldtian ethnolinguistics. *Word*, 1952, *8*, 95–105.

Beneš, B. *Wilhelm von Humboldt, Jacob Grimm, August Schleicher: Ein Vergleich ihrer Sprachauffassung*. Winterthur: P. G. Keller, 1958.

Boas, F. Introduction. In F. Boas (Ed.), *Handbook of American Indian languages* (Vol. 1). Washington: Government Printing Office–Smithsonian Institution, 1911.

Brinton, D. G. The philosophic grammar of American languages, as set forth by William von Humboldt, with the translation of an unpublished memoir by him on the American verb. *Proceedings of the American Philosophical Society*, 1885, *22*, 332–352.

Brown, R. L. *Wilhelm von Humboldt's conception of linguistic relativity* (Janua linguarum, Series minor, no. 65). The Hague: Mouton, 1967.

Brown, R. W. *Words and things*. Glencoe, Ill.: Free Press, 1958.

Brown, R. W., & Lenneberg, E. H. A study in language and cognition. *Journal of Abnormal and Social Psychology*, 1954, *49*, 454–462.

Burnham, R. W., & Clark, J. R. A test of hue memory. *Journal of Applied Psychology*, 1955, *39*, 164–172.

Carroll, J. B. Linguistic relativity, contrastive linguistics, and language learning. *International Review of Applied Linguistics in Language Teaching*, 1963, *1*, 1–20.

Cassirer, E. Die Kantischen Elemente in Wilhelm von Humboldts Sprachphilosophie. In J. Binder (Ed.), *Festschrift für Paul Hensel*. Greiz i. V.: Ohag, 1923, pp. 105–127.

Cassirer, E. [*The philosophy of symbolic forms*] (R. Mannheim, Trans.) (3 vols.). New Haven: Yale, 1953. (Originally published, 1923–1931.)

Cassirer, E. Structuralism in modern linguistics. *Word*, 1945, *1*, 99–120.

Chomsky, N. *Current issues in linguistic theory*. (Janua linguarum, Series minor, no. 38). The Hague, Mouton, 1964.

Chomsky, N. *Cartesian linguistics: A chapter in the history of rationalist thought* (Studies in Language, Noam Chomsky & Morris Halle, Eds.). New York: Harper & Row, 1966.

Church, J. *Language and the discovery of reality: A developmental psychology of cognition*. New York: Vintage, 1961.

Clark, R. T. *Herder: His life and thought*. Berkeley: University of California Press, 1955.

Condillac, E. B., de. [*An essay on the origin of human knowledge: Being a supplement to Mr. Locke's Essay on the human understanding*] (Mr. Nugent, Trans.). London: 1756. (Originally published, 1746.) Reprited with an Introduction by J. H. Stam, in R. W. Rieber (Ed.), *Language, man and society: Foundations of the behavioral sciences*. New York: AMS, 1974.

Cordemoy, G., de. [*A philosophicall discourse concerning speech, conformable to the Cartesian principles*]. Savoy: 1668. (Originally published, 1666.) Reprinted with an Introduction by K. Uitti, in R. W. Rieber (Ed.), *Language, man and society: Foundations of the behavioral sciences*, New York: AMS, 1974.

Cramer, J. J. *Ueber Herders Metakritik*. Zürich-Leipzig: Ziegler, 1800.

De Vito, J. *The psychology of speech and language: An introduction to psycholinguistics*. New York: Random House, 1970.

Diebold, A. R. A survey of psycholinguistic research. In C. E. Osgood & T. A. Sebeok (Eds.), *Psycholinguistics: A survey of theory and research problems*. Bloomington: University of Indiana Press, 1965.

Gipper, H. *Gibt es ein sprachliches Relativitäts-prinzip? Untersuchungen zur Sapir–Whorf*

Hypothese (Conditio humana: Ergebnisse aus den Wissenschaften vom Menschen; T. V. Uexküll and I. Grubrich-Simitis, Eds.). Stuttgart: Fischer, 1972.

Hamann, J. G. Aesthetica in nuce: Eine Rhapsodie in kabbalistischer Prose (1762a). *Kreuzzüge des Philologen*. In J. Nadler (Ed.), *Sämtliche Werke* (Vol. II). Vienna: Herder, 1949–1957. pp. 195–218.

Hamann, J. G. Versuch über eine akademische Frage (1762b). *Kreuzzüge des Philologen*. In J. Nadler (Ed.), *Säliche Werke* (Vol. II). Vienna: Herder, 1949–1957, pp. 119–126.

Hamann, J. G. (Review of *Kritik der reinen Vernunft* by Immanuel Kant, 1781). In J. Nadler (Ed.), *Sëliche Werke* (Vol. III). Vienna: Herder, 1949–1957, pp. 275–280.

Hamann, J. G. *Metakritik über den Purismum der Vernunft* (1784). In J. Nadler (Ed.), *Säliche Werke* (Vol. III). Vienna: Herder, 1949–1957, pp. 281–289.

Hamburg, C. H. *Symbol and reality: Studies in the philosophy of Ernst Cassirer*. The Hague: Nijhoff, 1956.

Harnois, G. *Les théories du langage en France de 1660 à 1821* (Etudes françaises, Vol. 17). Paris: Société d'édition "Les belles lettres" [1928].

Heider, E. R. "Focal" color areas and the development of color names. *Developmental Psychology*, 1971, *4*, 447–455.

Heider, E. R. Probabilities, sampling, and ethnographic method: The case of Dani color names. *Man*, 1972, *7*, 448–466.

Heider, E. R. Universals in color naming and memory. *Journal of Experimental Psychology*, 1972, *93*, 10–20.

Heider, E. R. (under Eleanor H. Rosch). On the internal structure of perceptual and semantic categories. In T. E. Moore (Ed.), *Cognitive development and the acquisition of language*. New York: Academic Press, 1973, pp. 111–144.

Herder, J. G. *Ueber die neuere deutsche Literatur* (1766–1767). In B. Suphan (Ed.), *Sämmtliche Werke* (Vol. I). Berlin: Weidmann, 1877–1913.

Herder, J. G. Versuch einer Geschichte der lyrischen Dichtkunst (1767?). In B. Suphan (Ed.), *Sämmtliche Werke* (Vol. XXXII). Berlin: Weidman, 1877–1913, pp. 85–140.

Herder, J. G. *Ueber die neuere deutsche Literatur: Fragmente* (2nd ed.) (1768). In B. Suphan (Ed.), *Sämmtliche Werke* (Vol. II). Berlin: Weidman, 1877–1913, pp. 1–108.

Herder, J. G. *Abhandlung über den Ursprung der Sprache* (1770–1772). In B. Suphan (Ed.), *Sammtliche Werke* (Vol. V). Berlin: Weidman, 1877–1913, pp. 1–147.

Herder, J. G. *Vom Erkennen und Empfinden der menschlichen Seele* (1778). In B. Suphan (Ed.), *Sämmtliche Werke* (Vol. VIII). Berlin: Weidman, 1877–1913.

Herder, Johann Gottfried. *Vernunft und Sprache: Metakritik zur Kritik der reinen Vernunft (1799)*. In B. Suphan (Ed.), *Sämmtliche Werke* (Vol. XXI). Berlin: Weidman, 1877–1913.

Herder, J. G. *Kalligone* (1800). In B. Suphan (Ed.), *Sämmtliche Werke* (Vol. XXII). Berlin: Weidman, 1877–1913.

Hoijer, H. (Ed.). *Language in culture: Proceedings of a conference on the interrelationships of language and other aspects of culture*. Chicago: University of Chicago Press, 1954.

Hook, S. (Ed.). *Language and philosophy: A symposium*. New York: New York University Press, 1969.

Hovelacque, A. [*The science of language: Linguistics, philology, etymology*] (A. H. Keane, Trans.). London: Chapman & Hall, Philadelphia: Lippincott, 1877.

Humboldt, W. von. Ueber das vergleichende Sprachstudium in Beziehung auf die verschiedenen Epochen der Sprachentwicklung (1820). In A. Leitzmann (Ed.), *Gesammelte Schriften* (Vol. IV). Berlin: Königlich Preussische Akademie der Wissenschaften, 1903–1935, pp. 1–34.

Humboldt, W. von. *Ueber die Verschiedenheit des menschlichen Sprachbaues und ihren Einfluss auf die geistige Entwicklung des Menschengeschlechts* (1835). In A. Leitzmann (Ed.), *Gesammelte Schriften* (Vol. VII). Berlin: Königlich Preussische Akademie der Wissenschaften, 1903–1935.

Hymes, D. H. On typology of cognitive styles in language (With examples from Chinookan). *Anthropological Linguistics*, 1961, *3*, 22–54.

Hymes, D. H. Two types of linguistic relativity (With examples from Amerindian ethnography). In W. Bright (Ed.), *Sociolinguistics: Proceedings of the UCLA Sociolinguistics Conference, 1964* (Janua linguarum, Series maior, no. 20). The Hague: Mouton, 1966, pp. 114–167.

Jost, L. *Sprache als Werk und wirkende Kraft: Ein Beitrag zur Geschichte und Kritik der energetischen Sprachauffassung seit Wilhelm von Humboldt* (Sprache und Dichtung, Neue Folge, no. 6). Bern: Paul Haupt, 1960.

Juliard, P. *Philosophies of language in eighteenth-century France* (Janua linguarum, Series minor, no. 18). The Hague: Mouton, 1970.

Kiesewetter, J. G. C. *Prüfung der Herderschen Metakritik zur Kritik der reinen Vernunft* (2 vols.). Berlin: C. Quien, 1799–1800.

Kroeber, A. L. (Ed.). *Anthropology today: An encyclopedic inventory*. Chicago: University of Chicago Press, 1953.

Kuehner, P. *Theories on the origin and formation of language in the eighteenth century in France*. Unpublished doctoral dissertation, University of Pennsylvania, 1944.

Langer, S. K. *Philosophy in a new key: A study in the symbolism of reason, rite, and art*. Cambridge: Harvard University Press, 1942.

Leibrecht, W. [*God and man in the thought of Hamann*] (J. H. Stam, Trans.). Philadelphia: Fortress, 1966.

Lenneberg, E. H. Cognition in ethnolinguistics. *Language*, 1953, *29*, 463–471.

Lenneberg, E. H. Color naming, color recognition, color discrimination: A re-appraisal. *Perceptual and Motor Skills*, 1961, *12*, 375–382.

Lenneberg, E. H., & Roberts, J. M. *The language of experience* (Indiana University Publications in Anthropology and Linguistics, Mem. 13). Baltimore: Waverly, 1956.

Mendelssohn, M. (with T. Abbt, G. E. Lessing, & F. Nicolai). *Briefe, die neueste Literature betreffend*. Berlin: Friedrich Nicolai, 1759–1765.

Michaelis, J. D. [*A dissertation on the influence of opinions on language, and of language on opinions*]. London: Owen and Bingley. Reprinted with an Introduction by J. H. Stam, in R. W. Rieber (Ed.), *Language, man and society: Foundations of the behavioral sciences* New York: AMS, 1973. (Originally published, 1759/1762.)

Miller, R. L. *The linguistic relativity principle and Humboldtian ethnolinguistics* (Janua linguarum, Series minor, no. 67). The Hague: Mouton, 1968.

Müller, F. M. *Lectures on the science of language* (2 vols.). London: Longman, Green, Longman, & Roberts, 1861–1864.

Müller, F. M. *The science of thought* (2 vols.). New York: Scribner's 1887.

O'Flaherty, J. C. *Unity and language: A study in the philosophy of Johann Georg Hamann* (University of North Carolina Studies in the Germanic languages and literatures, no. 6). Chapel Hill: University of North Carolina Press, 1952.

Percy, W. *The message in the bottle*. New York: Farrar, Straus & Giroux, 1975.

Porzig, W. Der Begriff der inneren Sprachform. *Indogermanische Forschungen*, 1923, *41*, 150–169.

Rink, F. T. *Mancherley zur Geschichte der metacritischen Invasion: Nebst einem Fragment einer älteren Metakritik und einigen Aufsätzen, die Kantische Philosophie betreffend*. Königsberg: 1800.

Sapir, E. *Herder's prize essay, "Ueber den Ursprung der Sprache," and its place in the discussion of the origin of language.* Unpublished master's thesis, Columbia University, New York, 1905.

Sapir, E. Herder's "Ursprung der Sprache." *Modern Philology*, 1907, *5*, 109–142.

Sapir, E. *Language: An introduction to the study of speech.* New York: Harcourt, Brace & World, 1921.

Sapir, E. The Status of linguistics as a science (1929). In D. G. Mandelbaum (Ed.), *Selected writings of Edward Sapir in language, culture and personality.* Berkeley: University of California Press, 1949, pp. 160–166.

Sapir, E. Language (1933). In D. G. Mandelbaum (Ed.), *Selected writings of Edward Sapir in language, culture and personality.* Berkeley: University of California Press, 1949, pp. 7–32.

Saporta, S. (Ed.). *Psycholinguistics: A book of readings.* New York: Holt, Rinehart & Winston, 1961.

Sayce, A. H. *Introduction to the science of language* (2 vols.). London: Kegan Paul, 1880.

Schmidt, S. J. *Sprache und Denken als sprachphilosophisches Problem von Locke bis Wittgenstein.* The Hague: Nijhoff, 1968.

Slobin, D. I. *Psycholinguistics.* Glenview, Ill.: Scott, Foresman, 1974.

Stam, J. H. *Inquiries into the origin of language: The fate of a question* (Studies in language, N. Chomsky & M. Halle, Eds.). New York: Harper & Row, 1976.

Steiner, G. *After Babel: Aspects of language and translation.* Oxford: Oxford University Press, 1975.

Steinthal, H. *Die Sprachwissenschaft Wilhelm von Humboldts und die Hegel'sche Philosophie.* Berlin: Dümmler, 1848.

Steinthal, H. *Der Ursprung der Sprache im Zusammenhange mit den letzten Fragen alles Wissens.* Berlin: Dümmler, 1851.

Steinthal, H. *Grammatik, Logik, und Psychologie: Ihre Principien und ihr Verhältniss zu einander.* Berlin: Dümmler, 1855.

Steinthal, H. *Einleitung in die Psychologie und Sprachwissenschaft.* Berlin: Dümmler, 1871.

Suphan, B. Einleitung (1881). In B. Suphan (Ed.), *Sämmtliche Werke* (Vol. XXI). Berlin: Weidman, 1877–1913.

Tax, S., Eiseley, L. C., Rouse, I., & Voegelin, C. F. (Eds.). *An appraisal of Anthropology today.* Chicago: University of Chicago Press, 1953.

Trier, J. Das sprachliche Feld. *Neue Jahrbücher für Wissenschaft und Bildung*, 1934, *10*, 428–449.

Turgot, A. R. J. Discours sur les avantages que l'établissement du christianisme a procuré au genre humain (1750). In P. D. de Nemours (Ed.), *Oeuvres* (Vol. II). Paris: de Delance, 1808–1811, pp. 17–51.

Turgot, A. R. J. Discours sur les progrès successifs de l'esprit humain (1750). In P. D. de Nemours (Ed.), *Oeuvres* (Vol. II). Paris: de Delance, 1808–1811, pp. 52–92.

Unger, R. *Hamanns Sprachtheorie im Zusammenhange seines Denkens: Grundlegung zu einer Würdigung der geistesgeschichtlichen Stellung des Magus im Norden* (2 vols.). Munich: Beck'sche Verlagsbuchhandlung, 1905.

Unger, R. *Hamann und die Aufklärung: Studien zur Vorgeschichte des romantischen Geistes im 18. Jahrhunderts* (2 vols.). Tübingen: Max Niemeyer, 1925.

Waterman, J. T. Benjamin Lee Whorf and linguistic field theory. *Southwestern Journal of Anthropology*, 1957, *13*, 201–211.

Weisgerber, L. Das Problem der inneren Sprachform und seine Bedeutung für die deutsche Sprache. *Germanisch-Romanische Monatsschrift*, 1926, *14*, 241–256.

Wheelwright, P. *Metaphor and reality*. Bloomington: Indiana University Press, 1962.

Wheelwright, P. *The burning fountain: A study in the language of symbolism* (rev. ed.). Bloomington: Indiana University Press, 1968.

Whitney, W. D. *Language and the study of language*. New York: Scribner's, 1867.

Whorf, B. L. On psychology [1927?*a*] In J. B. Carroll (Ed.), *Language, thought, and reality: Selected writings of Benjamin Lee Whorf*. Cambridge, Mass.: M. I. T. Press, 1956, pp. 40–42.

Whorf, B. L. On the connection of ideas [1927*b*]. In J. B. Carroll (Ed.), *Language, thought, and reality: Selected writings of Benjamin Lee Worf*. Cambridge, Mass.: M.I.T. Press, 1956, pp. 35–39.

Whorf, B. L. Aztec linguistics [1928]. Quoted in J. B. Carroll (Ed.), Introduction to *Language, thought, and reality: Selected writings of Benjamin Lee Whorf*. Cambridge, Mass.: M.I.T. Press, 1956, p. 25.

Whorf, B. L. A linguistic consideration of thinking in primitive communities [1936a]. In J. B. Carroll (Ed.), *Language, thought, and reality: Selected writings of Benjamin Lee Whorf*. Cambridge, Mass.: M.I.T. Press, 1956, pp. 65–86.

Whorf, B. L. The punctual and segmentative aspects of verbs in Hopi (1936b). In J. B. Carroll (Ed.), *Language, thought, and reality: Selected writings of Benjamin Lee Whorf*. Cambridge, Mass.: M.I.T. Press, 1956, pp. 51–56.

Whorf, B. L. Discussion of Hopi linguistics [1937]. In J. B. Carroll (Ed.), *Language, thought, and reality: Selected writings of Benjamin Lee Whorf*. Cambridge, Mass.: M.I.T. Press, 1956, pp. 102–111.

Whorf, B. L. Some verbal categories of Hopi (1938). In J. B. Carroll (Ed.), *Language, thought, and reality: Selected writings of Benjamin Lee Whorf*. Cambridge, Mass.: M.I.T. Press, 1956, pp. 112–124.

Whorf, B. L. Gestalt technique of stem composition in Shawnee (1940a). In J. B. Carroll (Ed.), *Language, thought, and reality: Selected writings of Benjamin Lee Whorf*. Cambridge, Mass.: M.I.T. Press, 1956, pp. 160–172.

Whorf, B. L. Linguistics as an exact science (1940b). In J. B. Carroll (Ed.), *Language, thought, and reality: Selected writings of Benjamin Lee Whorf*. Cambridge, Mass.: M.I.T. Press, 1956, pp. 220–232.

Whorf, B. L. Science and linguistics (1940c). In J. B. Carroll (Ed.), *Language, thought, and reality: Selected writings of Benjamin Lee Whorf*. Cambridge, Mass.: M.I.T. Press, 1956, pp. 207–219.

Whorf, B. L. Languages and logic (1941). In J. B. Carroll (Ed.), *Language, thought, and reality: Selected writings of Benjamin Lee Whorf*. Cambridge, Mass.: M.I.T. Press, 1956, pp. 233–245.

Whorf, B. L. Language, mind, and reality (1942). In J. B. Carroll (Ed.), *Language, thought, and reality: Selected writings of Benjamin Lee Whorf*. Cambridge, Mass.: M.I.T. Press, 1956, pp. 246–270.

Whorf, B. L. Grammatical categories (1945, posthumous). In J. B. Carroll (Ed.), *Language, thought, and reality: Selected writings of Benjamin Lee Whorf*. Cambridge, Mass.: M.I.T. Press, 1956, pp. 87–101.

Whorf, B. L. An American Indian model of the universe (1950, posthumous). In J. B. Carroll (Ed.), *Language, thought, and reality: Selected writings of Benjamin Lee Whorf*. Cambridge, Mass.: M.I.T. Press, 1956, pp. 57–64.

INDEX